LITURGY AND LIBERTY

Liturgy and Liberty

Combining the best of the old
with the best of the new
in worship

JOHN LEACH

MARC
Eastbourne

Front cover design by Vic Mitchell

British Library Cataloguing in Publication Data

Leach, John, *1953–*
    Liturgy and liberty.
    1. Christian church. Worship
    I. Title
    264

    ISBN 1-85424-016-1 (Marc)
        0-7324-0424-X (Albatross)

Copublished in Australia by Albatross Books,
PO Box 320, Sutherland, NSW 2232

Printed in Great Britain for
MARC, an imprint of Monarch Publications Ltd
1 St Anne's Road, Eastbourne, E Sussex BN21 3UN by
Courier International Ltd, Tiptree, Essex.
Typeset by Nuprint Ltd, Harpenden, Herts AL5 4SE.

To George and Edward—

'The "A" Team'

CONTENTS

FOREWORD

Expressions of worship continue to be reinterpreted and variously developed according to our changing culture. When we began urban church planting in Chile in the 1960s a new missionary named Daphne Richardson arrived and began composing music and paraphrasing psalms and other scriptures to be played on the guitar. National Christians there built on this inspiring start and began incorporating their own songs and music in the local churches. It seemed that we had stumbled on a whole new dimension in worship. We thought we were pioneering something in that small corner of God's vineyard – perhaps we were, though we later discovered that the Holy Spirit was doing similar things all over the world and has continued doing so since.

The priority of worship and the variety of it continues to be one of the most refreshing features in church life today.

'Choir walks out on note of discord' was a recent newspaper headline. Beneath this the wordline ran: 'The Vicar was accused by the organist of wanting to introduce "a lot of clap hands, here comes Charlie" services, addressing God as "you", and having little groups of people with guitars doing their nasty, folky stuff. All quite ghastly' (quoted by Andrew Maries in his book *One Heart, One Voice*). Clearly not everyone welcomes the changes, and quite possibly some of them are not for the better.

9

Today there is a plethora of new music books, new music cassettes and new books exploring the whole area of worship. I have about six on the subject. So why do we want another one? Why can't we just set to and get on with worship? Well, we can. But the subject is so alive, there's room for plenty of input.

John Leach articulates my own values in so many areas, and I find it exciting to read something which I would have liked to have said myself, had I had the time and skills. This book is brimful of guidance and has a real contribution of its own to make. It is by no means a stuffy book. John has the happy knack of combining humour, homely wisdom and illustration with technical know-how, deep understanding and an inspiring feel for his subject. It is written with the head, but from the heart. A single message comes across, but there is a delightful breadth to it.

Not many can combine a Baptist Free Church background with a good dash of Anglo-Catholicism in their spiritual pilgrimage. After serving a first curacy in Norfolk, John has been on the staff of a large and lively evangelical charismatic church. He has thought deeply about his subject, studying it in some detail, and writes out of his considerable experience in leading worship at St Thomas Crookes, Sheffield.

I am delighted to commend this wholesome book and pray that its influence may bring great blessing.

David Pytches
Formerly Bishop of Chile, Bolivia and Peru

ACKNOWLEDGEMENTS

All sorts of people have influenced me in my pilgrimage both towards worshipping and in writing about it. My special thanks go to my parents for bringing me up to know and love the Lord who is worthy of our worship; the leaders and people of all the churches in which I have served; musicians, both the famous who have given me a vision for what worship can be, and the unknown locals who have put up with me trying to work out that vision, and many in congregations around the country who have encouraged me and made me feel that I might be getting somewhere near realising it.

As far as this book is concerned, I would like to give particular thanks to the many friends, family and colleagues who have helped and encouraged me in its writing. The original vision for it came from Robert Warren, who didn't just leave it there but continually acted as a sounding-board for my ideas and sharpened up my thinking along the way. The three Worship Teams at my church, under the co-ordination of John and Janet Goepel, provided a creative medium in which to try out my ideas in real life—and a lot of laughs when they didn't quite come off. The Goepels themselves helped immensely in the process of articulating half-formed ideas to the point where they could be written down clearly and even used in the practice of worship week by week. Without the help of Liz

Harvey with the practicalities of using a word-processor, Duncan Twigg with the graphics, and Linda Russell-Ward with some of the typing, this book would have taken about ten times as long to write. I am also grateful to Lindsay Mitchell and all the staff at Whirlow Grange for peace, quiet and lots of coffee when I went there for uninterrupted stints of writing. Thanks are due again to the Goepels and to my wife, Chris, and sons, Steve and Paul, who between them were responsible for much of Chapter 12.

Finally, I need to thank the whole church family among whom I live and work for loving and encouraging me, and for providing such a creative medium in which my ideas could take root and grow. Special thanks and love go to my own family for their love and support throughout this project. For all these people I thank God, and pray that they and his whole church may be built up and encouraged by some of the material in this book as we all continue to grow together in that greatest privilege of the Christian life—worshipping and exalting the living God whose kingdom shall have no end.

INTRODUCTION

At the moment it's very fashionable to knock various models of training for full-time ministry. Personally, I am not one of those who enjoy that practice, but the sad fact remains that in my own five years at college I had no instruction whatsoever in the leading of worship, apart from the time when the organist at the church where I went for fieldwork spent five minutes before the service teaching me to sing the responses for Evensong (not, I might add, a happy experience for either of us, nor, subsequently, for the congregation). In the past, of course, it didn't matter too much, since if you were an Anglican you simply had to read through the service from the book, and if you were a non-conformist you had to pray and announce hymns, your only problems being respectively pronouncing 'inestimable', and understanding who or what 'runs' were and why reading a book might help them.

Now, however, things are different. Two distinct factors make leading worship a task which requires much skill and sensitivity. The first, affecting those from the Anglican and similar churches, is liturgical renewal. Out of the upheaval of the seventies has emerged *The Alternative Service Book 1980* with its plethora of options and alternatives, making a service no longer a trip from A to B as the crow flies, but much more a pleasant meander down various by-paths which brings you to the final destination of the dismissal via several 'pretty ways'. It is, of course, still possible to take a liturgical short cut, but churches which do so regularly are often left feeling guilty at missing so much.

The second factor, affecting all branches of the church, is charismatic renewal, with its emphasis on the immediacy of the Spirit and the expectation of his actually doing something during worship.

These two factors together mean that the leader of worship needs to combine an openness and spontaneity with a mental index of page numbers, and should, if possible, also be able to play the synthesiser or at the very least the tambourine. No longer is 'taking a service' enough; we really do need to be able to 'lead worship'. This book is an attempt to help those who have this task to look at it as a privilege. It tries to bridge a gap between material on the conduct of services and instruction on the musical side of renewed worship (precious little in either case), and it is as practical as possible so that it may be of real use to those who seek the skills it describes.

For whom is this book intended? For anyone, really, who is involved in the conduct of worship of whatever style. Clergy and ministers, lay people involved in leading worship (such as Anglican Readers), musicians and singers, those involved in planning worship: all may find material here which is relevant to their role. One of my main aims in writing this book is to attempt to redress a balance. Several books have been published recently on worship and worship leading, but almost all without exception have come from a house-church background. As an Anglican it is my desire to contribute something from my side, not as an exercise in point-scoring or flag-waving, but simply because worshippers in the Church of England and similar churches often have very different needs from those in house churches. While I have learned a great deal about worship from Restorationist teaching and praxis, it has little to contribute on the subject of liturgy, other than occasionally referring to it as 'dead', 'formal', 'empty' and so on, which of course it often can be. Most house church and non-conformist teaching will not help us in turning liturgy into worship—why should it, when they don't believe in the validity of liturgy in the first place?

The tension between liturgy and liberty is not new. It has been a problem to some degree throughout most of the history of the church, and it can, I believe, be detected in the Bible itself, even in the Old Testament. Throughout much of the history of Israel two distinct strands of spirituality coexisted, often uneasily, side by side. The 'prophetic' strand was marked by a 'charismatic' style, an immediacy in experience of God, many 'signs and wonders', a great emphasis on personal holiness, and very often a suspicion of those who were more structured in their spirituality and therefore prone to nominalism. Prophets leave us with the impression that they were often rather hairy, unpredictable people who did all sorts of weird and ecstatic things.

On the other hand, the priests were the height of respectability. They went in for liturgy in vast quantities and on vast scales, and seemed to have little respect for their unsavoury prophetic brothers-in-Yahweh. They were heavily into bureaucracy (as the priestly writings of Chronicles, Ezra and Nehemiah reveal), and liked things to be done properly and according to tradition, with careful planning and clearly-defined jobs for all. To be a priest was to be someone important in society, and the dignity of their calling was enhanced by their fine vestments.

I feel there are uncomfortable parallels with the house churches and the Church of England! Yet neither side has a monopoly on truth, and both sides are prone to their own particular dangers. Yes, the priests could and often did propagate nominal, meaningless worship, and those interminable lists of names are pretty boring. But prophets could go off the rails too, and prophesy what they or their audiences wanted to hear. Jesus flatly refused to be identified totally with one strand or the other, and worked within the best of both traditions. If we in his church are to follow him properly, we cannot afford to ditch half of his spirituality, whether that half consists of healing the sick or taking part in liturgical worship.

It is so sad that most of the history of the church has consisted in throwing babies out with the bath water. It would be tragic if, in this time of Spirit-filled renewal, this were to happen again with the rich and powerful tradition of the church's worship. It is my conviction that God is wanting to work with tradition, not in spite of it. He will work in spite of it if he needs to, but I believe that it is second best to do so.

It is not just tradition, however, which makes liturgy so important. There is a more fundamental fact which means that we ignore liturgy at our peril. Put simply it is this: life itself is liturgical. We function at many levels with a repeated set of actions and words which have got under our skins and which we feel secure and at home with. I remember my tutor at college beginning the very first liturgy lecture by speaking about 'personal liturgies'—which side of your face you shave first, the order in which you tie your shoe-laces, and so on; and 'social liturgies'—the sort of thing one might hear on the terraces at Carrow Road or Bramall Lane or at a student demonstration. We feel at home with these things, we know what we have to say or do, and we often say or do them unconsciously because they are so built into us.

It would be unnatural, therefore, if our worship of God were not to some degree liturgical in this way. And of course it is in most cases. I'll be noting later the fact that very often those churches which shout the loudest against 'dead, formalised liturgy' are the most liturgical of all.

Because liturgy is the built-in rhythm of life itself, there is a natural tendency to become liturgical in everything we do. The difference, it seems to me, between liturgical and non-liturgical churches has nothing to do with whether or not we use liturgy; we all do. It is about whether we use it deliberately and proudly, or accidentally and unconsciously. This book is written with the conviction that good things rarely happen by accident, and it is really a plea for all of us to become aware of what we do so that we can work consciously towards doing it better.

So, to whom is this book addressed? I suspect there may be three distinct groups. The first consists of those who have experienced personal renewal, and even renewal at a church level, but are still seeking to renew the worship of the church. How can we actually drag the services and the liturgy into the charismatic era?

Secondly, there may be those who have gone all out for renewal and in doing so have believed it necessary to abandon liturgy altogether. Perhaps even worse, there may be others who go through the motions because they feel they have to, while longing for the part of the service when they get into the 'worship time' and begin to do the 'real' worshipping. Some may have done this quite happily, but others may be feeling slightly guilty about it. The need for people in this group is not so much for a renewal of the liturgy as for a liturgising of the renewal.

Thirdly, and perhaps this is the largest group, there are those who fall in between these other two, and who feel as if they have renewal in one hand and liturgy in the other and don't know quite what to do with either of them. I hope that all three groups will be helped by this book as I discuss in some detail the practical outworkings of my convictions about liturgy and liberty, in the desire that the two may increasingly come together in the experience of many churches.

That may sound a difficult or even impossible hope, but the gulf between liturgy and liberty may not be so wide as some think. Both sides are on the move and are beginning to come together. Liturgical revision in the Anglican Church has brought in much more flexibility, and this trend is continuing in the thinking of the Liturgical Commission. Responding to documents such as *Faith in the City*,[1] they are increasingly thinking of liturgical texts as 'resource books' rather than as set and immutable 'orders of service'. Churches which are much more free in their worship have grasped something important about its liturgical nature through their use of modern worship songs. They are designed to be known and learned by heart, they are repetitive, and they are used to their greatest effect when they have gone so deep into one's being that they flow spontaneously out again in worship. This is exactly the way liturgy should be used, and 'non-liturgical' churches have a lot to teach about how to do it. The gulf is closing, and my hope is that this book may help close it a little more by enabling us to see the value of other traditions, or, in some cases, to see the value of our own and to learn to unite the best of both.

I am writing from the context of a local church moving on the same pilgrimage, as it tries to combine its Anglican heritage with the new life which God's Spirit is breathing into his church. We are in no sense a church which has arrived, so I write about past successes, present struggles and future uncertainties in roughly equal proportions. But my observations do come from real life.

I should make one important point. When I refer to worship leader as 'he' or 'him', I really mean 'or she' and 'or her', and my shorthand is simply an attempt at economy, not discrimination. There is absolutely no reason why women shouldn't take everything in this book as applying to them, apart from those parts which concern the celebration of the Eucharist, which they are not as yet allowed to do in the Church of England and other episcopal churches.

Where is this book coming from? In a church full of labels and parties, it is important to know whether or not a book has the right pedigree. Already some non-charismatics, lovers of the *Book of Common Prayer*, and opponents of women's ordination may have been put off. Perhaps it would be useful to know what the theologians call the *sitz-im-leben* or 'life-setting' of the book.

I am writing from the context of a parish church in the North of England which is an Anglican and Baptist Local Ecumenical Project. It would call itself an Evangelical church, although few of its members would go to the stake for any of the usual shibboleths like the integrity of Isaiah or the dating of Daniel. We would happily be described as a 'charismatic' church, and Anglicans would call us 'low' (although my own background is much more Anglo-Catholic, after my Baptist upbringing). We would also, I suppose, rejoice in the name of a 'signs and wonders' church, having been very much affected by the visits of John Wimber and others from the Vineyard Christian Fellowships in America, and having embraced much of his theology of the kingdom of God and its power available to us now.

I wouldn't want to apologise for any of this, but I do want to try to break out of any narrow mould in an attempt to provide a book which is useful in many different settings. In some parts, of course, I will need to deal with material only really applicable in the 'liturgical' churches (those which use set-service books); free-church readers are allowed to skip those bits. But in the last analysis, I am trying to help those of us, whatever denomination, theology or churchmanship we embrace, who want to be more in touch with God in our worship and seek to make it more relevant to the congregation.

With this end in view, I want to explore first of all a theology of worship which helps us to know what it is we're doing when we worship and how we can do it in different ways. The first chapter deals with the role and personality of the worship leader. Then we will look at the ingredients of a worship service and how a leader can deal most helpfully with the liturgical, non-musical and musical parts. This is followed by some thoughts on the planning process. There is a chapter on that increasingly common phenomenon, the worship group, and a section on how to help the congregation get the most out of and put the most into their worship. After a section which seeks to apply some of the insights so far explored to the area of worshipping with children, two final chapters aim to help churches seeking to introduce worship similar to that described in this book by dealing with change and conflict.

I have sought throughout to be practical, biblical and theological, and my aim is that after having read the book many people will be able either to take some first tentative steps in worship leading, or to move on from where they are at the moment. It is offered to the church not as a blueprint, but as a set of possibilities which reflect my own pilgrimage and some of the lessons I've learned along the way. My hope is that 'to him who is able to do immeasurably more than all we ask or imagine, according to his power that is at work within us, to him be glory in the church' (Eph 3:20)—glory both from the historic liturgy of that church, and from the liberty of his Holy Spirit.

Notes

1. *Faith in the City*, the Report of the Archbishop of Canterbury's Commission on Urban Priority Areas (London: Church House Publishing, 1985).

CHAPTER ONE

WHAT IS WORSHIP ANYWAY?

I. The Worship Cycle

IT'S AMAZING HOW QUICKLY you learn when you know you've got to teach. Facing me was the prospect of running a five-week course on worship, and as the time approached, I realised how little I actually knew on the subject. I quite enjoyed worshipping, but I'd never really thought about just what it was that I was doing. So I began to explore material.

First of all I dug out some notes I'd taken during a talk on the different Greek and Hebrew words used in the Bible. You know the sort of thing: this word really means 'shout', so we must all shout during Evensong. To be quite honest, I didn't find that approach too helpful. Having studied original languages, I knew how notoriously difficult it was to build a convincing case for very much at all purely on what words 'really' mean. Many preachers commit semantic murder each Sunday in the pulpit by failing to understand how words and meanings work. Take the oft-quoted example of the greenhouse. The word 'green' refers to a colour, while a 'house' is obviously something in which people live. Therefore a greenhouse is either a dwelling place of that particular hue, or possibly the abode of green people. However, 'green' also has connotations of envy and inexperience, so that a greenhouse now becomes a place where Martians, who haven't seen much of life but would desperately like to be those who had, hang out. One more 'green' nuance would mean that the aforementioned Martians were heavily into ecology. And finally the poor Martians, and no doubt most of us too at seeing such nonsense, would be feeling decidedly sick. See what I mean? Biblical terms can be useful, and certainly can make for interesting study, but to build a whole theology of worship on them is dangerous.

I began to search further afield. As I did so, two completely different strands emerged which seemed at first to be completely contradictory, but which later came together to form what I reckon to be a completely biblical view of worship—and one which excites me much more than knowing that the word *yadah* is used ninety-one times. The first strand came from hearing a talk at a conference which was basically making the point that worship is always a response to something which God has done. Worship starts with God and moves on from there. Fair enough, and not all that earth shattering, but then I read a book which contained a chapter on worship which seemed to be saying exactly the opposite. The author went back to the picture of the Tabernacle in the Old Testament, and noted that worship was actually something which produced a manifestation of God. The people worshipped in order that God would come among them in power, to be enthroned on their praises, and to manifest his glory. This left me in a dilemma. Which way round was it? Where did God fit in—at the beginning or at the end? Did we worship because he was there, or was he there because we worshipped?

It was obvious that both could be true. So I sat down with a large sheet of paper to try and work it out. The result was my 'Worship Cycle'. In spite of rude comments from friends about the suitability of bikes in church (they obviously didn't understand semantics either), I persevered until I had arrived at my own theology of worship.

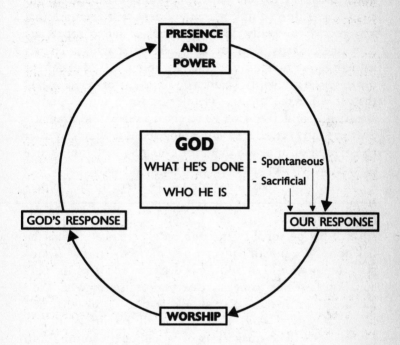

The diagram sets out my understanding of worship in pictorial style, and I'll explain what it means in the next two chapters. Basically there are two parts to it: the cycle itself and the side-effects that go with it. We'll begin with the cycle.

First of all, I agreed with my conference speaker that at the very beginning of worship is God. He is right in the centre of the cycle, and our response to him is to worship. Psalm 150:2 suggests that there are two things about God to which we respond in worship:

> Praise him for his acts of power;
> Praise him for his surpassing greatness.

In other words, we respond in worship to what God has done and also to who he is: to his works and to his character. I don't think it's an accident that they are that way round; we really do find it much easier to appreciate someone's deeds than we do their personality. There's something so much more concrete about it. It's easier for me to say to my wife, 'Thank you for that wonderful meal,' than it is for me to say, 'Thank you for being so understanding.' Similarly, if we've received a direct and dramatic answer to prayer, there's something about it which is easier to get hold of in praise than, for example, the omniscience of God which can appear rather vague at times.

Of course we can't separate God's deeds from his personality; his deeds are a reflection of his personality. Nevertheless, we enter much more easily into an experience of his personality through an experience of what he has done. We mustn't just stop with deeds (this is a constant temptation) but allow his deeds to show us his personality. It seems to be the case that praise for what God has done in a specific way should lead us on to what he's like in a general way. There's a lovely picture of this in Psalm 100:4. The imagery is of worshippers coming into the sanctuary and their progression is described thus:

> Enter his gates with thanksgiving
> and his courts with praise.

Actually, this is only an example of Hebrew parallelism (the way in which they wrote their poetry by saying the same thing twice), but it can be seen devotionally as a very common and regular experience for us as we worship. Thanksgiving for God's acts is the way in which we often come into the gates of the sanctuary, but with praise we enter right into his very presence. We must be sure never to stop in the gateway; appreciative though my wife is of my thanks for her cooking, housework, mending, etc, I do get the impression from time to time that she likes to be told how lovely she is as well as how useful! God is the same, and if we can never get past what he's done to arrive at who he is, there might just be something wrong with the way in which we view him.

God, then, is the centre and the beginning of the cycle, and as we begin to respond to him, we begin to worship. It needs to be said, though, that there are two routes we can take as we begin the journey. Sometimes our worship will be spontaneous. For some reason or other we'll feel particularly good about God or especially close to him, and it will be no problem at all for us to begin worshipping from the heart. We've come expectantly, almost impatiently, to worship, and we can't wait to get going. As soon as we hear the first chord or prayer, we're off, and there's no stopping us. Sometimes, however, things are not quite like that. We don't feel like it, we're not in the mood, we're too tired, we've got a headache, we're angry with God or even doubting if he's there at all, and the last thing we want to do is to make fools of ourselves with that clapping and gyrating crowd in whose presence we have for some unknown reason found ourselves. This is when we need to offer to God what has been called the 'sacrifice of praise'.

A sacrifice was something offered to God which hurt, which was costly, and which at times was no doubt a real nuisance, but which was offered because God was worth it. Mature Christians are those who have discovered the value of giving worship to God in spite of their feelings as well as because of them. We have a friend who lost a baby some years ago. This was at about the same time as the song 'Ascribe greatness to our God the rock' became popular, and it became for her an extremely meaningful song. It takes real maturity to be able to sing in worship, 'A God of faithfulness, without injustice,' under those circumstances; maturity which many of us who have not suffered so much pain find hard to achieve. But the fact is that God *is* faithful and *is* worthy to be praised, whether we happen to feel like it or not. The prophet Habakkuk, after a particularly disastrous year, said:

> Though the fig-tree does not bud
> and there are no grapes on the vines,
> though the olive crop fails
> and the fields produce no food,
> though there are no sheep in the pen
> and no cattle in the stalls,
> yet I will rejoice in the Lord,
> I will be joyful in God my Saviour
> (Hab 3:17–18)

'Hallelujah anyway', as the saying goes.

So we begin with God, and in response to him we enter into worship, whether we do so eagerly or with gritted teeth. Here my book author takes over from my conference speaker, and the cycle begins to swing into action. As we respond to God, he in turn responds to us. He reacts to our worship by coming among us. This is the real wonder and joy of worship—that we can, by our deliberate acts of will, build a throne on which the almighty God, King of glory and Lord of heaven and earth, comes and sits among us.

I am aware, of course, that to many Christians the idea of God *coming* among his people is a strange one. Isn't he already here? Since he pervades the universe with his presence, how can he come or go anywhere? And if he *comes* when we worship, does that mean he's not around the rest of the time when we're engaged in other activities like eating a Chinese takeaway, servicing the car or listening to the notices? The whole idea seems at best unusual and at worst bordering on the heretical. As is so often the case, it is actually experience rather than the Bible which leads us into new understandings of God and his ways. After we've had the experience, we go back to the Bible to find that it was there all the time.

The first time I went to a meeting held by John Wimber I was rather sceptical of the idea of God coming when invited, for reasons rather similar to those outlined above. But my theology was rather knocked on the head when God did come in a way in which I'd never experienced him before. Back to the Bible I went, to try and find out if God used to come then. I soon discovered that he did.

Many times in the Old Testament individuals or groups of people experienced the coming upon them of the Spirit of the Lord, with all sorts of interesting results. Commonly they began to prophesy, like the elders in Numbers 11:25, Balaam in Numbers 24:2, Azariah in 2 Chronicles 15:1, Jahaziel in 2 Chronicles 20:14, and Zechariah in 2 Chronicles 24:20. Slightly more unlikely people to be affected in this way are Saul in 1 Samuel 10:10, and three companies of his soldiers in 1 Samuel 19:20–21. Sometimes people were anointed for leadership by the Spirit. This happened to several of the Judges, for example, Othniel in Judges 3:10, Gideon in Judges 6:34, Jephthah in Judges 11:29 and Samson in Judges 13:25; and Kings Saul and David in 1 Samuel 11:6 and 16:13. This continued into the ministry of the prophets later on, notably Ezekiel. Clearly, there was one sense in which God was able to come upon or among people. Perhaps this was a forerunner of what we should expect in worship today, even if the occasional cutting up of oxen or dismembering of young lions which resulted then don't play a major part in modern-day Anglican liturgy. It is possible to argue, of course, that all that was in the Old Testament, but we now live in the era of the New.

No longer does the Spirit need to come upon us, because through the ministry of Jesus he is now given to live within us. What was for Othniel and his contemporaries a temporary anointing should be for us a constant reality. Dangerous though this would be for oxen and lions, there is truth in it, although my own experience tells me that I'm never too full of the Spirit to need a fresh anointing.

There is, though, in the Old Testament, another type of 'coming' by God among his people—one which is far more closely linked with worship. This is the appearance of the glory (later called the *shekinah*) of God, first on Mount Sinai, then in the desert at the Mosaic tabernacle, and later in Solomon's temple. This is a difficult concept for us to get hold of, but apparently the people would have been able to see when God was around because of what was described as a cloud, smoke or fire filling the sanctuary. It wasn't so much that God was somehow hidden in the smoke, but rather more that the smoke, like the flag flying on top of Buckingham Palace, was a sign that the King was in residence. When God came and sat enthroned between the golden cherubim on the lid of the Ark of the Covenant, the cloud of his glory would be clearly visible to the worshippers. This glory is seen in Exodus 16:10 for the first time, and manifests itself often, notably in Exodus 19:18; 40:34 and 1 Kings 8:10.

It is significant that Ezekiel, prophesying about the destruction of Jerusalem, sees in a vision the glory of the Lord leaving the Temple. It becomes a cry of the despairing psalmist, notably in Psalm 80, that God will once more shine forth from between the cherubim and come to save and restore his people. While there was in later Old Testament spirituality the clear belief that God was omnipresent, there were certainly times when it didn't *feel* as if he were there, and that he needed to be urged to 'return' (Ps 80:14), to 'come down' (Is 64:1), or even to 'remember' his people (Ps 74:2). Right at the end of the Old Testament period are some prophecies which anticipate the answer to these prayers, when Zechariah looks forward to the presence of the glory of the Lord in the New Jerusalem (Zech 2:5), and his contemporary, Haggai, speaks of a fresh coming of the Lord to his Temple, filling it with an unprecedented display of his glory, and with peace for the longing worshippers (Hag 2:6–9). In the Old Testament at least, it seemed to be the case that God could and did come among his people.

But what of the New Testament? Surely Jesus was the Person in whom God came once and for all? Surely the gift of the Holy Spirit (as we have mentioned) means that there need be no further divine comings and goings? In theory one would perhaps expect this to be true, but a closer look at the Gospels and Acts reveals the same sort of evidence as we have found already in the Old Testament. Individuals such as Jesus at his baptism and Stephen at his death were specially anointed by the spirit (Lk 3:22; Acts 7:55); he came upon groups and individuals bringing gifts including prophecy (Acts 19:6; 21:10); and there were clearly times when God was more present and active than at others, even during the ministry of Jesus himself (compare Mark 6:5 with Luke 5:17).

The primitive church clearly had both a theology and experience of God 'coming'. In Acts 4:31 the building itself shakes as God comes to equip his people in response to their prayer and in chapter 10 verse 44 God interrupts Peter's sermon by coming upon the people in Cornelius' house. This expectation continued in the church, and as liturgies began to be written down, a part known as the *epiclesis* appeared, first of all in the eucharistic prayer of Hippolytus, from the beginning of the third century. This was the 'calling down' of the Holy Spirit by the celebrant of Communion on both the elements and also the congregation. The prominence of the *epiclesis* has varied in different prayers down the centuries (it is to all intents and purposes absent from the 1662 Prayer Book, and only really hinted at in Series 2 and 3: 'as we eat and drink these holy gifts in the presence of your divine majesty') but in the Third Eucharistic Prayer of the *ASB* it is reinstated clearly and explicitly in words very similar to those of Hippolytus: 'Send the Holy Spirit on your people.' The same expectation, of God coming by his Spirit, is evident in the Anglican confirmation service where the Bishop stretches out his hands towards the candidates and prays: 'Let your Holy Spirit rest upon them.'

It is not just in the liturgical tradition that a theology of God 'coming' upon his people may be found. It is equally evident in hymnody. Even the most cursory glance through the 'Holy Spirit' section of a hymn book will prove this. Such words as 'Come, gracious Spirit, heavenly Dove', 'Come down, O Love divine', 'Descend, O heavenly Dove', 'Descend with all thy gracious powers, O come, great Spirit, come'[1] and many others, suggest that Christians down the centuries have had a theology which allows for the 'coming' of God by his Spirit. In spite of my original emotional resistance to the idea of God 'coming' on his people, all this evidence from Scripture, liturgy, hymnody and of course my own personal experience led me to the point where I couldn't help but conclude that God does come among his people at special times in a way in which he is not normally manifest, although of course he is never absent.

How are we to understand this? Clearly it is not the case that we cease to understand worship in the traditional way of God's people entering humbly into his presence since we can now summon him into ours. He is not at our beck and call. Rather, I think it is helpful to understand it in terms of invitation and enabling. God loves to be with his people; the problem is that all too often we simply don't allow him to be with us because we clutter our attention with so many other things. God is there; we just don't notice. At times he will sovereignly intervene and make his presence felt as he grabs our attention, but most often he waits to be given our attention. This is the theology behind both the evangelical 'quiet time' and much contemplative prayer; it is simply a slot of time during the day when we attempt to switch off from other concerns and give ourselves fully to God so that he may come and do something, speak to us, or whatever.

Maybe Jesus can help us to understand this more fully. In Mark's Gospel we read how Jesus goes to the synagogue and encounters a man whose hand is shrivelled up (Mk 3:1–5). Although Jesus is present in the synagogue, only later does he demand and receive the man's attention, allowing the healing to take place. In the same way God is present with us, but is not necessarily doing anything specific for us that we are aware of. Worship is a way of allowing his presence to become reality for us, simply by giving him our attention and expectancy.

Let me press the point home with one more illustration. Imagine my family seated together round the fire on a cold winter's evening. The boys are playing happily on the floor, and my wife is reading. I am just enjoying watching the scene. Suddenly one of the boys gets up and begins to walk across the room, and I can see in a split second that he is going to trip over one of the toys and may well bang his head on the fireplace. Quickly I get up and grab him, preventing the accident. Then I sit down and continue watching. Later the other, getting stuck with something he's doing, calls me over to help. I become involved in his game, and sort it out for him.

Imperfect though all our attempts to explain God are, I think this little scene illustrates well what I mean by God 'coming'. Like me, he is present and active in the scene. At times he can intervene, sometimes dramatically, without our asking (and sometimes without our knowing—how many times does he protect us from harm each day in situations where we are blissfully unaware of the danger?) but at others he waits to be invited in. He's happy to keep a fatherly eye on us, but also loves to be invited into a deeper level of involvement with us. Worship, focusing our attention on him, inviting him to 'come', enables this closer, more manifestly active presence of God by his Spirit.

With this, the worship cycle has almost gone full circle. We begin with God, and whether we like the idea or not, we begin to praise him. This produces some pleasant side-effects, which we'll look at in the next chapter, but the main thing is that he comes among us. When he comes he begins to act, and some more side-effects result. And we respond to his presence in the only way we know how: we worship. Hopefully this time it will be more out of spontaneity than sacrifice, but nevertheless, worship is the only appropriate response to the King present with his people. And so the cycle goes round again. I suppose that if I was pushed I would have to define worship simply as responding to God in order to have more of God to respond to.

This, then, is my understanding of worship, and the rest of this book will be built on it. Just one final illustration, though, gives a biblical example of exactly the same process we've been describing. In 2 Chronicles 5 Solomon has finished building the Temple in Jerusalem and is about to dedicate it. What happens is a clear working out of the main effects of the worship cycle. Let's have a look.

In chapter 5 verse 2 Solomon prepares to bring the Ark of the Covenant from David's tabernacle into the Temple. This is done with so many sacrifices 'that they could not be recorded or counted' (2 Chron 5:6) and is followed in verse 13 by choir and orchestra joining in a song of worship:

He is good;
his love endures for ever.

God responds to all this worship by coming to his Temple. In chapter 5 verse 13 the Temple is filled with a cloud of the Lord's glory of such intensity that the priests had to stop their ministry (if only that could be true for some of our ministers sometimes!). Solomon responds on behalf of the people with two long prayers which, like so many biblical prayers, are full of praise. In chapter 6 verse 4 he begins: 'Praise be to the Lord, the God of Israel, who with his hands has fulfilled what he promised with his mouth to my father David,' and the second prayer, in chapter 6 verse 14, starts on a similar note: 'O Lord, God of Israel, there is no God like you in heaven or on earth—you who keep your covenant of love with your servants.' This prayer ends with an apparently rather unnecessary invocation of God: 'Now arise, O Lord God, and come to your resting place, you and the ark of your might' (2 Chron 6:41). And once again, in response to Solomon's worship, he does just that—fire comes down from heaven and consumes all the sacrifices (2 Chron 7:1). The *shekinah* of the Lord once again fills the Temple, pushing the ministering priests out, and the people, seeing the fire and the *shekinah*, begin to worship again: 'They knelt on the pavement with their faces to the ground, and they worshipped and gave thanks to the Lord' (2 Chron 7:3). In chapter 7 verse 4 more sacrifices are organised, and so the cycle goes on.

When do we stop? I believe that's up to us. Perhaps heaven will be one long worship cycle which never ends. We may not achieve this here on earth, but there is one principle which I do think we should aim for. I owe this to Steve Gaukroger, who once gave what I think is just about the most sensible piece of advice I've ever heard for any worshipping community: always aim to begin your worship from where you usually end. You know the situation.

You stand up at the beginning of a service to lead worship; the church is cold and draughty, the people half asleep, your guitar has only five strings, of which only three are in tune, the pianist has flu and the bass player has just had a row with the churchwarden. And to make matters worse the relief PA operator is on duty, and he couldn't mix a sponge pudding, let alone your brilliant ensemble. Nevertheless, with the grace of God and several loud squeaks you get under way.

At first the whole experience feels rather like jogging through treacle, but you persevere and eventually someone in the congregation puts their hand in the air. This is all you need, and with great gusto you encourage and inspire the reluctant congregation into meaningful worship until the whole thing is actually beginning to feel OK. The singing stops for the sermon which, by some strange chance, is actually rather good and inspires people even further, so that when you come back to singing again the people almost seem keen on the idea. Off you go again, and this time it really takes off. The Lord is present, people are being touched, and there is a real sense of climax approaching as you work through a set of songs which accurately pick up from where the congregation is and lead further into the presence of God. Then, just as you are beginning to feel that you could almost reach out and touch the Lord, the service ends and everyone goes home.

Next week you come together again; this time it's you with flu and the pianist with only five strings, and the whole thing is right back to square one. If only we could pick up from where we left off last week. There's no reason why we shouldn't be able to, other than people's natural lethargy and laziness. Graham Kendrick has said that if people would only come to church as worshippers, they wouldn't need to be 'bump started' by the worship leader. What precious time we waste in the presence of God simply by our lack of commitment to worship. It should always be our aim to begin from the point where we left off last time. If we did that every week, there's no telling where we might end up.

Notes

1 Hymns 232, 235, 237 and 239 in *Ancient and Modern Revised*.

CHAPTER TWO

WHAT IS WORSHIP ANYWAY?

II. The Worship Cycle—Side-effects

IN THE LAST CHAPTER we looked at the Worship Cycle and saw that the main effect of our worshipping God is that he comes among us. In this chapter I want to look at some of the side-effects that take place when he does so. It's obviously important that we don't confuse the two, since an over-enthusiastic seeking after dramatic side-effects could divert us from our main purpose of seeking the face of the Lord. Nevertheless, they will happen, so we need to know what they are, understand them, and make sure we don't stop with them but move on round the cycle. I want to deal with them in two different sections: the side-effects of our worshipping God, and the side-effects of his coming among us. The diagram overleaf summarises this.

The side-effects of our worship, of course, we're all familiar with. The first is that we begin to enjoy ourselves. As we move into an awareness of God, even the most hard-hearted of us start to feel joy and excitement. Cobwebs are blown away from our minds, peace begins to fill us, and even when there is conviction of sin we can move easily into confession and the receiving of forgiveness, which in turn brings a renewed relationship with and closeness to

THE WORSHIP CYCLE

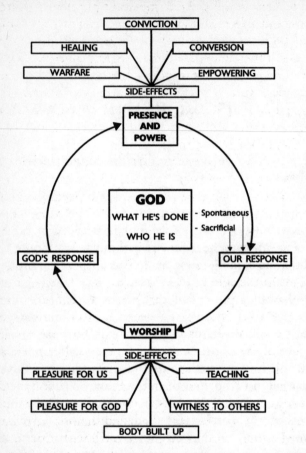

God. When worship is happening effectively, it takes a great amount of determination to stay outside. You have to be really angry or fed up not to get swept along in the flow.

Even more important than the enjoyment we receive from worship is the enjoyment God receives. To worship him is to bless him, to give pleasure to him. It's difficult to understand, from our human point of view, how a God who is unchangeable can be made more happy by our praises, but nevertheless it's true, and as we worship we need to bear in mind the tremendous privilege involved— that we can affect the way God feels. An illustration of this might be the way I feel when my boys tell me that they love me: if they understood the delight it gives me, I'm sure they'd do it much more often. For this reason alone we must make sure that we always offer our very best and highest to God. We're not involved in a dress-rehearsal where anything will do; we have a real live audience, and the King of kings is in the royal box.

So far we've only mentioned the individual dimension, but there is a corporate one too. In worship the whole body of believers is renewed, a sense of meeting with God together is achieved, and sometimes relationships are healed or strengthened. If the worship gets to the point where the congregation hears God's prophetic voice, there is much upbuilding as the body listens and responds. One of the charismatic movement's greatest strengths is the flesh that it has put on the bare bones of the doctrine of the body of Christ. No longer is worship a solitary experience, or the Lord's Table a table for two, as has so often been the case in the past. Now the whole thing is a family affair, as the whole body meets together with the Head.

Neither are the benefits of worship limited to those within that body. Any non-Christians who may find themselves among worshipping believers cannot help but be affected as they witness people in touch with God in a way which is probably totally new to them. One of the most frequent comments from newcomers to our church is that they have been deeply moved, or 'knocked out' (some of them literally) by the atmosphere of worship. Only the other week a visitor on her first trip to church experienced our worship and enthused after the service, 'This really means something to you lot. When can I come again?' Many have joined the church and the kingdom of

God because, like the outsider of 1 Corinthians 14:25, they sense that God is really among us.

Worship does not just affect us on the emotional level, though; it is also a tremendous method of teaching and learning. As we proclaim the timeless truths about our God, they have a habit of getting inside us and becoming a part of the whole way in which we function. Charles Wesley, arguably the greatest hymn-writer of all time, wrote his six hundred or so hymns around the time of the Methodist revival mainly as teaching vehicles, since he realised that most people learned their doctrine through what they expressed in song rather than what they heard in sermons. The same is very likely true today, and there is great potential for people to become firmly grounded in the truth if they are encouraged to worship with an articulation of that truth. This again emphasises the importance of liturgy as well as of hymnody. Words which we repeat regularly and become a part of our very being can plant truth in our lives in a very deep way; liturgical texts as well as hymns and songs are designed to do just that. Even those who, because of age (old or young), illness or handicap, find the logical processing of doctrine difficult can enter into and remember truth through the liturgical use of words and music. And, of course, the same is true for those as yet outside the kingdom. Much truth can be communicated and taken on board through the words which are sung.

So, good things happen when we worship. God enjoys it, we are drawn into the joy and peace of his Spirit and into renewed relationship with him, both individually and corporately, and those outside that relationship begin to get a glimpse of what it is that they are missing. Truth is proclaimed and learned and, most important of all, God comes to be present with his people.

His presence is the thing we desire most of all, of course,

but when he comes God begins to act among his people, and we experience another set of side-effects. I want to look at these in more detail than the first set, since they are less easily understood and, I regret to say, more rarely actually experienced. However, my conviction is that since God is God, he is likely to do the same sort of things whenever he comes. In other words, we ought to expect similar things to happen as happened when he came among us once before in his Son Jesus. In my experience this is true. So far I've classified five of them, but that's not to say that there might not be more.

1. Warfare

I can't claim to understand this fully, but I believe that when we worship in spirit and in truth we engage in spiritual warfare with Satan and his minions. It's certainly true on an individual level that people in some way affected by demonic forces are often brought to the point of release during worship. It's not an uncommon experience during a worship time suddenly to hear screams and shrieks from someone in the congregation, even when I'm not singing at that point, as a demon is forced to manifest itself. I think the example of the demonised man in Mark 1:21 ff illustrates this well. The *Good News Bible* translates verse 23 as meaning that the man 'came into the Synagogue', leaving one with the impression that he was some weirdo who simply happened to wander in off the street. However, there's nothing in the Greek to suggest that this is true. It's far more likely that he was already in there, an ordinary member of the congregation quite unaware of any problem—until Jesus arrives. He may even have been a synagogue-warden, if they had them then. Probably no one was more surprised than he was at his outburst. It wasn't as if he did it a lot. But when Jesus came into town, all sorts of hidden darkness was revealed and forced to manifest itself. The same happens in worship nowadays from time to time, and the common factor in both cases is simply that God is present in a way different from usual.

But I believe that there is more to worship than warfare against demonic forces which influence individuals. There is power in worship which works on a larger scale against the enemies of God in the spiritual realm. When we declare God's praises in worship, we are witnessing to the principalities and powers which affect various areas and realms of society that they are defeated, that their power is cut off, and that before the name of Jesus whom we worship and who is in fact enthroned on our praises and present with us, they must fall in cringing terror. This is the theology behind 'Praise Marches', like Graham Kendrick's *Make Way*, where the church invades areas where Satan has much authority and proclaims his defeat in worship to Jesus. There is an often-preached passage in 2 Chronicles 20 where a similar thing happens. King Jehoshaphat, faced with rather a difficult battle, decides to send out a group of singers before the troops to worship the Lord. The Hebrew here can mean that the singers were 'in splendid array'—perhaps they were the robed cathedral choir. Far be it from me to suggest that this is a scriptural warrant for dealing drastically with recalcitrant church choirs; in any case it didn't do the King any good because during the worship God came and finished off the enemy. No more Ammonites and Moabites, but he still had the choir!

In worship, therefore, we have a powerful weapon against the Enemy which can break down his strongholds in the lives of individuals and break his grip over whole areas, both geographical and social. As we declare the truth in worship, and focus on Jesus and his victory, God comes among us and uses that truth to bring victory and to set free those who are in the grip of evil.

There is a danger in this, of course, as there is in all warfare. I mean the danger of giving the Enemy too much attention so that he becomes more the focus of our worship than Jesus. Again, truth can help us. Orthodox Christianity has rejected the belief, known as 'dualism', that there are two equal and opposite gods, one good and one bad. Satan is a created being, and although he has superior intelligence to us, he is well and truly under the feet of God, and was so even before his decisive defeat by Jesus on the cross. He has a place in our worship, of course, since he is always there trying to pervert and spoil it, and we need to be aware of that and resist it, but he should never be the focus of our worship, and we should never take our attention off Jesus and give it to him. Warfare can be a by-product of our worship, and we can design a worship service to include warfare specifically, but it should never become an end in itself. We gain victory by keeping our eyes on the Victor and on him alone.

Again, liturgy has its place here. When at times Christians need to move in and minister directly to people or places under the influence of the demonic, worship is a prime weapon. Many old rites of exorcism exist in the liturgical tradition, especially the Roman Catholic, and the Eucharist is often central. This most dramatic proclamation of Christ's death, resurrection and victory seems through the ages to have been experienced as a powerful force in deliverance, and while at times there has certainly been superstition which looks almost demonic itself, there has often been freedom and release as Jesus is worshipped in the Communion. Even modern charismatic writers agree that the Eucharist is appropriate in deliverance ministry, especially that associated with buildings or places.[1]

Dualism is a danger we must avoid, but so is the far more common heresy that the Devil does not exist at all. For every demons-behind-every-bush charismatic there are probably several demons-are-really-your-subconscious liberals. To walk the tightrope of right belief, right living and right worship is difficult, but the surest way of doing it without falling off altogether is to keep your eyes on Jesus.

2. Healing

The second side-effect is that people are healed both physically and emotionally during worship. Healing formed a major part of the agenda of Jesus when he was physically on earth, and he loves to do the same today when he comes. I must admit that in my own experience this is nowhere near as common as I would like it to be, but I have known times when people have been spontaneously healed by the Lord while worshipping him. And on many other occasions the Spirit has come to rest upon individuals during worship so that those experienced in ministry can recognise God's touch on them and begin to pray for them. People may be touched on an emotional level too during worship, and receive some kind of healing or refreshment, or release from past hurts which are troubling them unconsciously.

3. Conviction

Jesus promised that the Holy Spirit, when he came, would convict of sin (Jn 16:8). He still does the same today, and it is during the course of worship that he does it most frequently and most strongly. In a sense that is only to be expected, since a glimpse of the living God in all his holiness and glory is bound to make us feel a little diffident about our own achievements in the sphere of righteousness. Isaiah found this to be true when he saw his vision of God (Is 6). The more the cherubim declared him to be holy, the more Isaiah was made aware of his own profound uncleanness and that of the people with whom he shared his humanity. It was only the Lord, and that on his own initiative, who could deal with this state of terminal unrighteousness. So as we worship today, and let God in close enough, as it were, to see the really mucky areas of our lives, he brings with him both the uncomfortable ability to spotlight just what it was that we were hoping to hide from him, and very often from ourselves, and the wonderful gift of free forgiveness through his Son's blood shed on the cross. In true worship we have no secrets from God; we withhold from him no area of our lives, however reluctantly we open up, and he withholds from us no measure of his cleansing and forgiving love.

4. Conversion

When the process described above takes place in the life of a Christian, it is like a cleaning out of the spiritual system, and is usually quite undramatic; a transaction that goes on in the mind and heart between the individual and God. At times, of course, quite a struggle may go on, for example if there is an area of sin which is quite deeply ingrained and over which the person has been arguing with God and their conscience for some time, but normally this is a fairly routine matter, not unlike the daily confession of sins secretly to God in prayer. But when non-believers find themselves under the same conviction, conversion is usually the result. This is the way in which the revivals of the past have worked; God seems suddenly to come upon an area and begins to break people's hearts wide open; first the believers, causing them to repent of backsliding and spiritual lethargy, and then on the community in general. My favourite account of this phenomenon concerns the Hebridean revival of 1949. Duncan Campbell of the Faith

Mission went to preach in the town of Barvas, near Stornoway. After the service, about thirty or so people went to a
nearby cottage to pray:

'God was beginning to move, the heavens were opening, we
were there on our faces before God. Three o'clock in the
morning came, and GOD SWEPT IN. About a dozen men
and women lay prostrate on the floor, speechless. Something
had happened; we knew that the forces of darkness were going
to be driven back, and men were going to be delivered. We left
the cottage at 3 a.m. to discover men and women seeking God.
I walked along a country road, and found three men on their
faces, crying to God for mercy. There was a light in every
home, no-one seemed to think of sleep.'

When Duncan and his friends gathered at the church later in
the morning, the place was crowded. A stream of buses came
from every part of the island, yet no-one could discover who
had told them to come. A butcher in his van had brought seven
men from a distance of seventeen miles: all seven were
gloriously converted. Now the revival was really under way.
The Spirit of God was at work. All over the church men and
women were crying for mercy. Some fell into a trance, some
swooned, many wept.

Campbell pronounced the benediction and almost all left
the chapel. Suddenly a young man began to pray. He was so
burdened for the souls of his friends that he prayed for almost
three-quarters of an hour. During this time the people
returned to the church, joined by many others, until there
were twice as many outside as inside. In some amazing way
the people gathered from Stornoway, and Ness and different
parishes. It was 4 a.m. the following morning before Duncan
pronounced the benediction for a second time.

Even then he was still unable to go home to bed. As he was
leaving the church a messenger told him, 'Mr. Campbell,
people are gathered at the police station, from the other end of
the parish; they are in great spiritual distress. Can anyone here
come along and pray with them?' Campbell went and what a
sight met him. Under the still starlit sky he found men and

women on the road, others by the side of a cottage, and some behind a peat stack—all crying to God for mercy. The revival had come.

That went on for five weeks with services from early morning until late at night—or into the early hours of the morning. Then it spread to the neighbouring parishes. What had happened in Barvas was repeated over and over again.[2]

Conversion, as well as the dramatic conviction of lukewarm believers, seems to have been a major hallmark of John Wesley's ministry in eighteenth-century Britain. In his *Journal* are many accounts of the direct action of the Spirit during services of worship and preaching. In July 1762 he received this letter from Ireland, where he had recently been preaching.

There is a glorious work going on at Limerick. Twelve or fourteen have a clear sense of being renewed; several have been justified this week; and on Sunday night there was such a cry as I scarce ever heard before, such confession of sins, such pleading with the Lord, and such a spirit of prayer as if the Lord himself had been visibly present among us. Some received remission of sins, and several were just brought to the birth. All were in floods of tears; they trembled, they cried, they prayed, they roared aloud, all of them lying on the ground. I began to sing, yet they could not rise, but sang as they lay along. Some of them stayed in the house all night; and, blessed be our God, they all hitherto walk worthy of their calling.[3]

Ten years later, in June 1772, the same phenomena were still continuing under Wesley's ministry, although he does seem to have had a knack of missing the best bits himself. Another letter describes a memorable evening in Weardale just after he had left for Sunderland:

On Saturday evening God was present through the whole

service, but especially toward the conclusion. Then one and another dropped down, till six lay on the ground together roaring for the disquietude of their hearts. Observing many to be quite amazed at this, I besought them to stand still and see the salvation of God, but the cry of the distressed soon drowned my voice. So I dismissed the congregation. About half of them went away. I continued praying with the rest when my voice could be heard; when it could not I prayed without a voice, till after ten o'clock. In this time, four of those poor mourners were clothed with the robes of praise.[4]

However, Wesley was to have some fun of his own the next night in Sunderland:

In the evening we mightily wrestled with God for an enlargement of his work. As we were concluding, an eminent backslider came strongly into my mind; and I broke out abruptly, 'Lord, is Saul also among the prophets? Is James Watson here? If he be, show thy power!' Down dropped James Watson like a stone, and began crying aloud for mercy.[5]

This process is not, however, limited to times past. Although we still await revival of that sort in our day in England, we are beginning to see glimpses of such phenomena. The American pastor John Wimber and his team from the Vineyard Church in California have held conferences throughout Britain, introducing the concept of 'power evangelism', where people are convicted and brought to faith by the direct working of the Spirit in some supernatural way, rather than by becoming convinced of the truth of the gospel by intellectual argument. Often this takes place in the context of worship, where people sense the presence of something the like of which they've never come across before, and also sense a change in themselves while being totally unable to articulate in precise terms exactly what has happened. Obviously there is then the need to explain the theology and to see if they still like it, but generally most people do!

A young couple turned up out of the blue to a church service in which I was involved. They weren't church-goers, but had been to a funeral during the week where the song 'Majesty' had been used, and something had got to them in such a way that they felt the need to pay a proper visit to church. I chatted briefly to them after the service, and thought nothing more of it until 11.30 the same evening when there was a knock on the door and I found the two of them on the doorstep in a state of great agitation. They had been fine, if slightly bored, in the service until we got to the point where we began to sing (it had not been that stunning a worship time, by my estimation) when the pair of them began, without any warning at all, to shake and quiver. The service eventually ended, but the shaking, unfortunately, did not. They had headed for the nearest pub, thinking that a couple of drinks would straighten them out, but they only ended up sitting in a pool of slopped beer. Eventually, still wobbling, they had come in desperation to see me.

'What's happening to us?' they wanted to know. I quickly and simply explained that God was touching them, that he had a claim on their live 0 which they needed to respond and that they could do so now. We went through *Journey into Life* together, and they went on their way rejoicing but no longer vibrating. Such spontaneous conversions, or 'kingdom births' will, I believe, become more and more common as the church increasingly rediscovers the power of the present Christ in worship. Obviously it doesn't do away with the need for personal evangelism and witness, nor does it undermine the importance of being able to give a good intellectual account of what and why we believe, but it certainly does make the task of evangelism easier.

It needs to be said, of course, that not every strange manifestation which may take place during worship is to be welcomed as a manifestation of the Holy Spirit. The Bible is clear on the need to test the spirits and to discern the

difference between divine, human and demonic manifestations. I'll say more about this later, but one of the most
important tests involves looking for the fruit which is
produced. It appears that churches which go in for 'power
evangelism' seem to have a pretty good record in this area.
If God genuinely chooses to bring people into the kingdom
in ways which seem strange, we would do well to get used
to it.

5. Empowering

As it is the work of the Spirit to convict us of sin, so also it
is his task to empower us for service. Worship is an ideal
context for this to happen, as we open ourselves up to God
for a fresh vision of his glory and offer ourselves once again
in love and service to him. Many people experience the
filling or baptism of the Spirit for the first time during
worship, and especially during times of singing in tongues;
others simply receive a new influx of power or boldness, or
a fresh vision of some area of ministry.

Returning to Isaiah's vision (Is 6), we can see that after
receiving cleansing from God he was then equipped by
being given the prophetic task and message. As we worship, we can expect to be given a fresh anointing for whatever it is that God has for us to do in his kingdom. Very
often this will come through the prophetic word as messages are given which not only call the church but which
also empower it to obey the calling. That is why spiritual
gifts play such an important part in worship.

These, then, are some of the side-effects of God's coming among his people as they worship. The sort of things
that Jesus and his Spirit love to do, they love to do especially when they come among us during worship. I'm not
saying that all this happens every time we worship—it
certainly doesn't when I'm leading—but we should expect

some of it to happen some of the time, and we should expect it to increase as we grow in our ability to worship in Spirit and in truth. It's very exciting indeed to be involved in a worship time when the Spirit really begins to move, and people all around are being touched in all sorts of ways. But we must never forget that these manifestations of the presence of God are only side-effects, marvellous though they are. The real point is that God himself is among us. That ought to be enough, though it is in the nature of God to do things for us and to us whenever he can get close enough. But if nothing at all happened, it would still be sufficient that the living God, Maker of heaven and earth, had come for a while to be enthroned on the praises of his people.

Notes

1. For example, Michael Green, *I Believe in Satan's Downfall* (Hodder and Stoughton: London, 1981), p142.
2. Colin Whittaker, *Great Revivals* (Marshall, Morgan and Scott: Basingstoke, 1984), p159ff.
3. John Wesley, *The Works of John Wesley*, Vol 3 (Zondervan: Grand Rapids, MI, 1958–9), p106.
4. *Ibid*, p470.
5. *Ibid*, p473.

CHAPTER THREE

TYPES OF WORSHIP

I N LOOKING AT THE Worship Cycle, we've said that the main effect of worship is to respond to God in order to have more of him to respond to. I want to go on further, though, and explore the different ways in which we do this. While this may be the aim of all our worship, we will have experienced times of worship which have felt very different from others. Sometimes the mood is one of gentle adoration, when we are content to gaze into the face of Jesus and offer him our love. At others we feel more like exuberant dancing, clapping and shouting. At other times again we may feel ourselves getting angry in worship as we think about the Enemy and some particular piece of havoc he has caused, while sometimes our overwhelming feeling is one of sorrow and penitence for our sins. I find it helpful in leading worship to try and identify these and other different moods, and to go with them. If we understand where the congregation is at and where the Spirit is wanting to take them, we can actually help this process by the sorts of songs we choose and the ways in which we treat those songs. Also we can let our spoken contributions reinforce this direction. I have identified five of these different moods. There may be more, but I find these useful as a general guide.

1. Adoration and love

This is perhaps the most intimate expression of worship. We simply stand before God, look him straight in the eye, and tell him that we love him. As with two human beings who are in love, it is an emotional rather than a rational experience. Although theological verbalisation is at a minimum, and in one sense it is a whispering of 'sweet nothings' in God's ear, our profound love for him is far from being a 'nothing'. Rather, adoration is the highest point of that relationship with God which gives all theology its meaning, although it is beyond theological expression. This kind of worship is commanded by God: 'Love the Lord your God with all your heart and with all your soul and with all your strength' (Deut 6:4–5), celebrated throughout the Song of Songs (although we mustn't spiritualise the primary meaning of this book, a celebration of human erotic love), and enjoyed by several of the psalmists, for example in Psalms 18:1; 42:1–2; 73:25; 84:2 and 116:1.

Whether we reach it during a quiet part of the worship, in a moment of profound stillness during silent contemplation, or at a climactic point in a service such as the *Sanctus* or the moment of receiving Communion, this most intimate place really is the 'Holy of Holies' where we meet God in a depth of relationship quite out of the ordinary. We may meet God in quiet intimacy, such as that reflected by Simeon in the *Nunc Dimittis*, or in awe and reverance, as Isaiah did in the Temple (Is 6) or in a mixture of both, as expressed by Mary in the *Magnificat*.

Similarly, the sort of music which is appropriate here can be soft and gentle, or occasionally strong and majestic, and songs which express this type of love might include 'I love you, Lord, and I lift my voice', 'Lord, you are so precious to me', and, in a slightly more majestic mood, 'God of glory we exalt your name' or 'For thou O Lord art high above all the earth'. Hymns are slightly less helpful for this mood of worship, because they tend to be too wordy and theologically complex, but some contenders might be 'Just as I am without one plea', 'O love that wilt not let me go' or 'King of glory, King of peace'. While simplicity in surroundings may help some to be drawn into greater intimacy with God, a sense of awe and reverence can be heightened by rich banners and vestments, incense and dramatic ceremonial. Worship seldom begins with this experience of love, but it should often arrive at this place.

2. Celebration and joy

This is a slightly less profound but much more exuberant form of worship. Their traditional reserve makes this type of worship slightly more difficult for Anglicans, but house-church people love it. Leaping, clapping, dancing and shouting before God—everyone has a really good time enjoying themselves, enjoying God and letting him enjoy them. There need be nothing irreverent about this type of worship; I believe God loves seeing his children having a good time just as much as I do mine. The impression one gets of God's people in the Old Testament is that they frequently indulged in such exuberant worship. When they brought the Ark to Jerusalem, David and the whole house of Israel celebrated 'with all their might before the Lord', with singing and all sorts of musical instruments (2 Sam 6:5), and after the return from the exile in Babylon, the restored community had such a good time of worship at the dedication ceremony for the walls of Jerusalem that 'the sound of rejoicing. . .could be heard far away' (Neh 12:27–43).

Note that here, as in many other places in the Old Testament, free, exuberant worship does not exclude careful planning, preparation, direction and liturgy, but happens within a structured context (all is not lost for Anglicans after all!). Many of the Psalms seem to reflect this type of worship, especially the 'Hallelujah' Psalms, (Ps 146–150), as do some of the canticles used in liturgical worship, for example, the *Venite, Te Deum*, 'Song of Creation' and 'Great and Wonderful'. In the Eucharist we celebrate with the offertory sentence 'Yours Lord is the greatness', and many hymns and songs such as 'And can it be', 'Hail thee festival day', 'To God be the glory', 'In the presence of your people', 'You shall go out with joy', 'Hosanna' and 'Be bold' would fit here. Congregations love the many Israeli-type songs which the resourceful worship group can play at ever-increasing speeds until even the most self-conscious worshipper can be seen going up and down on the spot, even if it is the floor-boards rather than he himself doing the propelling. Major festivals lend themselves to celebration, and flowers, banners, dance and an unrestrained dose of the 'Peace' can add to the mood.

3. Proclamation and witness

We have said that worship can have an effect on those outside the kingdom; we can design it specifically for that purpose, as well as for urging on reluctant believers into the presence of the Lord. Many songs announce the character and deeds of God, not just so that we can celebrate them but in order to draw others into an awareness of him. Sometimes we address God directly, so that others are somehow caught up in our worship. 'God of glory' would be a good example of this type of song, and 'Praise my soul the King of heaven' has the same mood. In other songs the words may express our corporate response to God, as in

'O Lord our God, how majestic is your Name' and its chorus 'We will magnify the Lord enthroned in Zion'. The creeds and the acclamations fulfil the same function liturgically. Sometimes our words are addressed directly to the outsiders, as we challenge them to see our God being worshipped and to join in. 'Make way!' would be a good example of this, especially the final verse:

> We call you now to worship him
> As Lord of all,
> To have no gods before him
> Their thrones must fall.

Make Way, by Graham Kendrick. Copyright © 1986 Make Way Music, administered by Thankyou Music, PO Box 75, Eastbourne, E. Sussex BN23 6NW. Used by permission.

Most of the *Make Way!* songs fall into this category. Old Testament passages like 1 Chronicles 29:10–20, where David praises the Lord for his provision for the building of the Temple, provide good examples of drawing others into worship, as do many of the Psalms, notably Psalms 95–100, three of which have found their way into Anglican liturgical worship as the *Venite* (Ps 95), the *Cantate Domino* (Ps 98) and the *Jubilate* (Ps 100). Revelation 19:1–9 provides a New Testament example of the saints and angels in heaven being drawn into the worship of God and the Lamb. Many of the evangelical mission hymns attempt to speak to outsiders. Examples might be 'We have heard a joyful sound' and 'Blessed assurance, Jesus is mine'. Any activity which gets the church out of its buildings can speak loudly and clearly to the world, whether it is a *Make Way!* praise march, a Palm Sunday perambulation round the church, or a Good Friday united procession of witness.

4. Declaration and warfare

Sometimes we may feel in worship that instead of pro-
claiming to people we have moved into declaration to the
Enemy. My dictionary didn't help me much with the difference between these two concepts: 'to proclaim' means
'to declare. . .' and 'to declare' means 'to proclaim. . .'. But
I certainly know what it feels like when I'm worshipping.
Sometimes when we approach God in worship it's as if he
invites us to come and stand where he stands, and then
shows us the world or different situations through his eyes,
as he sees them. This can often fill one not just with
heartfelt compassion, but also with a real sense of outrage
and righteous indignation. If you've never had this experience, pray for it.

I believe it's right from time to time to share our Father's
anger at the destruction and havoc wrought on his world
by the Enemy. The word 'rebuke', used throughout the
Gospels for Jesus' reaction to sickness, evil spirits, storms
and so on, reflects this sense of anger at the trouble caused
by Satan. We too must know this sort of sanctified anger,
and be able to express it and minister to others through it.

I remember on one occasion being asked to pray for a
sick baby. I went in with all the right prayers in mind, but
when I saw the poor little thing lying there, so small and
helpless, I was filled with a sudden rush of anger at the
Enemy who isn't content to harm and harass adults, but
enjoys attacking helpless children too. Before I had time to
think about what to pray, I found myself shouting out,
'Satan you. . .'. Now, that's not the way I pray normally,
and there's obviously a lot more to spiritual warfare than
name-calling, but I believe that on that occasion the Spirit
within me expressed something very close to the heart of
the Father, even if I vocalised it with rather unregenerate
terminology. It is the owning of that sense of anger which
I'm advocating, not the expression of it. We have already

mentioned 2 Chronicles 20 and the worship expressed in defiance of the enemy. Other examples might be found in Psalms 66:1–4 and 68, and Revelation 11:15–19. We've mentioned, too, the need to be careful so that we don't overstep the mark and become obsessed with the Enemy when we should be concentrating on God. Like the Archangel Michael in Jude 9, we mustn't take it on ourselves to enter single-handedly into battle against Satan. It seems to me that in the Bible it is the Lord who rebukes Satan, although believers can and should be involved in the rebuking and expulsing of lesser demons who are affecting people and places. But the sense of anger and outrage which calls on Jesus himself to march out against evil is something which we can bring to our worship, and which has a rightful place there.

My favourite song along these lines is 'For this purpose', but others might include 'Victory is on our lips and in our lives' and 'Let God arise and let his enemies be scattered'. Many older hymns, too, express this idea of warfare, although often in more indirect language, urging God's people on into battle. 'Onward Christian Soldiers', 'Stand up, stand up for Jesus' and 'Soldiers of Christ arise' would be good examples. This type of worship should not be the major ingredient in our services, but it should sometimes be there if we are to reflect a balanced view of what is dear to our Father's heart.

5. Intercession and penitence

When I first put together material on different types of worship, I stopped at the four types we've dealt with so far. I'd interceded, of course, and I'd even been penitent on occasions, but none of it really felt like worship. But now I'm becoming more and more convinced that these things have a place in our worship, and indeed will become increasingly important as we move on in time. One of the most powerful songs for me, and one of the few which I believe will stand the test of time and still be powerful many years from now, is 'Restore, O Lord, the honour of your name'.

There was a time in charismatic circles when this was just about the only song of its kind, calling on God for a fresh dose of his renewing and reviving power not just for the church but also for the world. But now I detect a trend in contemporary songwriting towards much more of this kind of material, and along with it an emphasis on our own crying out to God for mercy. I remember in my first parish, a rather Anglo-Catholic one where we used to follow strictly the church's liturgical calendar (a practice from which many other parishes could benefit greatly), remarking to a friend while trying to choose music for services during Lent, 'When is someone going to start writing some *miserable* charismatic songs?' Heartfelt penitence is, of course, far from a miserable experience, but the element of sorrow for sin seems to have been missing in much charismatic worship. I see it as a real sign of the maturity of renewal that we have at last come to the place where our intimate celebration of the glory of God has brought us to the point of needing to say, 'Woe is me!'

Several Psalms reflect this dual emphasis of a cry for mercy for the individual or community along with a pleading for the restoration of God's power among the people in general, notably Psalms 51, 57 and 60, while other prayers of profound penitence on the part of God's people are found in Ezra 9–10, Nehemiah 9 and Daniel 9. In each case there is a link between the people's sin and the lack of spiritual power which they have to ward off enemy attacks of one sort or another. Apart from 'Restore, O Lord', other songs and hymns which reflect this theme are 'O Lord have mercy on me, and heal me', 'We are your people', 'Lord, have mercy on us', 'O Lord, the clouds are gathering', 'O breath of life come sweeping through us' and 'Thy hand, O God, has guided'.

The church's year provides for two particular seasons of penitence, Lent and Advent, and there is much liturgy, hymnody and traditional ceremonial, which expresses the theme effectively. This material need not be used only during those times, however, but is useful whenever the Lord seems to be putting penitence on the agenda. The key verse for this whole emphasis in worship would be 2 Chronicles 7:14—'If my people, who are called by my name, will humble themselves and pray and seek my face and turn from their wicked ways, then will I hear from heaven and will forgive their sin and will heal their land.' Praise the Lord that at last his church seems to be moving into such repentance, because apart from the fact that repentance is generally healthy, revival has never started without such prayer and penitence. We may still be some way from revival, but if we continue to make repentance an important part of our worship, we may one day witness scenes like the one in Barvas described in Chapter 2 in the streets of our own towns and cities.

I wouldn't like to say that every last song or aspect of worship will fit neatly into one of these five categories. I may well discover a few more as time goes by, but this is where I am for now. I find this sort of classification helpful as a guide to understanding what's going on in a worship time, and in planning for worship. It helps you to decide prayerfully where the worship might go and how it might move through different types. Of course, you would be very unlikely to include all five types in one time of worship, but you would probably want to move through two or three. You might begin with celebration and move in closer to God in adoration, or you might progress from intercession to warfare and on to a celebration of the

Lord's victory. But understanding it first of all in broad outline will help you to avoid some of the directionless worship times which result when there is no clear purpose or progression. It may be useful for you to put together a list of songs in your church's repertoire, classified under these headings, and then maybe subdivide them further. I'll say more in greater detail later about putting together a worship time, but I find these categories helpful as a basic framework.

As well as knowing about different types of worship, it is helpful to recognise the different contexts in which we worship. They have to do simply with the number of worshippers involved, and the different dynamics which those numbers imply. I have called these three different sized groupings in church life celebration, congregation and cell. These correspond fairly closely to what sociologists would call tertiary, secondary and primary groups. These groups are differentiated largely on the basis of the types of relationships which people can have with others in the group. What might worship in these three groups look like, and how might it differ between the three? And finally, what are the particular problems and joys of worshipping alone?

Celebration

This is a gathering of 250 or more people, in fact the more the merrier, and the main characteristic of it is that there is very little relationship between people who are present. Some, of course, will have close friends there, and will have nodding acquaintanceship with others, but there will be many who are totally unknown. You simply cannot know all the other 11,000 people in the main arena at the National Exhibition Centre in Birmingham who have come for a *Make Way!* launch, or your thousands of fellow-pilgrims at the Walsingham Shrine. Yet you are still a group, because you are there for a common purpose. So how would such a group worship?

The emphasis, as you might expect, is often on jubilant praise—celebration, in fact. The dynamics of the meeting mean that it is very difficult for people to contribute much from the floor, partly because it requires a very high degree of courage to do something in front of that many people, and partly because even if you do, only a few of them will actually hear what you've said. Therefore the lead comes very heavily from the front, with little expectation of other contributions, although hopefully not a total ban on them. The larger the meeting, the more you can spend time simply singing to the Lord, one song after another, without the need for lots of interruptions from the leader.

It is important that the musicians give a good lead and that the volume of sound produced should be adequate, since 250 people will produce quite a volume themselves. They mustn't drown out the musicians, or the result will be anarchy. Celebrations are one of the most exciting situations in which to worship, but they do have limitations. The exuberant mood, the sense of occasion and the general atmosphere can make it difficult to sustain quieter adoration worship, and people will try to take off again into celebration given half a chance. Unless people know they're there specifically for a silent vigil or something similar, you may have trouble holding them down. Just like any human celebration, worship celebrations are an unreal context since they provide only one aspect of reality, whereas we need to experience a balance. Like good parties, they may be thoroughly enjoyable, but to live there would be another matter entirely.

Congregation

This provides the more usual weekly worship context,

where a group of 20 to 200, or, more commonly, 50 to 150 meet together. It is possible in a group of this size to know at least the faces of everyone present, and to know a high proportion of people to some degree of depth. So the whole thing is immediately much more intimate than the celebration. There is more space for people to feel involved and much more security in contributing, which means that the worship leader and group can afford to take a more low-key approach. The full variety of worship moods can be experienced here, and the people can be steered fairly easily from one to another. What it lacks in terms of the sheer exhilaration of being in a much larger group, it makes up for in terms of intimacy and flexibility. You cannot sustain so much continual music, but instead you can find lots of other ways of expressing worship and of listening to the Lord.

Cell

This is a group of less than twenty people, but often between six and fifteen, or about the size of the average house group or fellowship group. Here it is possible to be on close and even intimate terms with everyone present, and to have shared yourself deeply with the whole group. This is the context in which people are on one level most secure, and yet at the same time most vulnerable. It is a well-known fact that this is the most difficult place for worship, and certainly the most difficult context for the worship leader. People expect the fellowship group's worship to be at least a bit like the Sunday evening service when there were perhaps one or two hundred people present, and every week it is a tremendous disappointment as the seven of them croak and groan their way through 'Rejoice! Rejoice!' accompanied by a mouth organ and an inaudible five-string guitar. Somehow it just isn't the same as that last John Wimber conference. So they either give up altogether and move guiltily into praying instead, or bash on because they ought to, and breathe a sigh of relief when it's time for 'sharing' or whatever comes next.

Worship can be led successfully in very small groups, but it is not at all easy. First of all, the leader needs confidence in the singing and playing of the musicians. There will often be only one guitar and a flute or similar instrument, so it is important that a good clear lead is given. The louder the sound coming from the leader(s), the louder individuals in the group can sing without feeling that they can be heard by everyone else. The leader should also have done some work on planning the worship time since, as I shall say later, the so-called 'spontaneous' approach to worship almost always ends in disaster. However, he should not have everything sewn up and lead as if he were in a celebration. Songs should be chosen with care. Half a dozen people cannot really sing 'Shine, Jesus, shine' all that convincingly, and two-part songs such as 'For this purpose', 'May the fragrance of Jesus' and many of the Vineyard songs are unsuitable if you have nine people, only one of whom is male.

Whether your small group is primarily designed for prayer, intercession, Bible study or meditation, or perhaps an informal celebration of the Eucharist, the whole approach will be very different from the celebration or congregation. Singing takes on a much less prominent role, and spoken contributions and even silence play a more important part. The role of the leader is much more to facilitate the worship of the people, to make space for them and to gather together all that happens, drawing out from it what God is saying and doing among the group. And yet there can also be great similarities: worship, whether spoken, sung or silent can still flow in a small group, without the need for a stop-start style which simply announces each song in turn or leaves embarrassing gaps when no one is quite sure what is going on. The musician(s) can carry on playing between the items, and either lead into the next song or even allow space for a voice-over. In this respect worship in the cell need not be too different from that in a much larger group.

Generally speaking, the larger the group, the easier it feels to lead worship. It is important, though, to realise that there are real differences between the three groupings, and thus the ways in which worship will develop in each one. An understanding of this will help you to lead appropriately, so that you are not frustrated when each member of your 2,000-strong celebration does *not* contribute a prophecy, and so that your victims are not frustrated when you lead their fellowship group into vigorous warfare while all they want is to get a word in edgeways about how near breaking-point they are at work. I reckon that if you can lead successfully at cell level you can do it anywhere, vastly different though the approach elsewhere would be.

I do perhaps need to avoid possible confusion by making clear what I'm not saying in this context. It is unfortunate that the word 'celebration' is used in two different ways, and problems can arise by misunderstanding this. A celebration is a church gathering of more than 250 people, and used simply in that way the word implies nothing at all about what they do when they gather. It is a sociological term which deals with group dynamics and the way people in a group that size behave. It is distinct as a concept from celebration as a type of worship which is exuberant and joyful. Thus what I am not saying is that a group of six people will be unable to celebrate in worship until they increase their membership by a factor of forty-two, any more than I am saying that a gathering of 5,000 won't be able to adore the Lord or even experience corporate silence in worship. Group dynamics is one thing, and much research has established the validity of the concept of the three groupings, but the way those groups worship is another, although the atmosphere, dynamics and relationships will, as I've said, make some things easier in one context than in another.

Going solo

Finally it is worth saying that there is a fourth context for worship which in many ways is even more foundational than the cell. If you can worship alone, you'll immediately have many of the skills with which to lead others into God's presence. If you can't, the presence of other people, even a few thousand of them, will do nothing to hide that fact. So become competent there first, and then work on the other levels.

Solo worship can contain most of the ingredients of a collective worship time (although 'the Peace' might not take quite so long), but you will obviously handle things somewhat differently. Many people find that some form of liturgy, for example the Anglican or Roman 'Daily Offices' or even the framework suggested in some Bible reading notes, is a helpful structure to support individual worship. Music may or may not be important, and can be used in many different ways. You needn't just sing hymns or worship songs. Why not try singing Psalms or other biblical passages to tunes which you improvise as you go along (this is a good preparation for prophetic worship, which I'll be mentioning later), or spend time singing in the Spirit? Even if you're not brave enough to sing out loud, you can listen to tapes which draw you into God's presence (anything from the Vineyard to the *St Matthew Passion*), or simply play an instrument to the Lord. My favourite way to worship alone is simply to sit at the piano and play, even though my playing is of a standard which precludes any public performance.

This really is the main point about individual worship—it can and should be an opportunity for experimentation in areas in which you would never ever go public. You can do the most embarrassing things when you know that it is all simply between you and the Lord. The tone deaf can croak, the physically inhibited can dance, Anglicans can jump up and down on the spot, all content in the knowledge that God is really enjoying it, provided, of course, that it is being offered to him as worship. I believe there's even a sense in which he enjoys the cautious and self-conscious movements of the inhibited solo worshipper even more than a church full of enthusiasts who dance all the time, since he appreciates the cost and the commitment of will involved.

Really anything goes in individual worship, as long as it is God-centred, biblical and offered in spirit and in truth. And while it may be the case that some of the things which begin for you as individual expressions of worship will become a part of what you feel confident about doing in public, it doesn't have to be like that for everything you do. If your solo liturgical dance stays solo for the rest of your life it's OK—just something for God's eyes only. None of this is easy, but all of it can be extremely rewarding, both for you personally and for others whom you may subsequently lead in public worship.

So far we've tried to understand worship, not in terms of a list of words, but rather as a cyclical experience of our response to God and his response to our response which, if we let it, can lift us higher and higher into his presence each time we meet him. We've said that the main reason for worship is for us to build a tabernacle in which the Lord can come and meet us, and we've noticed that as we do that various other things may happen which, although pretty wonderful things in themselves, are not the main reason for our praise. We've also identified five different ways in which we can worship (or five different moods in which we may find ourselves as we worship), and four different contexts for worship with regard to the size of the gathering. That's all the theory, the theology, but how do we actually do it? Perhaps even more fundamentally, *can* we do it? And if we can, what sort of people should we be in order to do it effectively? In the next chapter, we'll move on to explore what makes a good worship leader.

CHAPTER FOUR

A JOB DESCRIPTION:
WHO IS EQUAL TO THIS TASK?

I F THE PREVIOUS CHAPTERS accurately describe what we expect to happen when we worship, and some of the ways in which we may expect it to happen, it is clear that the role of the leader in worship is a very important one indeed. A tremendous amount hangs on his ability to handle things well, and at the very least not to get in the way of what God is trying to do. In this chapter we'll spend some time looking at the worship leader himself, first at just what the role involves, and then at what sort of person he must be to succeed within that role. I want to suggest, in fact, that a worship leader, whether an ordained minister or a lay leader, has not one role but nine.

1. Figurehead

Those who have been on special management training courses and gone through the exercise of being left in a group without a leader will know just what an uncomfortable position that is. Valuable though it may be in some settings, it is certainly not what we want worshippers to experience. If I had to identify one thing which makes for successful worship, it would be security for the congregation, both in God himself and also in the leader. Therefore the leader needs to inspire that sort of confidence in people, and needs to be in a position, both physically and spiritually, to be seen to be able to inspire it.

On a purely physical level, he should be in a place where all can see him, as he will provide a focus of attention, at least for the beginning of the worship time, and he must never desert his post while the worship continues, since if anything untoward happens, all eyes will instantly be on him for direction. If, because of an interruption, you open your eyes and return from a state of deep worship to find that the leader is somewhere in the fifteenth row, this won't help your security one little bit.

On a spiritual level, if the leader is not the vicar or minister he must be known to be a person of maturity who is held in esteem by the church leadership.

2. Host

Whether you are talking about a regular Sunday church service, a Saturday night ecumenical celebration, or a small fellowship group in someone's front room, somebody needs to be seen to be hosting the occasion. This may involve such things as welcoming people, making sure they are comfortable, having all the right books, knowing where the loos are and so on. This won't always fall to the lot of the lay worship leader, but it may well do occasionally, especially in a gathering which begins with a time of worship. If he is the first person to be seen or heard on the platform, the congregation will look to him for some kind of practical help to feel a part of what is going on. Like any good host, he needs to be polite and attentive to people's comfort while at the same time resisting the temptation to become the life and soul of the party.

3. Articulator

By this rather ugly term I simply mean one who says for people what they are thinking or feeling in order to establish some kind of bond between himself and them and between different members of the congregation. This may range from, 'Isn't it good to come together to praise the Lord?' at one end of the spectrum to something like, 'Many of us may be finding it difficult to think of praising God after those tragic riots in our city last night. This kind of thing raises all sorts of questions for us, but we're here today because we know that only God can make any sense at all of the evil in our world. So let's offer him a sacrifice of praise.' It really involves catching the mood of the gathering, being aware of what may be going on for people, and making sure that we worship through these feelings, not simply laying them aside if they don't seem to fit. A good vicar or minister should naturally have this pastoral feel for the congregation, but a lay leader, or any leader who is working in a context other than his own church, may find it more difficult. This task, if done sensitively, can free charismatic worship from its bugbear of triumphalism, but if it is ignored it can leave people behind or alienate them totally.

4. Encourager

After articulating for people the position they are at, the next task is to move them on into worship. Many people will come feeling that worshipping is only a marginally more attractive prospect at that moment than setting fire to their trousers. Many will come full of inhibitions and self-consciousness. Some will be there for the first time and will feel very uncertain of the whole situation. All will need to be encouraged to enter fully into the experience of worship, not just once at the beginning, but often, as new depths of intimacy with God are reached. Whether the need is for encouragement to relax physically, to sing in the Spirit or to contribute prophetically, the leader is the person to do it, with gentleness and tact.

5. Leader

This aspect of the role almost goes without mention, but not quite. The point needs to be made that a leader is someone who goes out first into the fray in order that others may follow. Yet one occasionally meets clergy and worship leaders who, like the Duke of Plaza-Toro, prefer to lead from behind, finding it easier that way. Some clergy may tend to 'preside' over the gathering in a way which suggests that they are not really involved at a grass-roots level. It's important to lead people, not push or manipulate them, in all sorts of areas of leadership. In worship, it's absolutely essential. You always need to lead by example. People will not relax and enter into worship simply by being told to. What will help more than anything is for them to see the leader relaxed and enjoying himself. As a general rule, you won't get people to go anywhere you're not prepared to go yourself.

6. Protector

People approach worship, perhaps especially charismatic worship, with all sorts of anxieties and fears. These are mostly unnamed and unfaced, but if really pressed people might admit to worrying in their weaker moments about things like false manifestations of gifts, demons appearing (perhaps even in them!), other interruptions in the service from disturbed people or, more vaguely, about things getting 'out of control' in some unspecified way. The congregation need to feel protected from anything which they conceive of as being potentially harmful to them, and the leader needs to give them this security. Again, lay leaders may have to work harder here than clergy, since they may not immediately command so much respect. Also, since people's fears are not all of negative things, there is the need for the leader to take on the role of what I call the 'priest'.

7. Priest

It can truly be a fearful thing to fall into the hands of the living God. Those who have experienced charismatic worship will find that their expectations about what might happen in worship have been raised to include such physical manifestations as screaming, weeping or resting in the Spirit, so it can seem frightening at times when God gets his hands on you. Thus the leader, in the twin role of protector and priest, must understand the ways both of God and the Enemy (as well, of course, as the disturbed or even just over-enthusiastic human spirit). He must discern which is which, and help the people accordingly to resist or go with whatever is happening. If anything untoward or unplanned occurs, the congregation will immediately look to the leader to see how to react.

Therefore he must above all be someone who does not panic, since there are few things more infectious in a group. He will need to be able to deal quickly and decisively with an unhelpful contribution in worship, while at the same time dealing gently and lovingly with the person who made it. He will need to be able to show that he understands what God is doing in dramatic events, and that he is happy to be a part of that. He will also need to have the help of a ministry team experienced, as he is, in dealing with people under the unction of the Holy Spirit or in the grip of the demonic, since he must not leave his position up front to deal with crises in the congregation. His other roles don't stop just because someone screams, and it will make people feel very insecure indeed if there is no figurehead.

I feel that I need to emphasise what I don't mean by the word 'priest' in this context. Of course Jesus is our great High Priest, and we have no need of any other mediator between us and God. Neither am I referring specifically to the ordained clergyman. This will of course be part of his priestly role, but I will say more about him under the next heading. What I mean is simply that the worship leader, whether lay or ordained, is one who fits in with the Old Testament picture of the priests who were those who understood what God did since, to put it simply, they spent time with him for a living. This concept is one which I find helpful. The Shaman or witch-doctor fulfils this role in other religions and cultures, and despite the accessibility of our God to all his people, I feel that there is still a role for those who especially understand God in interpreting for less mature believers exactly what is going on. This role will be especially important as God's people gather for worship with the express aim of experiencing his presence and power among them. And we mustn't forget that at times the power of God will be so strong that even the priests are sent scuttling out of the way!

8. President

Tied in very much with the role of the priest is that of the 'president', a term used helpfully in the *ASB* to describe the role of the priest in the celebration of the Eucharist. The background for this is the Jewish celebration of the Passover, where the family patriarch would naturally assume the leading role at the head of the table, presiding over the ceremony and holding the different contributions together. Particular prayers and actions would appropriately be his alone, and he would provide some sort of focus for the whole group. I find it helpful to think of the priest celebrating the sacraments as having a similar role, coming both from his position with regard to God because of his ordination, and his position with regard to the congregation because of his pastoral care and leadership. And I would see this role extending to those types of service which, although not classed by the Thirty-Nine Articles as sacraments, nevertheless have something sacramental about them. The minister officiating, for example, at weddings or funerals still has the job of presiding over the event in a way which facilitates worship among those present. Even in non-conformist churches where less emphasis is placed on the sacramental side of worship, there is still the need for someone to preside at the Lord's Table, either the minister himself or a deacon or elder. So the president's role is an important one, whether or not it is seen directly in terms of priesthood and ordination.

9. Prophet

I mean by this term the ability to function 'prophetically' rather than simply to function as a prophet. In other words it's not so much about contributing a prophecy from time to time, although this is an important part of it, but more about the much broader prophetic ability to convey the heart of God to his people. I see it in the much more 'Old Testament' sense of the prophet who was able to read the signs of the times and see them from God's perspective. There need be no tension here, however, between the concepts of Old Testament, and New Testament or charismatic prophecy. Although there are some obvious differences, the overwhelming similarity seems to be the ability of the prophet to hear from God about how he sees things and to communicate that sense to the people.

Whether he shouts at the king, writes it in a book, or offers it at a charismatic prayer meeting seems to me to be secondary. A leader needs to be able to feel what God is doing during a time of worship, where he is taking people, and how confidently they are following him. This may then need to be communicated to the people in such a way that they are put in touch with the mind and purposes of God. If we were working with a very simple model of worship like equating it, for example, with adoration only, there would be little need for this role to be fulfilled. But since in this book at least we are thinking of a very diverse set of pathways down which we may be led by the Spirit during a worship time, we do need someone who, under the anointing of that Spirit, can act to some extent as a guide for the journey.

In our church at the moment we are going through the process of writing job descriptions for each person involved in any ministry within the life of the church, from the vicar to the deputy-washer-of-tea-towels. Not only does this help people to know exactly what they are committing themselves to when they take on a job, but it also gives a clearer picture of the sort of person who might do that job successfully. If the roles we have described above form part of the job description of the worship leader, can we now move on to see what sort of person might be right for the job? If these are the tasks, who might be equal to them? Again, I've identified several different characteristics of the good worship leader, and I have made no attempt to tie them in properly with the roles above. The fact that once again I've managed to think of nine is purely coincidental.

1. He must be mature

It will be clear from what we've said before that leading

worship will not be a new Christian's first task after coming to faith. Clergy and lay leaders alike will need a thorough biblical grounding, a sound knowledge of theology, and a real live experience of God in their own lives. In worship we are dealing supremely with a God who reveals himself in truth, and we will need to be dealing with truths as we worship. Doctrine is important, therefore, not as a dry academic study to keep the cupboards in our brains well stocked, but as a living knowledge of just who God is so that we can encounter him in truth as well as in spirit. The need for this kind of deep understanding is especially reinforced when we realise that it's not just God who is involved in our worship; the Enemy is there too, flitting around the edges, trying to see if he can get a grip in order to pervert us and lead us off into erroneous side-lines. As the leader is involved in encouraging others in worship, he constantly needs to apply the plumbline of good biblical doctrine to every contribution, including his own, in order to ensure that everything is straight. I'm not saying that you need a PhD in theology before you can be a good worship leader, but you do need the depth of understanding and knowledge which takes years rather than weeks to acquire. A faithful walk with the Lord over a long period, and a steady growth in biblical study and understanding are vital here, and will prevent a congregation being led off into side-lines or even error.

2. He must be experienced

I'd always wanted to be a van driver in my youth, but whenever I applied for a job it was always the same: 'Have you got any driving experience? No? Sorry.' Only when I had broken into the business by devious means, which need not concern us now, could I hold my head up in van-driving circles as a fully experienced member of the club.

These catch-twenty-two situations can be avoided in the church if we take seriously Jesus' method of discipling. In our church we've recently introduced a rule which we're still trying hard to begin to keep: no one from the vicar down does anything without having someone else there who is being trained to do it themselves. This rule certainly ought to apply in the worship group, and even in the leadership of the whole service. It may not be appropriate or even legal for lay people to lead every part, but there are things which they can do, and potential leaders should be given training in doing them.

John Wimber has helpfully spelt out what he considers Jesus' method of making disciples. Although he gleans this primarily from the healing ministry in the Gospels and Acts, it can be applied to just about any area of church life. First Jesus did it, then he did it with trainees watching, then they did it with him watching, and then he left them to do it on their own. Perhaps the most striking example of this in action can be seen by comparing the accounts of Jesus raising Jairus' daughter (Lk 8) with the raising of Dorcas by Peter in Acts 9. Peter is clearly following the example of Jesus. If we are to take this method of discipling seriously in our church life we must beware of two common errors: we mustn't forget the need for feedback and critical assessment of the trainees' performance, and we must be prepared for the fact that sometimes the trainees we're working with will reach the point when they begin to do greater works even than we can manage. To be good trainers we need to be non-threatening and non-threatened.

If we follow this method of discipling, the new worship leader standing up to guide worship for the first time will not be beginning from scratch, but will already have served an apprenticeship equipping him to deal positively with anything which may happen during worship. If the Spirit falls on someone and they begin weeping, the leader will know what to do since he has seen other, more experienced leaders handle the same thing before. If a demon manifests itself, he will stay calm, since he knows from past experience of seeing someone else handle it that there is nothing to be afraid of. And, most importantly of all, he will have learned from others not just a troubleshooting manual of what to do in 527 different unexpected worship situations, but the skill of listening to God and discerning from him what's going on and how to respond to it. If you are a worship leader, you need to ask yourself *now* who it is that you are training up to take over when you move on to higher things, and if you are the leader or minister of a church, you might do well to look for other areas where this method of discipling could usefully be employed.

3. He must be submitted

If the worship leader is not the overall church leader, vicar or minister, he must be someone who is and is seen to be under the authority of that leader. This may sound obvious, but if you stop to think about it, it is in this sort of area that music in worship has had most of its problems historically. If you were to do a survey among Anglican vicars as to who was public enemy number one in their church, how many would say the organist or the choirmaster? I suspect a very high proportion. I'm not sure whether the same is true in non-conformist circles, but in the Church of England there is often a fierce rivalry between the musical side of the church and its vicar; a rivalry which has been responsible for more than a few nervous breakdowns on both sides. What's the problem?

Leaving aside the personalities involved, and trying not to paint every situation in too black-and-white a way, it seems to me that in a large number of cases music has ceased to be a servant and has become the master. The idea, surely, is that music is used within the service to heighten the liturgy, to raise people's spirits to God, and to provide a vehicle through which people may come in worship before the Lord. But simply because the musical staff *are* musical, they want things done properly; and because the vicar is perhaps not musical, he abdicates responsibility and lets them get on and do what they want. In the quest for higher musical standards the congregation is left behind as both music and words become more and more complex and Latinate respectively. In the end you have an esoteric club of musicians, and a congregation whose idea of worship is that of simply sitting back and letting it all wash over you (a valid way of worship sometimes, of course, but one which if indulged in too often tends to generate the same passive attitude in other areas of church life, such that the whole Christian faith is a matter of letting things wash over you). Music now becomes the ruling force in the church's life and the servant role which music ought to have is totally reversed. (I even know one church where the clergy had to ask the choirmaster whether or not he wanted them to preach a sermon during the service. You can guess what the answer usually was!)

It would be tragic if within renewed worship the worship group took on these negative traits previously belonging to the church choir, yet in some places I can detect this beginning to happen in very small ways. We must resist it at all costs, and we can do that if worship leaders are in a relationship of submission and love with the church leader, and always see their work in the context of that servant role, even if this means at times laying aside some of their artistic integrity. We do, of course, want a good standard of music, and I'm not saying we should encourage anything in our worship to be second rate, but 'good' in the context of worship doesn't mean 'complicated'; it means first and foremost 'accessible'. And just as the music needs to be a servant, so does the music leader. A visiting pastor said in our church, 'If you're not committed to the leader and his wife, and if you don't love and respect them, then you should leave the church and find one with leaders whom you can respect.' While this might be a recipe for an ecclesiastical 'all change', there is certainly truth in it, and I can think of many hassles which could have been avoided if this advice had been heeded. Certainly, if the music is not going in the same direction as the rest of the church, trouble is on the horizon.

I realise that by now many lay worship leaders, or aspiring ones, will feel like throwing in the towel since they are in situations where the musical status quo is so entrenched and supported by the church leadership that their attempt to help the advent of renewal is one long battle. How can we be in relationships of submission and love with leaders who don't seem to want to know about anything which we hold dear? I'll enlarge on this in the final chapter, and in Chapter 13 I'll have some things to say to clergy and leaders fighting against entrenched congregations, but for now I'd want to say first that it is possible, although very difficult at times, to love and honour those wanting to go in directions different from our own, and second that being in submission doesn't mean that creative shaping of one another's views and ideas is impossible. I actually believe that there is much more potential for changing recalcitrant leaders within that relationship than there is in a constant pitched battle.

Since the lay worship leader's role is such a public one, the relationship between him and the church leader will often be on display. He will need not only to be submitted, but to be seen to be. If, for example, the minister needs to step in and take over during a time of worship, the worship leader must be seen to be quite happy for this to happen, rather than scowling or grumbling about it. If you do think it was a mistake, talk about it after the service, don't moan about it at the time. This public face of your relationship is one of the most important aspects of submission.

4. He must be dedicated

The worship leader's tasks require that he is someone who is committed to the job, to those working with him, and to the moving on of the whole church in worship. The church needs to know that he will be there, that he will be there in good time, that he will come prepared, both personally and practically, and that he will put everything he's got into the task in hand, even if he feels that he'd rather be at home watching *Songs of Praise*. Clergy, of course, have little option here, since they are paid to be there, although it is possible to lead worship looking as if you would rather be at home watching *Songs of Praise*. If someone can't be there, the church needs to be sure that he has arranged for the job to be covered adequately. All this, of course, is true for just about any job in the life of the church, but for some worship leaders, especially those with an artistic temperament, this day-to-day dedication can sometimes be a problem. You may need to redefine your sensitive and creative personality as awkward and sinful at times, and commit yourself to the task anyway.

5. He must have presence

I find this a very difficult concept to define, although we all know it the instant we see it. It's about the sort of commanding aura that someone either does or doesn't have around them as they stand up in front of a room full of people. Many different things contribute to it: physical size and shape, tone and volume of voice, body language, clothing, confidence and so on. Unfortunately, we have no control whatsoever over some of these. Someone who is six feet four inches tall, with a rich booming voice and a shock of red hair, will naturally tend to have more presence than a five-feet-two-inch balding midget with a squeaky voice, a lisp and a Wolverhampton accent. However, the good news, especially for those in the latter category, is that there are some things which you can do to help.

But do you want to? If you must do things to yourself to make yourself more conspicuous, isn't that a denial of the whole role of a worship leader? What about 'I must decrease, and he must increase'? There's a real tension here, because while the latter is obviously true, we want the congregation to feel as secure as possible during worship, and the more the leader inspires confidence in them the more secure they'll feel. It's not so much a matter of making yourself conspicuous as of coming over confidently and authoritatively. If you naturally have difficulty in doing that, then it seems right to do anything you can which will help. It is possible, as any actor will tell you, to learn not to show nerves, to learn to project your voice, to use your body more effectively and so on. You might try wearing clothes you feel most comfortable in (within the bounds of what is appropriate, obviously!), and you might like to get some friends to give you an honest opinion of how you come over publicly so that you will know which areas need special care. Clergy may need help here too. There is a popular move, at least in some church circles, away from any clerical 'uniform', including even dog-collars, but there is the need to weigh up the gains in informality against the losses of presence. When all is said and done, a gold cope or chasuble can certainly help people to notice that you're there.

I suppose the most helpful definition of presence was one given by a friend who described it as the ability to stand up in public without making the audience feel nervous for you. I know that our help is in the name of the Lord, but that of itself won't make us immune to normal human nerves. Since anxiety is both so contagious and so counterproductive in worship, we have a duty to do all we can to prevent it from showing.

6. He must be attractive

It is just worth mentioning that presence in itself isn't necessarily a positive characteristic. Count Dracula and Hitler were both oozing with it, but almost certainly wouldn't be the sort of people who could helpfully lead worship in your church. So our presence must have a positive, attractive quality. There's one key to this, and it never fails: smile a lot. A genuine, open smile can transform any face into a picture which is lovely to look at. If you've had a bad day and can't think of anything to smile about, just concentrate on the goodness and grace of God. You might find that will help your worship in other ways too.

7. He must be musical

If the sort of worship you'll be leading involves any music at all, you need at the very least to have some sort of musical feel by which you know whether or not something seems to be right, even if you don't understand why it is right. Certainly if you are going to be leading singing it will be most helpful to the congregation if you are not tone deaf, and if you have the sort of voice which is not that much like a walrus with sinusitis. You certainly don't need to be another José Carreras, but you do need to stay in tune. If you use an instrument you obviously need to be sufficiently skilled on it so that your playing doesn't get in the way of people's worship.

8. He must be a worshipper

It seems to me to be axiomatic that you won't lead people any further than you've been yourself. In a very real sense it's true to say that a church's worship will only be as good as that of the worship leader, and that what the worship leader does on the platform or in the pulpit on Sunday will only be as good as he does the rest of the week at home on his own. There is another real tension here, though. The most effective way for a worship leader to encourage a congregation to worship is for him to stand up and put all he's got into worship. Yet at the same time he must fulfil a servant role for the rest of the people by being attentive to God and to them and by concentrating on his singing, playing, communication and so on. So he may need to sacrifice some of the wholehearted personal entering into worship in order to meet the needs of the other people present. Yet at no time must he be standing on the side-lines cheering people on without playing the game himself. And if he is conscious of the sacrificial nature of the role, he must make opportunities to worship without being in charge, so that he doesn't forget how to do it freely. The most important things, though, are a heart overflowing with love and praise, a frequent entering into the presence of God devotionally, and an infectious enthusiasm both for the Lord himself and for the practice of exalting him.

9. He must be anointed

Anointing is the special equipping of someone by God for a particular task. It seems to be a function of God's sovereign choice and grace. God chooses who he is going to anoint, and he then gives them the supernatural ability to carry out the task for which he has sovereignly chosen them.

It is seen most clearly in some of the Old Testament

characters we mentioned in Chapter 1, people upon whom the Spirit of the Lord came, giving them special power and authority for the task he had for them. This is perhaps the most important element of all, not just in leading worship, but in any area of ministry. You may be a highly-trained and theologically-equipped minister, with all the skills in the world, more presence than Superman, a voice like Stevie Wonder's, musicianship which would put Beethoven in the shade, and a profound love for the Lord, but simply be the wrong person for the job, and therefore have no anointing from the Spirit. Or, more encouragingly, you may not have any of the right abilities, and yet be chosen and anointed by God such that you can do it anyway.

1 Samuel 16 tells the story of the choosing of David, and of Samuel's natural assumption that the person who most looked the part would get it. But God had another man for the job; someone so unlikely that he didn't even turn up for the interview. Samuel anointed him, 'and from that day on the Spirit of the Lord came upon David in power' (v 13). What we need is not so much skilful worship leaders as anointed ones.

My own story may be encouraging here. My first exposure to charismatic renewal left me absolutely terrified, and even after several years of experience within it I felt very uncomfortable indeed during worship. I was the sort of person who would be the only one in the meeting without my arms in the air because I didn't want to look unusual. Even now I'm not the most liberated of worshippers, finding moving and dancing in worship very difficult. But after going to Spring Harvest for the first time, I caught a vision of what worship could be like and became determined to do something about it.

Around this time my Vicar and I decided to start a second evening service as an alternative to the 1662 Choral Evensong which we held at 6.30 pm, so it seemed an ideal opportunity to introduce some 'charismatic'-type worship. We planned carefully, bought some copies of a song-sheet with a more 'charismatic' flavour, and tuned the church piano. Then all of a sudden, a shocking realisation hit me with the force of a sledge-hammer – someone was going to have to lead the worship. Someone from our little church in East Anglia was going to have to stand up in front of everyone and do what Graham Kendrick and Dave Pope did. An even worse realisation followed—it was going to have to be me.

I didn't even really like charismatic worship, and now I was going to be leading it, saying things like, 'Let's lift our hands to the Lord in worship,' and, 'There's no need to be frightened or inhibited,' and other such phrases which made me squirm to hear, let alone say! I remember praying in despair (and I think it was more of a bowing out rather than a genuine request for help), 'Lord, if you want me to do this, you'll have to provide everything I need, because I've got nothing to contribute at all, and I don't even want to do it.' I suppose I thought God would become angry at my response and call someone from Spring Harvest to come and live in our patch, but I should have known better; that's just the sort of prayer he enjoys the most, expressing utter dependence on him.

I believe I received something from the Lord that day which far surpassed any skills I have been able to muster or any natural abilities which may have been latent in me. It didn't happen magically overnight; I had to get my guitar out and start practising, I had to go to workshops and learn practical skills, and I had to make many, many mistakes. A lot of healing in my personality had to take place, but I did learn, and I am still learning today. But on that fateful day of my prayer, I never imagined that I would one day be writing a book about leading worship. The moral of the story is: be careful what you pray, or you may have to buy a word-processor. And, more seriously, don't think that because you have all the skills you must automatically be the right person for the job, or that if you haven't got any of the skills you'll never be able to do it. Seek the Lord for his anointing. If you receive it, others will soon start to tell you. It's not so much the ability that counts; availability and anointing are worth far more.

Does all this sound a tall order? Don't despair; the Lord loves to work with people on the way rather than with those who've arrived. I've not met the perfect worship leader yet, and I doubt I ever will this side of heaven.

CHAPTER FIVE

THE RAW MATERIALS

HAVING LOOKED AT THE worship leader, let's move on now to see what he has to work with. What are some of the ingredients which go together to make a worship service, and how can we make the best of them? I've managed to identify twelve different ingredients, some of them subdivided. Let me begin simply by explaining what I mean by these terms.

1. Liturgy

I want to use this term in its narrowest sense to mean simply material which is set to be used in the service. The most common material which I'll refer to will of course be the set prayers, creeds, canticles, lections and so on which make up the various rites used in Anglican-type worship, and which are printed out, for example, in the *Alternative Service Book* or the *Book of Common Prayer*. But non-printed material can also be liturgical. Any ceremonial which we use (any physical movement which we make during services, even bringing the offering plates to the front, is strictly speaking ceremonial), or any words which though not written down are a regular part of our worship week by week, would be included in liturgy.

2. Rubric

This word comes from the Latin for 'red', and it refers to those parts printed in red in the old Roman service books. They were simply instructions about what to do next or how to do it. Anglicans who use the *ASB* will be familiar with them as 'bluebrics' since they are now printed in blue. I want to adapt this word to mean anything not printed in the set liturgies which we say in order to help people through the service. This might range from very simple commands like, 'Please be seated,' or, 'Let us pray,' through to more extensive suggestions like, 'Let's spend a few moments in silence before we join in the confession, to allow the Holy Spirit to bring to mind any particular things for which we need to ask God's forgiveness.' Lest free-church readers think that rubric and liturgy are things which don't affect them, there is a great tendency in non-liturgical worship (and sometimes in liturgical) to do a transforming act whereby rubric becomes liturgy. In the Baptist church I used to attend, you could rely on one thing in particular in the service: the way in which the notices were started. Week in, week out the secretary would stand up and say, 'We do extend a very warm welcome to all in church this morning/evening, especially any visiting friends.' Secretaries came and went, they had weeks off through illness or holidays, stand-ins were found, but the words were the same. If that isn't liturgy, I don't know what is. This tendency to fossilise rubric into liturgy besets all of us who lead worship. We must fight it at all costs and find different ways of communicating what is essentially the same information each week.

3. Notices

Sometimes it is very difficult to feel that the notices are part of worship; they seem rather to be a break from it or an intrusion into it. But as the worshipping community comes together, practical details of its shared life should be given. I suppose there are three rules here: decide where to have the notices, give them out as creatively as you can, and keep them as short as you can. I have experienced about four different placings for notices: right at the beginning or even before the service starts, at the start of the sermon, at some other point in the service, or right at the end. You will know which is the best placing for your service. Personally I prefer them right at the start, though that does have the disadvantage in our church that only about thirty per cent of the congregation hear them since most people seem to like to arrive during the first hymn.

Dealing with them creatively might involve humour; people might actually look forward to the notices if they know how entertaining they will be. The added advantage of this approach is that people are far more likely to remember what they've heard if they enjoyed hearing it.

Something else we try to do is involve the congregation in things in which they are not actually involved. During July, for example, Anglicans have to sit through up to twenty or so sets of banns of marriage. I often remind the congregation that these people are not just names on a list, but real individuals about to take an incredibly important step in life. I might say, 'They need our prayers, so as I'm reading the list, why not pray for them?' People will often latch on to one or two couples whom they know personally, or who live in their street, or who have the funniest middle names and pray for them, not only then but perhaps during the week too.

Even with creativity, brevity is still important, so do all you can to be crisp and efficient in notice giving. Many busy churches now print out some kind of notice-sheet or bulletin. This is often a good idea, as long as you don't then go and read the whole thing out as well. One final suggestion: why not try to find someone in the church who might have a real gift for notice giving? Don't laugh, I'm serious—someone who is good with words, has a quick wit and pleasant personality, and who will come over well not just to the congregation but also to any visiting friends. Perhaps Anglicans could learn from many non-conformist churches which, like the Baptist church I used to attend, have a secretary whose job it is to give the notices. There might be a real ministry there for someone.

I've gone into notices here at some length because they won't get another mention anywhere else in the book. They do need care though if they are to take their proper place in worship. I well remember one service of an hour's duration when the notices took twenty minutes. I think we'd all agree that that wasn't an ideal state of affairs.

4. The offering

Not every service will include the taking up of a money offering, and not every church will do it in the same way, but if it is done, it ought to be seen as an important part of our giving to the Lord in the context of giving ourselves to him in worship. So whether we actually take up a collection, during a hymn or as part of the service in its own right or simply by having a plate at the door which is then brought up as part of an offertory procession, we have a potentially powerful visual aid which expresses some important things about the whole nature of worship. The only thing we have to be careful to avoid, for the sake of visitors, is giving undue emphasis to this part of the service, otherwise we might reinforce in them the commonly held view that the church is only after people's money. At carol services and other services where we know there are likely to be plenty of visitors, we often ask people *not* to put anything in, and tell them they can 'have this one on us'. People generally like that idea very much.

5. Prayer

By this I mean those times in the service when we address God directly. Obviously there are many subdivisions in this category. Prayer can be silent or vocalised. If vocalised, that can be done by the leader alone, by members of the congregation individually or by leader and congregation together, either from a book or from memory (for example, the Lord's Prayer or the Grace). We will look at prayer in greater detail in Chapter 7.

6. Preaching

In many churches the sermon is the *bête noire* of the service, but it can and should be a very important part of what happens when God's people come together. Through preaching we are instructed in our faith, we increase our knowledge, understanding and, hopefully, our living out of the Bible. We are challenged or comforted according to what we most need and, at times, we hear the very voice of God speaking directly into our situation. John Stott, defending the role of preaching in worship believes 'that nothing is better calculated to restore health and vitality to the Church, or to lead its members into maturity in Christ than a recovery of true, biblical, contemporary preaching.'[1] It would be very dangerous indeed if, in a renewed church which placed all its emphasis on singing, dancing and spiritual gifts, we lost sight of the absolute necessity of the preaching and teaching ministry.

This is not a book on preaching, so purists must forgive

me for including under that title any activities during the service designed to teach or apply God's word. Drama, dialogue, interviews of some sort, audio-visual aids and even videos are increasingly being used in worship, and I would want to include them here. I must add my own personal conviction that these things, while extremely useful, can never and should never replace the straightforward preaching of God's word by a gifted and anointed preacher.

7. Testimony

For many years of my own Christian experience, the only thing God did was convert people. At least, that's the impression you got if you listened to what people talked about. Whenever anyone 'gave their testimony', it was a story about how they'd lived a life of sin and degradation, plumbing all the depths of human evil and filth, until they met the Lord at the age of twelve and now were saved and on their way to heaven. Everyone listened intently while they whipped through their catalogue of sins, but switched off when Jesus came along and rather disappointingly cleaned things up for them.

I do not in any way want to deny the glorious reality of what the saving power of Jesus can achieve, but it is true to say that we haven't always been at our most helpful in the ways in which we've shared it with others. Nevertheless, testimony is an important part of our worship, and should be increasingly so as we move more and more into times when we expect God to be among us doing things. No longer are we restricted to telling about what God did when he saved us forty-three years ago; now we have a living relationship in which we meet with God daily and often dramatically. There is much to share in terms of healing, empowering, our witness in power evangelism and so on. Again, I'm not saying that these things never happened in the past, but it does seem to be the case that God is anointing his people in a tremendous way at the moment, and in a way which means that we experience him doing all sorts of things. So what better place to share our experience of God than when we gather for worship.

A powerful testimony, given honestly, coherently and humbly, can give a real boost to our faith and expectation of God. I can remember a meeting where I was just about to start the worship time when someone asked if they could 'just give a notice'. I agreed, slightly reluctantly, but was thrilled when the notice turned out to be about someone healed of a very serious illness as a result of prayer at the last meeting. You could actually feel the faith level rise, and we went straight into the first song full of praise and gratitude to the living God who is still pleased to work among us today.

8. Music

To many people music is synonymous with worship. It has the power to lift our spirits to God, inspire our praise and adoration, and at times break us down in tears. Worship without music is possible, but it is extremely difficult. Much of this book will deal with the skills needed in leading musical worship, whether by an individual, a worship group, a choir and organist, or simply your own wonderful voice. I want to identify five different types of music in worship, all of which are self-explanatory. They are hymns, what I would loosely call 'choruses' or 'worship songs', liturgical elements (for example, sung settings of the *Gloria* and *Sanctus*), music 'performed' rather than for congregational participation, and finally 'singing in the Spirit'. Each of these types requires something different from those involved, and they will be dealt with in more detail in subsequent chapters.

9. Spiritual gifts

Many of the gifts listed in the New Testament—tongues, interpretation, prophecy, discernment, healing—are seen most often in the context of worship. We must remember David Pytches' dictum that 'the meeting place is the learning place for the market place'. In other words, spiritual gifts are really for use in our evangelism out in the world, but we should still expect them to be manifested when we meet together in Jesus' name. The leader has a threefold role here: he needs to lead and encourage others by his example, he needs to test and deal with what is less than the best, and he needs to know how to help the congregation respond to what the Lord is saying or doing. The larger the congregation the harder it will be for anyone to risk giving a prophecy or something, so there is a real need for leadership in which the congregation feels secure and safe.

10. Silence

There is an interesting reaction going on in Christian circles: the more noisy and exuberant and dramatic charismatic worship becomes, the more people become interested in contemplative prayer. Joyce Huggett's *Listening To God* (London: Hodder and Stoughton, 1987) was number one in the Christian books' top ten for weeks and weeks in 1987, just as John Wimber's *Power Evangelism* (London: Hodder and Stoughton, 1985) had been two years earlier. Many people at my church are telling me they long for more silence in the services, but when we try to have some, people can't cope with it and feel the need to fill the space we've created with 'a scripture the Lord's given me' (ie Psalm 119: 76–132, or something similar). The Anglican *ASB* specifically allows for silence to be kept in nine different places during the Communion service, but gives no indication as to how to use it, such that I have experienced very few places where any use at all is made of it.

In a world where noise is increasingly available to us, we need to help congregations find and use silence. And in a world where we separate ourselves continually from one another, we need to help people towards the thrilling experience of shared silence. I suppose the ultimate in worldliness in this area is the Walkman which enables us to shut ourselves in with our own personal noise. I once taught a healing course and noticed one of the punters sitting throughout with a Walkman on; it turned out they were listening to John Wimber teaching tapes. (I bet nobody goes to the Vineyard and listens to tapes of me!) What we need, certainly in my church, is not so much silence, which although difficult to achieve is just about possible, but stillness, which is next to impossible. It reflects the frenetic pace of the life we're used to that we find stillness so hard. We need to give people permission in worship by saying, as it were, 'Don't just do something; sit there!'

11. Ministry

In our church we offer prayer for healing at every Sunday service, and although most of it goes on after the service has ended, we still see it as part of our ministry to the Lord that we minister to each other. I won't say much about it, since it isn't the main purpose of this book, but if we really are going to understand the worship in our churches as providing God with the opportunity to come and reign among us, we will need people skilled in ministry, in recognising the Spirit's touch on people, and in prayer for healing, inner healing and deliverance.

While it is true that God often intervenes sovereignly in people's lives and works a miracle without any specific prayer or ministry having taken place, it is nevertheless observably true that more people are healed or touched by God when there is a competent ministry team in action than when we simply 'leave it up to the Lord'. I'm sure that is because God enjoys co-operating with us in what he wants to do. I often wish that were not the case, but I'm certain it is.

One of the things I enjoy doing very much is washing my car. It's a real family occasion, and my two boys put on wellies and coats, grab their sponges, and attack the grime with great enthusiasm. However, as is often the case with young children, their enthusiasm soon gets diverted elsewhere. Before long they decide that the pavement is much more dirty than the car, so they give that a good wipe over. Then they remember that it's the car they're supposed to be washing, so the sponges go straight back onto the bodywork. Then they decide to wash the flowerbeds in the front garden, and again the accumulated soil on the sponges is transferred back to the car. This goes on until the job is finally finished and we all get into the car, go down to the local garage, pay £1.75 and go through the car-wash. Why do I do it? And why does God choose to work with us when he could do things so much more quickly and efficiently without us? I do it because I love seeing my boys enjoying themselves helping me. I'd rather spend the time with them inefficiently than do it on my own with much less mess. In short, I value the relationships more than I value the end product.

God is the same. I often wish he wasn't, but I believe he is. He has chosen to set this world up as a partnership; just as he asked for Adam and Eve's co-operation in Eden, he invites ours now. I don't think it is without significance that so many of Jesus' parables about the kingdom were taken from the farming world: the partnership of human sowing, tending and reaping, and divine life and growth seems to be a perfect picture of a kingdom which is brought in sovereignly by God, but also as a result of his people praying, 'Your kingdom come.'

If we are to work in partnership with God we must take our responsibilities seriously. In the area of healing and ministry we need to become proficient in praying for those with whom God is working in healing power. We have looked largely to John Wimber's teaching on healing in our church, as I've already mentioned, but whatever your understanding of healing, make sure you put it into practice. If your worship deepens as you hope it will, you'll need to.

12. One another

This ingredient isn't quite in the same league as the others, but it needs to be mentioned since it is increasingly being given liturgical significance, and not only in liturgical churches. In the past, worship was often seen as a very individualistic and private matter. Anglicans, certainly, spoke of 'making my communion', and in most branches of the church one regarded one's fellow-worshippers as intruders rather than as valued companions (and often glared at them accordingly!). But now there's much more of an emphasis on the fact that we come together as the body of Christ into God's presence. Anglicans recognise this liturgically in the 'Peace', which is hardly the most peaceful time during the service, when everyone wanders about greeting their fellow-worshippers with anything from a polite handshake to an enthusiastic bear-hug, depending on the degree of renewal to have hit the church so far. Non-Anglicans are not slow, either, to take this up in various ways, perhaps by having the Peace without necessarily calling it that, or by looking at one another as we sing songs addressed to others rather than to God, or in other creative ways. One excellent song which can be used as a 'sung Peace' is from Graham Kendrick's Christmas *Make Way, The Gift*. The tune and words are very simple:

> Peace to you,
> We bless you now in the name of the Lord,
> Peace to you,
> We bless you now in the name of the Prince of Peace,
> Peace to you.

One of the most moving worship experiences I've ever had was singing this song in a crowd of 11,000 people. We sang it through a few times, and then simply began wandering around, hugging friends and strangers alike and singing to each other. In print it sounds terrifying; at the time it was truly beautiful.

This relating to one another, however we do it, is an important part of worship in the body of Christ. Even if we don't build it into the service itself, it will still happen before and after, so we may as well include it in the list of things involved in worship.

Here, then, are twelve things which may make up our worship services. Maybe I haven't covered every last jot or tittle of the service, but these seem to me to cover most of it. How can we make the most of these ingredients and mix them together in a way which makes a mouthwatering offering for our God? I'll be looking in much more detail at the whole process of planning in a later chapter, but it is worth introducing it now in a basic way. I believe that two matters are important here: integrity and direction.

Integrity

By this I mean the fact that all the ingredients in the service are in some way linked. Most of the time this is obvious: we choose hymns which are connected with the theme of the service, and readings and prayers which reflect this too. But there are other more creative things we can do to make the service feel like a whole unit. Omission of some items is allowed: we don't have to use every last bit of the liturgy (written or unwritten) at every service. It can be great, at times, to omit one part and really concentrate on another which ties in with the theme much better. As long as the congregation has a balanced diet over a long period of time, it doesn't have to be fed every single nutrient at every meal. (I'll say a bit more about this, including its legality or otherwise, in the next chapter.) So, for example, a service on the theme of the character of God may elaborate on the Creed or some other statement of faith, while keeping the penitential section as simple and brief as possible; whereas in another service where 'world mission' was the theme, we may want to do without some of the music in order to give more time for prayer and intercession. Similarly, the type of music we choose may vary according to what we're emphasising. We've already seen that worship can include such things as intercession and warfare, so we may choose to cut down our spoken prayers and give time for a real crying out to the Lord in song. Non-musical items similarly need to be thought out: there's not much you can do about the notices, but testimonies can be chosen with care to reflect God's working in an area relevant to the subject matter of the service.

The key to integrity is probably to have a theme for the service and to make sure that everyone knows what it is. To some this may be a radical thought; they haven't bothered with that sort of thing before, so what's the problem? The problem is that people need to feel part of something they understand in order to get the most from and give the most to worship. A seemingly random collection of hymns, prayers and readings, thrown together with no visible thread running between them, will simply confuse people and alienate them from the task in hand. Even if the hymns and prayers took you seven hours of determined prayer and preparation to throw together, it does people no good if they can't detect the obscure link which your incredibly creative but rather too complex mind has used to hold the whole thing in place. A simple sentence at the beginning of the service can let people into the secret in such a way that they rejoice in your creativity as the service unfolds rather than feel baffled by it.

Direction

If a theme ensures integrity in a service, an aim is essential for direction. Just as the worshippers need to feel that the whole service holds together, so they also need to feel that it is not a static unity but a dynamic one, moving from a starting point towards a clearly visible goal. The service leader needs to ask two questions: where will people be starting from as they come to worship, and where do I and God want them to be by the end? A subsidiary question, once these two have been answered, would need to be asked: if that's where we're moving from and to, where will we be going on the journey? To think through these questions carefully in preparation is to provide some sort of map for the service which may prevent it from becoming hopelessly lost in the uncharted sea of charismatic spontaneity or compulsory liturgy.

Let's take an example. During the summer just after I began this book, I preached on the life and character of Elijah. It was part of a series designed to encourage the congregation. Thus my overall aim was to make them feel that like Elijah they are men and women precious and important to God in weakness as well as in strength. What took us towards that goal?

First of all, I needed to know where they'd be coming from. Many people were approaching the summer holidays in a state of near exhaustion, and saw August as a brief reprieve before we began, in September, a major upheaval in the life of the church which involved everyone in twice as much work. I was also aware that there were some people who, in the past, had been very heavily involved in major projects but who then took a well-earned rest and never really got back into the centre of things again. Another factor was that people came to the August services with a much-lowered expectation level since the worship group was off duty, the Vicar on holiday, and the Curate had to do the lot.

I wanted to begin the service with a sense of us all being in this together, and, yes, it is a real pain and a struggle at times. I chose for an opening hymn 'Praise, my soul, the King of Heaven', reflecting God's care for us in that situation.

> Father-like, He tends and spares us;
> Well our feeble frame He knows;
> In His hands He gently bears us,
> Rescues us from all our foes.

I then wanted the service to move through the penitential section with an awareness of our own sin and weakness, especially in the areas of defeat and discouragement, and an acknowledgement of these things as sin, at least in part. In the prayers we concentrated especially on those under strain and stress, either in the church or community or in the news. We also picked up another theme from Elijah's story and brought political and social awareness to bear on our intercession, using that, as God did with Elijah, as a corrective to an over-introverted spirit. In the sermon I expounded 1 Kings 19, looking especially at God's care and provision for his prophet on the physical level (verses 5–7), the spiritual level (verses 11–13), and the vocational level (verses 15–17). (Can't you just hear the three points?) I wanted people to feel really wrapped up in the arms of the Lord by the time I'd finished, and refreshed and renewed for further service. We ended the service with 'Dear Lord and Father of mankind', and afterwards some of us prayed for individuals about different pressures, worries or areas of depression in their lives.

The service had both a distinct theme and a definite direction. The more minor parts of the service were chosen to fit in as well as possible. For example, we interviewed a family from the congregation who were leaving us as the father was going to college to train for the ministry. It actually added to the theme for us to pray for them and send them out with a new anointing for the Lord's service and his protection against the pressures of a completely new lifestyle. Each ingredient should contribute something to both the integrity and the direction of the service.

I've given here a few guidelines for the best use of some of the service ingredients, and subsequent chapters will deal in further detail with more of them. I've also said a bit about putting together the service as a whole in order to make it feel like a whole. I wouldn't want to leave the impression, though, that all there is to a successful worship service is clever planning. Like a recipe, there's much more to it than a list of ingredients, even if you do choose the right ones and add them in the right order. There's a method as well, and I want to end this chapter with a brief look at it. I'll do this by changing the metaphor from cooking to smoking, and use an illustration which I hope will clarify the relationship between these ingredients, the worshippers and the service as a whole. For my illustration, I want to look at incense.

It is a well-known fact that many Anglo-Catholic,

Roman and Orthodox churches use incense in the course of their worship. However, not many people know exactly how it works. Probably not many people have much of a desire to know, but for the purposes of this analogy, I'm afraid you'll have to find out. I leave aside the vexed question of whether we ought to use incense, I'm simply mentioning it to illustrate a point.

To be a successful thurifer (that's the person who swings it around and is otherwise generally responsible for it), you need first of all two ingredients. The first is the incense itself, which comes in small globules rather like little bits of a rather disreputable brand of demerara sugar. This is slightly smelly, but nothing to write home about as yet. The second is charcoal, which looks like a much larger version of the sort of tablets you take with you when you go on holiday to Tunisia or wherever. The idea is to put the incense on the charcoal, which then makes it give out its smoke and fragrance. But one vital thing is still missing, without which the whole exercise is futile: fire. The charcoal must first be ignited; in fact it must be blown or fanned to glowing heat before it will do anything at all to the incense.

Let me explain my analogy. It helps me to think of the ingredients listed above as individual grains of incense, each with their own particular fragrance to offer, but at the moment sitting there doing nothing. There is no particular delight for the Lord in a printed prayer shut between two pages of an *ASB*, or a song sitting silently in a closed *Mission Praise* or wound round and round on a piece of magnetic tape. The ingredients need more than their own intrinsic value to turn them into worship. Secondly, I can easily imagine many worshippers as being like charcoal— dull, dusty and, like their smaller counterparts, capable of stopping anything. Even though it is a start, those two things together won't achieve much without the third: fire.

For worship to be successful, the fire of the Holy Spirit needs to come and ignite the hearts of the worshippers first of all, until we are glowing hot in our love for the Lord. Then, and only then, are we capable of taking the different ingredients in the service and offering them as a gift to the Lord to rise fragrant before him, blessing him and giving him delight in his children.

I find this a helpful analogy, since it explains our responsibility in worship to be prepared and in tune with God. Churches which use incense need to light the charcoal about fifteen minutes before the service begins so that it has time to catch and grow hot. When we rush late into church more hot and bothered than on fire with the Lord, it is no wonder that our worship often fizzes, smoulders a bit and then goes out. Preparation of the worshippers is perhaps the most serious lack in worship today. We wander into the Lord's presence with little care or attention, and then blame the leaders because the worship didn't take off or because the sermon or the prayers didn't do anything for us. To go back to my analogy, the incense will only be as smelly as the heat of the charcoal allows it to be. All the ingredients we've listed are simply means to an end. It's up to us to make the right use of them in a way which is anointed by the Spirit of God.

Notes

1. John Stott, *I Believe in Preaching* (London: Hodder and Stoughton, 1982), p. 338.

CHAPTER SIX

HANDLING THE LITURGY

I'VE ALREADY MENTIONED the fact that I am an ardent lover of liturgical worship, and believe that it provides the best framework of all for freedom in the Spirit and spontaneity in responding to him. You can imagine, therefore, how deeply it upsets me when I find Anglican churches where the liturgy is regarded at the very best as a necessary evil, and where no care is given either to using it effectively or to training others to get the most out of it. This chapter is offered in an attempt to encourage some leaders of liturgical churches to rediscover this most tremendous resource and to renew it, along with other areas of their churches' life, so that it becomes a means through which the Holy Spirit may flow in his invigorating power. I write not just to clergy, but to all who have the responsibility of leading others in liturgical worship, and also to those whose privilege it is week by week to join in with the forms of worship which have been used by God's people in one way or another for many hundreds of years. In this chapter I want to make six suggestions about how to approach liturgy.

1. Respect it

The *ASB* is the culmination of a long process stretching back for centuries. The church has been seeking the best ways to formulate its public worship down the years, and a tremendous amount of hard work and prayer has gone into the evolution of the liturgy we now use. The creativity of scholars and poets, some no doubt more and some less devout than others, the doctrinal sharpening up of truth by theologians, the discussions and disagreements which have been resolved into consensus—all these have left us the legacy through which we can now meet God in worship. To ignore this legacy is not only blindness, it is also dangerous. Any generation which thinks that it is self-sufficient and has no need to learn the lessons of the past or to rejoice thankfully in its inheritance is heading for trouble. And yet, sadly, it is all too common for us to undervalue the past. As someone once put it:

> History repeats itself.
> Has to.
> No one listens.

I went through a stage recently where the Lord began to speak to me about historical continuity. It suddenly struck me that when I used a Psalm to express my feelings to God in a particular situation, I was using the same words which had been used by countless people down the centuries in many different or even similar situations. I already knew this, of course, but one day it really struck me in a way which went deeply into my heart and has affected the way I pray ever since. As I read, for example, Psalm 103, I really began to get in touch with others who may have used the same Psalm in the past. I could picture myself joining with the Israelite community in the Temple in Jerusalem, being there as a young boy called Jesus learned the words with his father Joseph, attending a Mass celebrated by Thomas à Becket (my favourite historical character) in Canterbury Cathedral, and so on down the ages until I arrived in an urban parish in the North of England at the end of the twentieth century, still using the same words. Our worship can be greatly enriched if we get in touch with other worshippers, both worldwide and down the ages, by sharing with them in the liturgy.

This continuity reaches its climax in that most central aspect of Christian worship, the Eucharist. In a beautiful and well-known passage in his book *The Shape of the Liturgy*, Gregory Dix, an Anglican Benedictine monk, describes the same experience I had when reading the Psalms. Commenting on Jesus' command to 'do this in remembrance of me', he asks:

Was ever another command so obeyed? For century after century, spreading slowly to every continent and country and among every race on earth, this action has been done, in every conceivable human circumstance, for every conceivable human need from infancy and before it to extreme old age and after it, from the pinnacles of earthly greatness to the refuge of fugitives in the caves and dens of the earth. Men have found no better thing than this to do for kings at their crowning and for criminals going to the scaffold; for armies in triumph or for a bride and bridegroom in a little country church; for the proclamation of a dogma or for a good crop of wheat; for the wisdom of a Parliament of a mighty nation or for a sick old woman afraid to die; for a schoolboy sitting an examination or for Columbus setting out to discover America; for the famine of whole provinces or for the soul of a dead lover; in thankfulness because my father did not die of pneumonia; for a village headman much tempted to return to fetich because the yams had failed; because the Turk was at the gates of Vienna; for the repentance of Margaret; for the settlement of a strike; for a son for a barren woman; for Captain so-and-so, wounded and prisoner of war; while the lions roared in the nearby amphitheatre; on the beach at Dunkirk; while the hiss of scythes in the thick June grass came faintly through the windows of the church; tremulously, by an old monk on the fiftieth anniversary of his vows; furtively, by an exiled bishop who had hewn timber all day in a prison camp near Murmansk; gorgeously, for the canonisation of S. Joan of Arc—one could fill many pages with the reasons why men have done this, and not tell a hundredth part of them. And best of all, week by week and month by month, on a hundred thousand successive Sundays, faithfully, unfailingly, across all the parishes of christendom, the pastors have done this [for] the holy common people of God.[1]

Whatever I may feel about some of the theology implied in this passage, I still find it intensely moving to read, and it restores in me a sense of proportion when I'm tempted to think that the twentieth century in England is all that has ever really existed. To approach the liturgy with this sense of awe and respect for its background is a most positive way to begin to appreciate it.

Having said a little about the formation of the *ASB*, the Church of England Liturgical Commission (who were responsible for its publication) offer it humbly to the church with these words:

Those who use [the words of this book] do well to recognise their transience and imperfection; to treat them as a ladder, not a goal; to acknowledge their power in shaping faith and kindling devotion, without claiming that they are fully adequate to the task. Only the grace of God can make up what is lacking in the faltering words of men. It is in reliance on such grace that this book is offered to the Church, in the hope that God's people may find in it a means in our day to worship Him with honest minds and thankful hearts.[2]

It seems to me that this is exactly the sort of respect one should have for the liturgy. Those who receive and use the *ASB* (and, of course, other liturgical texts) in the spirit in which it is offered will not go far wrong.

2. Learn it

One of the first Anglican services I ever went to was a
rather elaborate 'Mass' at the local parish church. My Baptist sensibilities were offended, not so much by the hordes
of servers mincing around the sanctuary, nor by the can-
dles which seemed to sprout from every available crack in
the stonework, nor even by the quantity of smoke which
almost totally obscured the back wall, but simply by the
fact that people not only had service books, but they didn't
even use them. People closed their eyes and carried on
through the service without once looking to see what was
going on in the book. This just proved what I had always
been taught about the C of E, and more so: not only were
they into 'vain repetition', but they were so far into it that
they'd learned the whole thing off by heart.

Yet now, after a fifteen-year love affair with the Church
of England (which began that day and grows daily more
intense for me), I have come to see the value in learned
liturgy. When the words are so deeply entrenched in our
minds, we are free to use them from the heart. There is no
need to fumble for the right page or even hold the book;
we can simply close our eyes, lift our faces to God (and our
hands as well if we choose), and worship him with body,
mind and spirit. Similarly, when other moods are appropriate we can be free to express our devotion physically as
well as vocally, and make our bodies say what we want to
say to God without demanding that they act as a personal
lectern as well.

Learning the words does not just free our bodies in
worship, but also our minds. Those of us who were
brought up to memorise Scripture know how deeply it
penetrated into our very beings by the frequency with
which verses pop up at appropriate times. Liturgy works in
the same way, and can be a treasure store of the grace of
God, not just during public worship but at odd times

during the rest of the week too. When we use the words in the course of a service, we are using something which comes not from a book but from somewhere deep within us. We have already taken it on board and digested it, so that when we use the words, we are using something which is already dear to us, something which is already a part of our devotional lives. Yes, of course there is a danger of vain, mindless repetition, but in my experience this is far more frequently a product of vain, mindless worshippers than of the liturgy itself. Learn the liturgy and encourage others to do so too. You'll notice the difference in the feel of your worship very quickly.

I think there is much value in those who lead services learning part of the text too. A pet hate of mine is being given the Absolution or the Blessing by someone with their nose in a book, their hands in their pockets, and their mind, by the sound of it, on the latest cricket score. I don't suppose forgiveness is affected objectively one little bit, but I certainly feel more forgiven when the Absolution is given by someone who looks at me and tells me with authority in their voice of the Lord's mercy and grace (it's an added bonus for me if they use the sign of the cross to remind me of the basis of that free forgiveness). For that reason I've learned the *ASB* Absolution as well as many of the Blessings, Peace introductions and Eucharistic invitations off by heart, so that I can actually say the words to people rather than read them into the air somewhere.

3. Worship with it

I was once helping a mission team on a weekend in another parish. Because of the rather elderly, conservative congregation normally present at the evening service, the Vicar asked if I wouldn't mind saving the more outrageous aspects of my ministry until a sort of continuation meeting after the service had finished. Ever happy to oblige I agreed, but I couldn't help feeling that there was a kind of sad, ironic truth in the announcement he made to the people that 'after the service has finished there will be a time of worship'. We've already mentioned the fact that the whole service should be worship, but very often this just doesn't work out in practice.

In a good charismatic church you can get a crude but reliable guide to what is worship and what is not by counting the number of hands in the air. If your church is anything like ours, you'll notice very quickly that worship songs are worship, but that notices, hymns (apart from 'O for a thousand tongues to sing') and above all liturgical bits are not. When we reach the *Sanctus* in the middle of the Eucharistic Prayer ('Holy, holy, holy Lord, God of power and might'), there is not an elevated digit to be seen, but if we then go on to sing a song with almost identical words such as 'Holy, holy, holy is the Lord', everyone's away and you can't see the front of the church through the forest of hands which suddenly sprout up. Now, there's more to worship than raised hands, but why do we make it look as if we switch on for songs and off for the rest? And why does liturgy appear to be the biggest turn-off of all? I suspect there are two primary reasons.

The first has to do with *permission*. Do people know that they are allowed to worship through liturgy? If you are a leader, maybe you could give specific permission during teaching or preaching on worship, and back it up by showing some physical involvement and by saying your parts of the liturgy as if you were worshipping. This simple step could go a long way towards making the whole service seem more like worship.

The second reason, I suspect, is about *instrumentation*. In many churches where traditional music coexists peacefully (or otherwise) with more modern songs, the musical parts of the service are often allocated so that the organist and choir handle hymns and liturgy (if any of it is sung) while the worship group handle the 'charismatic' songs and choruses. This way of doing things indirectly tells people that they are only allowed to worship when the group is playing, not the 'proper' musicians. If we want worship to pervade the whole service, we need to explore the possibilities of mixing things up a little so that organ and group play together occasionally, the group alone handle some parts like the *Sanctus* or *Gloria*, and some of the worship songs are arranged in parts for the choir. This will confuse the congregation thoroughly, but hopefully it will lead them to the point of worshipping throughout the entire service rather than switching off completely at certain points.

The ultimate responsibility lies with the leader, not just to teach people how to worship through liturgy, nor even just to show them how themselves, but also to lead the liturgy in such a way that people are inspired to join in with the worship they are already offering as they take the service.

4. Jump off it

This section applies more to members of congregations than those up front during the services. The liturgy can be used as a springboard for your own prayers and meditations. If, as you are proceeding through the service, something strikes you which you want to dwell on for a while longer, stay with it, and let the rest go on for a few minutes without you. For example, if during the introduction to the penitential section you suddenly remember an old friend from way back with whom you have an unresolved conflict, or that GBH charge which you'd quite forgotten about since you became a Christian, it may be more positive all round if you treated those thoughts not as a rather tiresome interruption to what you're supposed to be concentrating on, but as a prompting of the Spirit to prayer and even possibly action. Again, if one line or phrase from, say, the *Gloria* or a collect suddenly strikes you in a new way, stay with it and meditate for a while on the new facet of truth which has been revealed to you. Let the liturgy flow on around you while you deal with what the Lord has on his agenda for you, and catch the rest of the people up a few prayers later. It's fine to do that; a liturgical service should not be seen (or led) as if it were a route march, but rather as a ramble with plenty of time to stop and enjoy what you encounter on the way, be it a panoramic vista which suddenly opens up or a tiny flower which someone spots. It is sad that the rubrics which allow for silence to be kept several times during the course of the Communion service are so seldom heeded, but it is permissible for you to switch off for a while and create your own private silence.

5. Take it home

I don't mean the service book itself, of course; you should already have one of your own. I refer to the value of picking up insights gained during worship and staying with them during your own private or family devotions. I am serious about owning your own book. My *ASB* is second only to my Bible as a book which I value and treasure, and along with Shakespeare (why always Shakespeare?) and, if I could swing it, Fritz Perls' *Gestalt Therapy Verbatim* (Moab, Utah: Real People, 1969) it would undoubtedly accompany me to any desert island on which I was fortunate enough to be marooned. There is something about your own copy of a book which makes it special to you; I would want to encourage people to feel the special nature of liturgical texts too.

One way of using the liturgy during the week is to make it the basis and framework for your own prayer life. Anglicans know this as 'saying the Daily Office', and many people find that the services of Morning or Evening Prayer form a helpful and comprehensive framework for them. Even on less ambitious levels it is possible to incorporate parts of the liturgy which you use on Sunday into the way you pray during the week. For example, the *Gloria* could be used occasionally, or possibly the Confession or the Creed. In the chapter on 'children and worship', I suggest that this is an especially helpful thing to do as a family with young children. It is undoubtedly the case for all ages that use of the liturgy during the week enhances our appreciation of it on Sundays and vice versa. If the Lord speaks to you particularly through one of the texts during Sunday worship, it is valuable to stay with it and see if you can get more out of it by giving it time during the week. If something really hits you during the week and you have time to take it on board, you will come to the same text with a whole new appreciation next Sunday.

6. Experiment with it

This section is especially for those who are responsible for the formation and/or leading of a service. I have subdivided it into a further seven parts.

(i) Explore it

One of the controlling factors in the whole way the *ASB* is put together is flexibility, and yet in many churches the liturgy is about as flexible as the pews people sit in to do it. How many people have actually explored all that the book has to offer? Very few, I suspect. We tend to stick to what is familiar, and in doing so miss out on a whole wealth of alternatives, each of which can add a new flavour and richness to worship. The Propers set for each Sunday are designed to fit in with the subject matter for the week and can, with judicious use of the index, be used just as effectively for those who preach on themes rather than from the lectionary. It's even permissible at times to make up your own Propers if none of those provided exactly fits the bill. For example, in Lent Three, with the theme of suffering, you could use these words lifted more or less straight from John 16:33 for the introduction to the Peace: 'I have told you these things so that in Jesus you may have peace. In this world you will have trouble. But take heart—Jesus has overcome the world. The peace of the Lord be always with you. . .'

People probably avoid using alternatives because they are not always easy for the congregation (or the celebrant) to find. The compilers of the *ASB* were faced with a straight choice of putting alternatives side by side (as in the old Series I/II booklets) or putting them separately at the end. Both have advantages and disadvantages, and they plumped for the latter course of action which means that a straight service is easier and one which uses alternatives is more difficult but need not be impossible. During the penitential seasons of Lent and Advent, I often plump for the latter position for the penitential section, using the brilliant form of the Commandments on page 161, followed three pages later by Confession 'C', and then on to page 170 for the alternative Humble Access prayer and the Peace introduction. I do not find it too intrusive to turn people to the relevant pages as this is moving through the book, not nipping backwards and forwards.

As a really radical alternative, why not get copyright permission and put some of the prayers on OHP slides so that no one needs to bother about page numbers? In my first parish I spent a long time writing out on bits of Filofax paper (I need to put it on record that I am a pre-Yuppie

Filofax user) all the Propers for each Sunday in each year, as well as Saints' Days and so on. I then filed them so that each week I had one sheet, containing all the extra material, to use with my *ASB*. This meant that I had no flipping about of pages to do during, for example, the Eucharistic Prayer. You can even get Filofax paper in the correct liturgical colours, if that sort of thing turns you on, and apparently someone somewhere produces continuous Filofax stationery for computer printers.

It is slightly more difficult, then, to use the text creatively, but I reckon it is well worth the slight inconvenience to enrich the worship and give it integrity. Explore fully what you've got and use more than just a few little bits of it.

(ii) Sing it

It used to be considered the sole preserve of the Anglo-Catholic branch of the church to use sung liturgy, but fortunately all that has changed now, and many churches are experiencing the value of singing parts of the service. There are many settings of, for example, the Communion intended for a range of instrumentation and in a range of styles and complexities. There are even some with a good charismatic pedigree. Many are available on tape, so you can hear what it ought to sound like before committing yourself to using it, and learn it much more painlessly once you have. It is worth a church having two or three settings in its repertoire, and it is best to use them in blocks rather than week by week. For example, a good use of two different settings would be to use a slightly more meditative one during Lent and Advent, and a celebratory one for the rest of the year. In my experience the use of a different setting each week on a rota confuses people. Criteria for choosing a setting would be its simplicity and singability together with its ability to stand repeated use over a long period.

There is a lot to be said for home-grown settings if anyone in your congregation writes music. The most successful ones use a simple melody line which is treated slightly differently in each part. If you are writing for a worship group as opposed to an organ, there is much scope for orchestration, and a congregation can get much more excited about something which it knows has been composed from within the context of its own life, rather than by some Oxbridge professor. Nevertheless, most churches will have to rely on something composed by a 'proper' composer, and there are plenty of lovely ones on offer. For the record, my own favourite is Patrick Appleford's *New English Mass* (London: Josef Weinberger). Since this setting doesn't have a Creed, I would add the one from Betty Pulkingham's *King of Glory* (Yeldall: Celebration Services, 1975) setting which I think is superb. But in the end it is all a matter of personal taste, and a church needs to find one or two settings which are acceptable.

Having chosen a setting it will need to be taught. This will take at least three months, and it is better to do it gradually, beginning perhaps with the *Gloria* and then moving on to the *Sanctus* and including other parts as people become more confident. Many churches take five minutes or so before the service starts to begin to teach what the people will then use liturgically later on in the worship. It may help to issue music copies to people, but this can be counter-productive. We have our words complete with music written on OHP slides, and one terminally non-musical member of the church was heard to comment, 'I don't know why they've written all those dots and lines all over the words; it's hard enough trying to work out how it goes without all that in the way.' In the end, though, if the music is simple enough it can be easily learned and will stay in people's minds very successfully. If you don't sing your liturgy, why not give it a try? And if you do, how about experimenting with singing some bits that are not usually sung? I've already mentioned the possibility of a sung Peace; another option which can be very powerful at times is to sing some sort of a prayer of confession, for example that by Chris Rolinson from his album *Lighten our Darkness* (Kingsway: Eastbourne, 1987).[3]

(iii) Do it

Liturgical purists will know that what we say in services is the ritual, while what we do is the ceremonial. Ceremonial is, of course, a dirty word in many evangelical circles but, like non-conformists and their liturgy, we all have it. If the vicar walks in at the beginning of the service and out at the end; if the offering is brought forward and received; if people kneel (or sit) for prayer—all this is ceremonial, just as much as genuflection and making the sign of the cross. We all have ceremonial parts in our worship, so let's acknowledge the fact and make the best use of it.

Trevor Lloyd's excellent booklet *Ceremonial in Worship* (Grove Books: Nottingham, 1981) is well worth reading. Each minister as well as each local church will have different ideas about what is appropriate or otherwise, but some guidelines might include doing what has to be done decently and in order, but not doing for the sake of ceremonial anything which does not need to be done; making sure that your ceremonial does not communicate something which you do not actually believe theologically, either in terms of doctrine or, more subtly, in terms of priesthood; and making sure that it adds to the worship of the living God rather than detracting from it and becoming an end in itself. Again, just for the record, my own personal list of babies thrown out with the 'low-church' bath water would include the sign of the cross given during the Absolution and Blessing and made by the people in response, processions (Graham Kendrick's *Make Way* [Eastbourne: Thankyou Music, 1986] has helped a lot here), and kneeling for prayer. It's good that many churches are very relaxed and charismatic in their worship nowadays, but it would be sad if charismatic Christians forgot how to get physically on their knees before the Lord.

I could say a lot more here about the environment for worship: banners, vestments and robes, liturgical colours and so on, but I'm not really very qualified in those areas, although I know what I like. These things are important, though, and need to be thought through seriously, especially by those whose more low-church background makes them put such things fairly near the bottom of the list of priorities for the life of the church. I'll simply leave you with two comments from friends who have stayed with me and have been very important in my own pilgrimage.

The first was from a young Anglo-Catholic curate whom I met shortly after I began to become interested in the Church of England's way of doing things. He was a bit of a country bumpkin who had come up to London. Explaining why he liked liturgical colours, he said they reminded him of the seasons of the year, and the way that nature and the countryside change colour according to the season. To see the same happen in church spoke to him of the marvellous creativity of God. The other comment was from a friend who taught English and drama. He described the celebration of the Eucharist as the most incredible piece of drama ever. Something about both these ideas grabbed me, and has deeply affected the way I feel about, and celebrate, Communion. It upsets me when the Eucharist is handled with about as much dignity as the celebrant would use when making himself a bacon sandwich at the kitchen table. Ceremonial matters; let's work at getting it right.

(iv) Select and emphasise

In Chapter 9 we will see this principle worked out more fully. But briefly, I feel that it is a mistake to go straight through everything in the book on every occasion. When different themes are being emphasised in the preaching, why not emphasise them liturgically too? Why not spend some time really making something of the Creed, perhaps by singing it or a song with similar content, or by taking it apart clause by clause and meditating on it quietly? Then you could make up for the time by simplifying the intercessions into nothing more than a minute or two for silent prayer.

During Lent and Advent you may want to take more time over the Penitential Section and omit a hymn, one of the readings or the Creed. I find it helpful to think of the balance which a liturgical framework for the service provides as being worked out not over a period of one service but during a month or two. Thus it is possible to miss out the Prayer of Humble Access for one or even a couple of weeks, as long as it isn't absent for months at a time. Taken over a longer period every part of the service is there, although not every part will be there every week.

(v) Replace it

This simply means using songs which have similar sentiments to certain parts of the liturgy rather than those parts themselves. Many of us, of course, have been doing something like this for years with material from *Psalm Praise* (London: Falcon, 1973) which, as well as containing up-to-date (or at least up-to-1973) versions of many of the Psalms, also has settings of the non-Eucharistic canticles. The most famous and widely used today is probably 'Tell out my soul' (the *Magnificat*), but others have caught on and are still popular.

Although our modern worship songs are not generally

settings of the exact words of the liturgical texts, it is still possible to use songs which are close in vocabulary and feel. So, for example, you might replace the *Gloria* with 'God of Glory', the *Sanctus* with 'Holy, holy, holy is the Lord' or 'Holy is the Lord', the *Creed* with 'We believe', and so on. Used sparingly this can be a very effective way of linking liturgy with modern worship. You could even use one of these songs to replace a liturgical text and then lead into other songs in a time of worship.

Replacement can also occur in spoken rather than sung texts. Prayers from other traditions can be used, via the OHP or on printed sheets, and whole sections of the liturgy can be fitted together creatively to follow a particular theme where no such provision is made in the *ASB*. *Church Family Worship* (London: Hodder and Stoughton, 1986) is particularly helpful here, and as parts of the charismatic song-writing scene become increasingly 'liturgical', you could occasionally include parts in weekly worship. In *Make Way!*, Graham Kendrick borrowed from the Anglican liturgy the Eucharistic Prayer's acclamation 'Christ has died, Christ is risen, Christ will come again'. In *Shine, Jesus, Shine* he has a beautiful credal part as well as a moving prayer of confession which I think could be successfully used in normal worship. It is also possible to move in another direction and find much that is helpful. One Advent we replaced our intercessions with a responsive version of the Roman Advent Antiphons based on the text from *Prayers for Alternative Services*.[4]

I wouldn't like to see substitution happening to the extent that the normal liturgy becomes redundant and people never know what they are going to get each week. A careful use of replacement, however, can be very effective now and again.

(vi) Regroup it

In Chapter 8 I'll be talking about the problems with the

'hymn sandwich' approach to worship structure, but for now let me say that it is possible, and at times very effective, to use all the set parts, but in a different order. This happens to some degree in Rite A with the movable penitential section, and also in the Initiation services, but it is in the non-sacramental services that it is most useful. The first part of Morning and Evening Prayer is rather an up-and-down affair with readings, canticles and a Psalm coming hot foot after one another. Why not have a Psalm and the readings together, as in the Eucharistic Ministry of the Word, with space for meditation in between, and then respond to the readings in worship, perhaps beginning with a canticle and launching off into a time of worship? Alternatively you could use the responses ('O Lord, open our lips') as a very appropriate lead in to spoken and sung worship, which then moves into hearing the Bible readings. This is all fairly simple, but it seems that clergy actually need permission to feel they can do this sort of thing. It's OK, you can.

(vii) Add to it

Comprehensive though the *ASB* is, it totally misses out one worship ingredient—the chance for a good long time of worship with several songs one after the other. Yet within the overall framework, for example of Rite A, there are several places where such a time might be added in a way which contributes positively to the flow of the service. How about the following?

- For five minutes before and ten minutes into the service, in place of the opening hymn.

- Instead of the *Gloria*, leading into the Collect and readings.

- Launching off from the Creed.

- Beginning from the Peace instead of the offertory hymn, and leading up to the climactic 'Yours, Lord, is the greatness'.

- Launching off from the *Sanctus* in the middle of the Eucharistic Prayer.

- Building slowly from the quietness of the administration of Communion and ending exuberantly with the Blessing and Dismissal.

If all this fails, you could always have a time of worship after the service has ended!

But what about the legality of all this? While many Anglican clergy have no conscience whatsoever about doing anything they feel like in worship, others may regard the suggestions I've made as outrageously illegal and therefore quite unacceptable. There is in fact nothing in what I've said which transgresses Canon Law, and a careful reading of the *ASB* rubrics and *The Canons of the Church of England*[5] can help salve the consciences of the scrupulous.

First, the *ASB* itself allows for the omission of many sections, in fact any with numbering in blue rather than black. Along with this go the rubrics allowing 'other suitable words'[6] and the very important permission given in Canon B 5 to the minister to 'make and use variations which are not of substantial importance in any form of service prescribed'.[7] In extreme cases it is up to the Bishop to decide whether or not the alterations are of 'substantial importance', but I doubt if he'd want to know about your using 'Lord, have mercy on us' instead of the Kyries (which you are allowed to omit in any case). Personally I reckon that one service which I attended where they dispensed with the Eucharistic Prayer and went straight to the breaking of bread had overstepped the mark, but the Canon is gloriously vague and can cover a multitude of things which are therefore not sins. The only stipulation is that any variations made 'shall be reverent and seemly and shall be neither contrary to, nor indicative of any departure from, the doctrine of the Church of England'.[8] Between them these allowances give permission to do quite a bit with the Communion service.

The Offices are slightly more difficult, but the way to cope is to obey Canon B 5 again, where the minister is allowed 'on occasions for which no provision is made. . .[to] use forms of service considered suitable by him to those occasions'.[9] This is the Canon which allows such things as family services, sacramental confessions, and so on, and could equally well apply to a more informal 'praise service' or whatever you want to call it. And having set up your praise service, you are of course perfectly entitled to use parts of existing texts during the course of it, for example some parts of Morning or Evening Prayer.

All this may appear to be a rather questionable exercise in bending rules in order totally to break the spirit of the law, but in fact it is the very opposite: an experimentation within rules which seeks to make worship more appropriate for God's people. And it is this very exercise which the Liturgical Commission themselves are engaged in. There is a constant process of restructuring and experimentation going on, and they are aware of the widespread use of different forms of service. Rather than making people feel guilty and secretive about what they are doing, they are often glad to hear about examples of creative liturgy and about how they were received by the congregation. The liturgical books of the future are likely to be much more open and flexible, even than the *ASB* as they opt for a resource book approach rather than a straightforward set of rites. The days of fossilised liturgy are over, and the creative use of words, music and action in some of the ways I've suggested, far from being frowned upon as illegal, is actually being acknowledged as pioneering for the future.

What matters supremely, however, is that those who work creatively with the liturgy do so carefully, appropriately and with great understanding of the principles involved. One of my hobbies is Indian cookery, and it is a cuisine based on the delicate blending of spices and flavours. An experienced chef will never use recipe books, but will work by instinct and tradition. But, as I have found to my cost, attempts to emulate the masters can either work or not. Too little spice leaves a flat, bland taste, and too much can create an overkill effect. Getting it just right takes great skill, and I fail as often as I succeed. Spicing up the liturgy is a similarly skilled process. The master chefs of the Liturgical Commission know what they are doing, and have served us up a real feast in the *ASB* and their other publications. To try to improve on it is fine, as long as we don't spoil it in the process.

I hope you can see, then, that I am not one of those who consider it clever to play fast and loose with the law of the church, but I do believe in using to the full the opportunities it allows me to work as skilfully as I can at making the worship of the people in my care more and more appropriate, and more and more a vehicle through which they can meet God.

Notes

1. Gregory Dix, *The Shape of the Liturgy* (Dacre: Westminster, 1945), p 744.
2. *The Alternative Service Book, 1980* (SPCK: Cambridge, 1980), p 11.
3. A lead-sheet for all the songs is available from The Rainbow Company, PO Box 77, Hailsham, East Sussex BN27 3EF, and the Confession mentioned in the text is in NS 88/89, no 2.
4. David Silk, ed, *Prayers for Alternative Services* (Mowbrays: London and Oxford, 1980), p 25.

5. *The Canons of the Church of England* (SPCK: London, 1969). For a useful commentary on the Canons as they relate to worship, see Michael Perry, *A Handbook of Parish Worship* (Mowbrays: London and Oxford, 1977), pp 1–8.

6. For example *ASB* p 128 section 30 at the Peace. I don't believe this rubric refers solely to the alternatives provided at section 83.

7. *Op cit*, p 9.

8. *Ibid*, p 9ff.

9. *Ibid*, p 9.

CHAPTER SEVEN

HANDLING WORSHIP

I. Verbal

S O YOU'RE GOING TO LEAD WORSHIP. How do you do it? Having looked specifically at liturgy, I now want to move on and look at two further aspects of the service and how they might be handled. For convenience I've split it into two different sections: this chapter will deal specifically with non-musical parts, and then we'll move on to look more closely at music. Once again I want to try to help people involved in different styles of worship, so if some sections don't apply to you, feel free to give them a miss. But first, some general comments:

1. Preparation

Before you get anywhere near the service, you should have prepared for it adequately. Personal preparation is important. Are you OK with the Lord or out of touch? Have you just had a row with your wife and kids? Have you come straight from a heavy session of counselling, with someone reliving their birth experiences all over your floor? How much sleep did you get last night? All these factors and many more besides will affect not just the way in which you may 'perform' up front in a service, but also the way in which you'll plan for it in advance. You'll be able to deal with some things through prayer and repentance, but others will mean that you need an even greater degree of reliance on God's grace. I find it a helpful insight, and one which I owe again to John Wimber, that we can function 'in role' as well as 'under anointing'. Sometimes you will be aware of the Spirit resting powerfully on you as you minister, but at others you will feel nothing at all or even worse. In those instances God honours the 'role' you have in that context, that of 'service leader' or whatever, and great things can still happen.

What about those times when you feel so out of touch with God that you hardly even believe in him any more? We may have talked with people who have told us that they feel totally unable to come to church any more since it has all become so unreal to them. Taking part in a service would simply feel like going through the motions, and would surely be nothing short of hypocritical. If such feelings make it difficult for people in the congregation, how much worse it is when the worship leader loses his faith.

If this is an ongoing problem, it may well be right to take some time out of ministry for as long as you are able, and to seek help from someone you trust. But for those times when our depression is simply a phase through which we are passing, there is real merit in keeping going and putting on a brave face. First, the discipline is very helpful at such times, and can stop a dangerous and insidious process of drifting out of attendance. Secondly, it is often the case that our own 'hypocritical' worship leading can be the very thing which lifts our spirits up to God again. As we're exhorting and encouraging the congregation to worship, we may suddenly find that we've talked ourself into it too. I find it more positive at such times to think not in terms of hypocrisy, but rather of offering a sacrifice of praise to the Lord. It was John Wesley who said, 'Preach faith until you have it;' the same principle is behind worship leading too. And thirdly, when all is said and done, if every minister who was feeling out of touch with God were to stop functioning until they felt better, the whole of Christendom would collapse within about three weeks. The Enemy knows how fragile we are emotionally, especially when we're about to go out on public view. That's why he always makes our spouses or friends function at their most abrasive just as we're leaving home for the service. Many worship leaders begin to praise the Lord with the sound of angry words and a slammed front door still ringing in their ears. If we give in too easily to the Enemy, he's got us just where he wants us. So deal with what you can. What you can't deal with, forget for now and get on with the job in hand, which is to glorify God.

Another part of preparation is planning the service. This is so important that I've given a whole chapter over to it, so I won't say a lot more now. But it should go without saying that a service can very often tend to run better if we've not only chosen the hymns, readings and so on beforehand, but also communicated that fact to the organist, readers and other interested parties.

Finally, and this is the most neglected part of the preparation, you need to do the last-minute getting together of everything you're going to need. All the necessary books should be ready, with markers in the appropriate places. The hymn book should be open at the first hymn you're going to use, and the scraps of paper people have handed you with notices on should be neatly clipped together. Other people taking part should be aware that you're expecting them, and of when you're expecting them. All this is obvious, but we still don't do it. We nip back into the vestry during hymns to get things we've forgotten; we have times of silence not so much so that the Spirit can move, but so that we can find the right page; we forget to read the Banns; all this can be avoided if we take time before the service to prepare. One Anglican clergyman, baby in arms, suddenly realised with horror that he'd forgotten to fill the font. Pondering momentarily on a theology of dry-cleaning rather than baptism, he decided that the only way to redeem the situation was through sheer bluff, so he ordered the congregation, 'Please stand for the ceremony of the fetching of the water!' and proceeded in a dignified manner to the tap. I doubt whether anyone even noticed, but such situations are not really ideal. I find it helpful to think through each part of the service, checking that I've got everything I'm going to need.

2. First impressions

I've already mentioned my difficulty in defining 'presence', but I do know some things I can do to help, and I need to make sure I do them very quickly as the service begins. One of my special responsibilities is to be in charge of all our weddings. As I stand up at the start of each one, I'm aware that I'm faced with a church full of people with all sorts of things going on in their heads. The vast majority of them are not Christians; they may be feeling horribly out of place in church; they will have expectations about how the service will feel, what a vicar will be like, how long they have to put up with this before they can get back to the beer, and so on. I'm also aware that their impressions will be confirmed or shattered within a very short time of the start of the service, perhaps even a matter of seconds rather than minutes. So I go all out to be the best I can be right from square one. I look round, I smile at them, I open my mouth to speak, and I make sure they can hear right from the very first word. Drawing myself up to my full height, I boom out with the butchest and most unparsonical voice I can manage: 'Welcome to St Veggieburga's. . .' I want to get people to relax by letting them know they're in my hands and that I can handle it. Whenever people tell me later what a 'nice service' it had been, I believe I convinced them of that within the first thirty seconds of it. By contrast a weedy, uncertain, inaudible start can lose people in a way which makes them next to impossible to recapture. What is true for outsiders at weddings is to a lesser extent true for all services. Presence is nowhere more essential than at the very start.

It's worth saying something briefly at this stage about microphone technique since most churches today use PA. By far the best system for the service leader is to use a radio microphone. This means that you are totally free of wires and can wander about at leisure with no drop in sound volume, but it does have several drawbacks. Radio mikes are notoriously unreliable, and can fizz and crackle throughout the service, especially if you have something metal too near the transmitter. Anything from chair legs to loose change can make the service sound as if it is being broadcast live from Leningrad. And of course they are very expensive. The PA operator needs to be on the ball, since the only time they are absolutely guaranteed to work is before the service starts, and it can be most unedifying if the waiting congregation picks up at full volume everything from the prayer in the vestry that God will give the so and sos a good shaking tonight to the pre-service trip to the loo.

The next best thing is a trailing halter mike, which is considerably cheaper but does limit mobility. The ceremonial unplugging at the chancel step and replugging at the altar can add something to the liturgy (usually two loud thumps), but once again an operator who is on the ball can switch the mike off during the process. If you use ordinary stand mikes, you need to make sure that you are the right distance and direction from them when you speak. Different mikes vary, and you will need to get to know yours, but on average your mouth should be about six to eight inches away from and three to four inches above the end of the mike. If you are too close the congregation will hear your heavy breathing, and if you are not far enough above the mike, there will be a clap of thunder every time you use a word with a 'p' in it. Some mikes have a built-in 'pop shield' to prevent this; if not, you can get external ones—little sponge rubber hats which fit over the business end (you can even get them in the correct liturgical colours). Having positioned yourself correctly, the art is simply to forget that the mike is there and speak as normally as you can. It is not enough just to be able to use mikes correctly; you also need to train and practise with anyone who will speak into one during the service. Lesson readers and intercessors can be notoriously bad at it.

Good PA is very important since it is an unchangeable law of the church that those with the most severe hearing difficulties always sit nearest the back. The sound level should be comfortable for everyone. If you do have an elderly congregation it may be worth considering an induction loop system in a part of your building. This is basically a loop of wire under the floor or around the walls which gives a signal which many hearing aids can pick up. Specialist firms will be glad to advise you about a system like this. But whatever you use, it should be as unobtrusive as possible so that it adds to rather than detracts from the sense of worship.

3. Body language

The general rubrics to the *ASB* Rite 'A' Communion Service specify that 'the president may use traditional manual acts during the Eucharistic Prayers' (*ASB*, p 117). I've said a bit about this in the previous chapter, but it is worth making the point that a good worship leader will be physically as well as verbally involved in the service. Whether or not you go in for the works in terms of ceremonial, it is important that what you are saying with your body backs up and illustrates what you are saying with your mouth. Many people lead worship with their hands in their pockets, as it were, and this cannot help but communicate to the congregation that they are not really interested in what they are doing. In whatever way is appropriate for your setting, you need to communicate involvement, excitement and participation in worship. In this way you will give a good lead to the congregation to become fully involved. This applies not just during the Eucharistic Prayers, but throughout everything you do.

4. A service, not a meeting

There is all the difference in the world between 'taking a service' and 'leading worship'. The former implies that there are certain things to be got through during the next hour, rather like items on an agenda, whereas the latter implies that everything we do and say should be aimed at leading people into the presence of God so that he can be lifted up among us. It is a rare skill to be able to make everything, notices and Banns included, into part of an act of worship, but it can be done, and it should be our aim to do it. The way in which we conduct things, including ourselves, should point to God and should express some truth about him which people, whether they know him or not, should be able to take on board. So how might we do it?

The welcome and introduction

These should be welcoming and introductory, since they

are the first things people will hear you say. I have taken many services where the very first thing people have heard me say (or rather sing) was, 'O Lord, open thou our lips'. Let's just stop for a moment and listen to what I was actually saying.

O Lord, open Thou our lips. . .
Well, here we all are again. We're starting on page nineteen, but there's no need to tell you that because you all know it. You're the same people who were here last week when we started on page nineteen, and in fact every week since 1662 when the words were first said. You know you're welcome, so there's no need to spell it out, although it would have saved us all a lot of bother if you hadn't come. Never mind, here you are, so we'd better get on with it. If by any unimaginable chance you're new here and don't know what on earth is going on, tough. You'll just have to feel welcome and try to peer over to the nearest person five pews away to find out what page we're starting on or even which book we're in.
And our mouth shall shew forth thy praise.

Hardly welcoming or introductory, is it? This whole approach works on the assumption that no one will ever be present at a service who is not a regular attender. Very often it is a true assumption, and it is easy to see why. So let's take the trouble to welcome people if they really are welcome, and to give them at least a vague clue as to what they might expect to happen and how they might join in if they feel like it. Sometimes it is a good idea to begin with what Anglicans call the Peace and to give people a chance to greet one another. This establishes a corporate feel to the service right from the start, and in my experience lifts considerably any singing which is to follow.

Hymns

There seem to be two equal and opposite errors in the announcing of Hymns. The first is simply to say, 'Hymn number 239,' and the second is to preach a sermon about the theology of the hymn, the biography of its author, the musical merits of the tune, and how you like it because you had it at your wedding. There is probably a middle way which gives some idea as to why you have chosen this particular hymn and how it reflects the theme of the service, but which doesn't make the actual singing of it seem like a bit of an anticlimax when you finally get round to it. Your introduction should help people to experience singing the hymn as a part of their worship, as they realise how it moves them further along and deeper into the unfolding theme of the service. It also helps if instructions about posture are given as the last thing you say before they start, and not the first. If you say, 'Let's stand to sing "Great is thy faithfulness",' and then go on to say a bit about it, you leave people hovering somewhere between sitting and standing, which is not only embarrassing for them but also very bad for the posture. So say what you want to say, and then round it off with, 'So let's stand to sing.' That way everyone knows where they are.

Prayers and parts of the liturgy

There is a variety of ways of getting people to begin speaking at the same time. The most widely practised is for the leader to begin with the first line, speaking in a slightly slower and more emphatic tone of voice, so that people can join in with the second phrase:

Leader: Almighty God
All: to whom all hearts are open. . .

But there are other ways of doing it. You can announce the fact that you are going to use the Collect for Purity, and then give a cue for people to begin:

Leader: Together.
All: Almighty God, to whom all hearts are open. . .

The disadvantage of this model is that it sprinkles the liturgy with several 'together's' which, after a while, take on an almost liturgical feel themselves.

The other main way of doing it is for the leader to say the first line, which the congregation repeat after him:

Leader: Almighty God
All: Almighty God, to whom all hearts are open. . .

This works fine as long as everyone knows the rules, but if you have in your midst anyone who is used to the first and by far most common model, you set up a wonderful fugal effect as he carries on from line two while everyone else goes back and repeats line one. In the end, the majority tends to win, but it can be rather unseemly for a few seconds while the competition is going on. All in all I prefer the first way which, although it has the disadvantage that the people never get to say 'Almighty God', seems to me to outweigh the other models, not least because it is the most widely practised.

It is important to be consistent so that, as it were, everyone knows the rules. Once the prayer gets going, the leader needs to make sure that he leads clearly and avoids idiosyncratic pace or phrasing, but sets the speed and follows the natural rhythm and pauses of the words. Clergy seem to be notoriously bad at this, and they get worse as they get older. Not only should the leader be leading the people, he should also be listening to them, and listening especially for any tendency to leave them behind or drag behind them.

When everyone is joining together in a piece of liturgy, it is good to encourage them from time to time to say it as if they mean it. Experiencing a 'performance' of *Shine, Jesus, Shine*, the follow-up to *Make Way!*, profoundly affected the way in which I lead liturgy. It contains several 'liturgical' passages, some of them lifted straight from Anglicanism, but rather than being used as bits to say together, they are used as triumphant shouts or as heartfelt prayers. It made me realise how unconvincing much of our liturgy must sound to God, and the following Sunday I led the congregation at my church in 'shouting' Psalm 96 together. This was obviously a new idea, but I could see from people's faces how much they were enjoying it. I certainly found a new depth of meaning in the words as they were spoken with the gusto which they deserve.

Congregational praying

This can also be handled in different ways. How can you pray together as a church in a way which feels together, but which also allows for maximum participation? There is a fundamental tension here, and it is one which increases with the size of the congregation. We use a variety of models, each of which has strengths and weaknesses on both counts.

(i) The 'Keswick' model Here each subject for prayer is introduced, and then one person will pray about it as fully as possible. This may be the leader, but it may equally be someone from the congregation, sometimes previously briefed. The strength of this is that it scores high on togetherness, as there really is the feeling of one person articulating for everyone what they would like to be saying. But participation by everyone is at a minimum, and the prayers can often take on a rather samey feel as predictable people come out with their own predictable prayers. So the final score for this model would be—togetherness: *****; participation: **.

(ii) Small groups In this model the congregation is invited to turn around and form groups of four to six, and to pray in those groups about whatever is on the agenda. The great strength of this is that in theory at least everyone can pray if they want to, and any subject will be covered from many different angles and points of view. The disadvantage is that it can be very off-putting for the first-timer, the visitor, the couple who've come to hear their Banns, and so on. We always give a get-out clause with this one, and allow people just to sit and 'pray quietly on your own'. Even when it does work properly, it can feel rather fragmented as you have no idea what anyone else apart from those in your group and the lady with the loud voice in the next one is praying. Togetherness: **; participation: *****.

(iii) *The cathedral model* This is where one person leads intercession from the front, and everyone else listens and, hopefully, meditates and prays silently around the subject. It is worth saying that this model is not only found in cathedrals; it is also the way in which the non-conformist churches usually handle intercession, the only difference being in whether you say 'Amen' once at the end or several times as you go along. If it is done well it can give a good whole-church feel and sum up the prayers of all the people, but it is weak in that it can encourage passivity in the congregation. One wonders how people who have nothing but this diet fare in their own prayers at home. Togetherness: ****; participation: *.

(iv) *The 'Yonggi Cho' model* We don't use this very often, but in the Full Gospel Central Church in Seoul, Korea, they do it all the time. On the word 'go' everyone begins to pray their own prayers, out loud, all at the same time. The advantage of this is that participation is total, and so is togetherness, because everyone is doing the same thing and you are only too aware of it. Its weakness lies in the fact that British congregations would generally rather be dismembered than do such an outrageously embarrassing thing. People need a huge push to get into it, and some loud background music helps considerably. Some might feel that it offends St Paul's injunction that everything be done 'in a fitting and orderly way', and I might well agree with them. However, when you look at the size of Yonggi Cho's church, it doesn't seem to have done much harm there. Togetherness: *****; participation: *****; embarrassment: *****.

(v) Medium-sized groups Because we have quite a large membership, we have recently split the church into several different 'congregations' which meet not in different venues but at different times in the same building. Each congregation is a self-contained pastoral unit, and it means that when we come together as a whole church to pray we can conveniently spend part of the time in congregational groups. Your church may not be of a sufficient size to warrant more than one such group, but to split into groups of between twenty and fifty people and then to have open prayer within the groups probably provides the best balance overall. This will probably not be all that useful during Sunday services, but it is ideal for other prayer meetings. The amount of upheaval caused by moving people around means that it is worth spending some time in the groups once you've got there. But subjects for prayer can be covered fully and effectively by several such groups, especially if there is some built-in specialisation (one group pray about the missionary's family, another group about his church, and so on). It is essentially a compromise, and so achieves neither aim completely, but it is probably the best compromise available. Togetherness: ***; participation: ***.

The way in which we handle the spoken parts of the service is vital if it is to lead people deeper into an awareness of God. I want to end this section by quoting a passage from a Roman Catholic book on worship, which sums up beautifully much of what I have been trying to say. If you haven't understood so far, I hope this will help.

God is dead!

God is dead. . .when the priest, praying to God, looks at the congregation as if to persuade them that he is.

God is dead. . .when soloists, or the choir, sing words to God and make music without being involved in what they are singing.

God is dead. . .when the reader reads from the Bible as if it were a telephone directory, without pausing for breath and without allowing the Spirit to breathe.

God is dead. . .when the assembly recites the Lord's Prayer or sings a hymn as if it were a popular song.

God is dead. . .when hymns no longer know how to speak to God and only aim to question a new moralism.

God is dead. . .when the priest raises his arms to shoulder height in a mechanical gesture, no longer towards a symbolic otherness, or holds out his hands over the offerings in a mechanical gesture, and not under the weight of the Spirit.

God is dead. . .when people speak of God, carp at God, always refer to him as 'he' and not as 'you'.

God is dead. . .when the word of God is not in the words, the ineffability of God is not in the silences, the Spirit is not in the bodies.

No, God is not dead, but appearances—and liturgy is all about appearances—are sometimes able to make us doubt his presence.[1]

Notes

1. Jean Lebon, *Understanding the Liturgy* (London: SCM, 1987), p 58.

CHAPTER EIGHT

HANDLING WORSHIP

II. Musical

WE'VE TALKED ABOUT the liturgical and verbal parts of the service, and how to help them feel more like worship; now we turn to the more specifically musical parts. We hope, of course, that the whole service will be worship, but for many people music is at the heart of their response to God. I don't want to get into any arguments about terminology, so I will use the word 'worship' in two distinct ways: to describe the service or meeting as a whole, but also that part of it commonly designated a 'time of worship'. In concentrating now on music, I do not mean to imply that anything else that happens is less glorifying to God (although it may well be in practice).

The idea of being in any way involved in leading music will, of course, give many ministers or service leaders a sense of foreboding horror as they exclaim, 'But I'm not musical!' While this may in many cases be true, it need not actually matter too much if there is someone around who is musical and who knows how to lead in such a way that the unmusical service leader can trust them. You can simply hand the leadership over for the duration of the worship time and take it back again at the end. It is also worth investing a lot of time in your musician, since he will be a very important right-hand person to you, and you will need to build up a really empathic relationship with him. Get him to try and drum some kind of musical 'feel' into you, and at the same time you teach him some of the rudiments of leadership which we discussed in the last chapter. You should both benefit from the relationship in the long run, although it may take years rather than months. It also needs to be said that even if you are musical, there may still be someone else better equipped to lead the worship time than you are, and you may need to relinquish some of your responsibility to them from time to time.

What exactly is a worship time, and how can you lead one? Perhaps it would be helpful to look at some different ways in which this is done in different settings, in order both to identify what it is we're talking about and to look at different 'models' which, no doubt, will all have strengths and weaknesses. You will have discovered by now that I have the sort of mind which works with lists and sub-headings, so it will come as no surprise to you that I have identified six different models for a worship time.

1. The 'hymn sandwich' model

This is not really a model for a worship time as such; rather it is the very antithesis. Both liturgical and non-liturgical churches can fall into this trap in different ways. Basically it is the use of music as a set of bridges to get from one item in the service to another. It could, of course, be seen the other way round, that the sermon, readings, notices etc are the bridges to get from one hymn to the other, but either way it gets you nowhere, since you are not doing anything in the service for long enough at a time. The Baptist church in which I was brought up probably typifies this approach. We were definitely not liturgical, but every week without fail the service went like this: Hymn — Prayer — Reading — Hymn — Notices — Collection — Very Long Prayer — Hymn — Sermon — Hymn — Benediction (of the non-conformist, not the Anglo-Catholic variety, of course). Liturgical services can be just as bad, though. As I've already mentioned, I was once involved in starting a new evening service in the parish church, which was to be 'charismatic' in nature. I am basically a liturgical creature, so I was adamant that we had to use the framework of the *ASB* Evening Prayer service. It wasn't very many weeks before we discovered the same thing as our Baptist friends—that music broken up into little bits tends to produce worship broken up into little bits, moving and wonderful though the *Magnificat* and the *Nunc Dimittis* are. So we held onto the framework but put all the music together and then had the readings, canticles and so on. It made a tremendous difference to the whole service to do it that way round.

The problem is that if we want to get the worship cycle going, and expect God to come among us and meet with us, we have to cycle very fast indeed to get there in the space of one hymn or song. Yes, the readings are still worship, but unless we are very tuned in to God, we are bound to experience a slight dropping off in the intensity of our devotion when we move from the last chorus of 'Rejoice, rejoice' into Leviticus chapter 13, verses 47 to 59 or whatever the first reading happens to be. We're only human, and it takes time to get in touch with Almighty God, especially if we really do want intimacy with him in worship. This model allows no time, and it needs to be adapted for renewed worship.

2. The 'community singalong' model

Here the mistakes of the 'hymn sandwich' model have been rectified, and plenty of time is allowed for a good sing. Under the direction of an enthusiastic song leader, who is determined that everyone *will* have a good sing, the congregation goes through one piece after another while the leader tests his ingenuity, and at the same time seeks to prevent boredom, by thinking up as many different interesting ways of singing as he can. Meanwhile, either because he thinks they need it, or because he is cold or has circulation trouble, he conducts the congregation vigorously. Like a frenetic windmill, he encourages the singers on: 'Now, the ladies only for verse eight'; 'The men this time, very quietly'; 'The chorus again, this side of the aisle'; 'Right, this side, let's see if we can do better than that'; 'The next song—only people called Arthur or Tracey', and so it goes on. This may be great fun, especially for the leader, but it has one major problem: it has nothing whatsoever to do with worship.

Whatever words the people may be singing, it is very difficult for them to take on much worship content while the singers are watching a gymnastic display, listening to a shouting contest, and trying to guess whether or not they are likely to be allowed to join in next time round. The best hope for a worshipper caught in such a session is *not* to be called Arthur or Tracey and to sit the whole thing out completely and practise his Ignatian contemplative prayer exercises while the singing goes on around him. You may laugh, but there is truth in this. It is only too easy for the worship leader to get in the way and prevent people meeting with God, however well intentioned he may be. Although there is danger in a leadership style that has too little rather than too much visibility and verbal encouragement, personally I would rather err on the other side than on this.

3. The 'songs of fellowship bingo' model

This one is the favourite of informal small groups, college CUs and house fellowships. There are two variations. In the purest version, the leader simply says, 'Er, has anyone got a song they'd like to sing?' After an embarrassed silence, broken only by the frantic rustling of song-book pages, someone says, 'Could we sing number seventeen?' More rustling as everyone else finds number seventeen, then off they all go. At the end of the song there is a bit more silence and rustling, then, 'Number 127,' which they dutifully sing. By now the group has got over its self-consciousness, and the real bingo begins as people all over the room remember what number *their* favourite is and shout it out with great fervour: '28!' '354!' '182!' Then the group's equivalent of the village idiot, who *always* picks number 469 every week without fail, gets to place his order amid polite but scarcely disguised groans. So the meeting goes on until the leader thinks that everyone has had enough. He is probably right.

The second variation, for the more liberal rather than the purist, tries to inject a little objectivity and direction into the proceedings. Obviously some prayer and planning has gone in here, as the leader confidently announces, 'I thought we'd begin with number 511.' At the end of 511 he leads smoothly into his next choice, number 217, and thence into 86. At this stage the inexperienced worshipper may begin to feel that he has accidentally stumbled upon a proper worship time which has direction and is actually going somewhere. However, his fears are soon allayed as, just as the group is beginning to get in touch with God, the leader asks the fateful question, 'Has anyone got a song they'd like to sing?' For details of the rest of the meeting, see variation 1 above.

What's the problem? This model ought to work, yet it seldom does. Surely if everyone is choosing songs which are important to them, there must be at least one person enjoying themselves at any given time? The difficulty lies in the flow of the songs. Just because number 392 is my favourite it doesn't mean that it has any connection in mood, theology or key with number 142, which was the last person's favourite, or number 5, which is going to be the next person's. A worship cycle using this model would be a very rough ride indeed, rather as if it had square wheels. Before long all but the most ardent gripper of the spiritual handlebars would have fallen off into the mud. If the leader goes for the second variation it's almost worse, since you begin to get somewhere and are then disappointed. With the first, at least you're sure from the start that you're in for a flop.

4. The 'spontaneous' model

This model enshrines the belief that all planning is sinful, worldly, faithless and restricts the Holy Spirit. Failing to notice that they have a pretty restrictive view of the Spirit if they think he can be limited by their plans, aficionados of this model turn up to worship with nothing but an open mind, and wait for the leading of the Lord. At first sight this seems to be a very biblical model; the expectation is that everyone will come along with a contribution of some sort and that all the different contributions will flow together into a pleasing whole. And, it must be said, this does sometimes happen. The problem is, though, that it doesn't happen very often. What in fact tends to happen is that you get a combination of the Bingo model, or nothing at all of any lasting devotional use. If indulged in frequently enough, the spontaneity takes on a remarkably predictable, even 'liturgical', feel with the same songs, verses, prayers and so on coming out week after week. I am a firm believer in careful planning, because I think that in the end it allows more actual spontaneity to take place. And, I believe, it is by far the most biblical way of going about things. The spontaneity model is built on one verse from 1 Corinthians chapter 14; planning and preparation seems to me to be the hallmark of vast sections of the Old Testament, as we've already mentioned.

5. The 'Vineyard' model

When I first attended a conference run by John Wimber of the Vineyard, and experienced their worship, I soon became aware that not only was I in for a completely new collection of songs, but also a completely new way of worshipping. Since John's first major public exposure to English Christians in late 1984, his style of music, and many of the Vineyard songs, have become extremely popular in our churches. He has a carefully thought out theology of worship; he knows exactly what he expects to happen and how to help people let it happen. And for thousands of people, it has happened. As one friend told me, 'Vineyard worship took me to a place I've never ever been to with the Lord before.' What is this marvellous way of worshipping? Is it really as brilliant as all that?

There seem to be two keynotes: simplicity and intimacy. The aim of worship is to bless God, to let him enjoy, and find pleasure in our praises; to reach the point of intimacy with him and, as in our own worship cycle, to have him come among the worshippers and meet with them in power. To do that, you have to strip away everything extraneous which could be a distraction from that goal of intimacy. You simply sing to the Lord and move gradually deeper and deeper into his presence. The songs are simple, repetitive and full of emotion, and much use is made of men's and women's voices singing in canon, with the accompanying climactic points when both join in together.

The worship leader's job is simply to murmur, 'Number 7,' before the next song (not always number 7, of course—it's not that simple!). Apart from that there are no verbal interjections. (I discovered on a subsequent visit to America that even 'number 7' is a concession for the benefit of British audiences. Over there the songs are not announced at all.) The music rolls along with no perceptible direction, not even the shortest of breaks, and no sense of an approaching climax for anything up to forty-five minutes, then it stops.

Clearly this model is a contender for a successful worship time. The exact antithesis of the 'community singalong' model, it allows the worshipper space and time with the Lord and provides music which cannot, by its complexity, get in the way, but is intended to carry the singer along in its flow as smoothly as possible. For many people this model has provided a way to God which is both real and exciting; for that I praise the Lord. But, without wishing in any way to detract from what has become a very important strand in British worship, I want to make some more negative comments about it. The problems seem to be connected to style of music, understanding of worship and expectations of the worshippers.

The problem with the music (or the strength of it, depending on your point of view) is that it is all very similar. If cathedral choirs are 'Radio 3' worship, and much modern British material is 'Radio 1', Vineyard songs are definitely 'Radio 2'. As I say, this may be good or bad for you personally, depending on whether you like Derek Jameson or not, but Vineyard songs have nowhere near the range of feel, colour and tempo as a selection of our songs. The lyrics may seem simple and intimate to one worshipper, while slushy and theologically bereft to another, especially if you have been singing them for forty-five minutes. This limiting of musical style is tied in, I think, to a limited understanding of the purposes of worship. To go back to our five categories, Vineyard music is very good on adoration and love, and there are at least two songs of celebration and joy, but that's about it. Particularly noticeable by its absence is any hint of the victorious mood of many of our spiritual warfare songs such as 'Let God arise' or 'For this purpose'. I feel that this is a serious lack, one which seemed like a real missed opportunity at a recent Vineyard conference on spiritual warfare.

But for me the most serious problem lies in the expectations that this model seems to have of the worshippers' spiritual stamina. The very thing which is designed to leave space for them to meet with God can in fact be that which leaves them to their own devices. No doubt you get better at it with practice, but I find it very hard to concentrate in worship for over half an hour at a time, especially when the music is so unvaried and the direction so unspecified. I think that congregations need more help than the Vineyard would give them. But, let me say again, this is only my personal opinion. If you really love this style, praise the Lord! If you feel it could be right for your set-up, go for it!

6. The 'Spring Harvest' model

I'm slightly embarrassed by this name, but I don't really know what else to call it. I'm sure Spring Harvest isn't the only place they do it, but for me this tremendous Easter-time conference-cum-festival epitomises a way of worshipping which, while not being perfect, is the next best thing. Those who are Spring Harvest veterans will know exactly what the worship is like; for those who are not, I'll attempt to pick out some of the distinctive qualities. You'll see very quickly that I'm sold on this model, and to some extent have used it as a yardstick against which to measure the other models. That's why I've been so rude about some of them. I'm not totally uncritical of it, of course, but I do feel that it combines the very best of lots of other strands, and provides the most helpful model for many of our needs in the church today.

There is, first, an extremely wide range of songs and musical styles. Traditional hymns sit comfortably alongside the most rowdy of modern choruses, and pieces of such theological stature as 'Meekness and majesty' walk hand in hand even with—yes!—Vineyard songs. There is a clear worship leader whose job is not just to announce the next song, nor whip up human enthusiasm, but rather to encourage the worshippers by his words, to suggest new direction for their meditation or praise, to use the words and music to greatest effect, to highlight and articulate what he feels God is especially doing at the moment and, above all, to guide and lead the worship time, under the direction of the Spirit, in the way and towards the end which God has for it.

The music, as in the Vineyard, is 'seamless', but this is achieved not by non-stop singing, but by skilful and sympathetic instrumentalists 'laying down a carpet' of extempore music while the leader speaks, prays, prophesies or just asks for stillness in the congregation. One song flows neatly into the next with no awkward pauses, and the direction is maintained. Should the leader feel that the Spirit is taking them off in a new and unexpected direction, there is built-in flexibility to allow for this, but it is always flexibility within a framework rather than the complete spontaneity which so often leads nowhere at all. If this model has dangers, they lie in two different areas: first, the temptation, which the leader must resist at all costs, to preach a twenty-minute sermon before each song, and secondly, the almost total lack of complete silence which ought to feature in our worship from time to time. But these are not intrinsic dangers in the model, they arise simply from bad use of the model and needn't be too much of a problem for the well-trained and experienced leader.

One variation from 'pure' Spring Harvest praxis which we use at our church, and which we can use because we don't yet have five thousand in the congregation, is what we refer to as the 'PSH'. This stands, rather irreverently some feel, for a 'Planned Spontaneous Happening'—in other words, an opportunity in the middle of a worship time for us to open for contributions from the floor, as people are invited to express their worship in prayers or songs, or to bring a prophetic word or picture. We will deliberately build in a PSH at a climactic point in the worship, and we use it either to continue and reinforce the same direction or alternatively to change direction.

So, for example, in between singing 'For thou, O Lord' and 'I love you, Lord', it might be appropriate for people to express their love for the Lord out loud as an encouragement to others. When after a few minutes the prayers stop flowing, the worship leader would either announce, or better simply lead into the next song so that the flow continues. If the musicians can manage it, they could be improvising quietly under the congregation's contributions and following the mood of what was being expressed (some of the skills of the old 'silent movie' pianist come in very handy here).

Alternatively, the PSH can be a useful way of changing direction slightly. Recently we moved from 'Jesus put this song into our hearts' to 'I give you all the honour', something which ought not to work at all, by inserting between them an opportunity for people to express their praises to God out loud. This began, as you would expect, quite exuberantly, but soon calmed down and deepened so that it felt appropriate to encourage people to look more closely at what God had actually done in their lives. Singing words like

You have broken chains that bound me,
You've set this captive free.

seemed to fit perfectly after the corporate and joyful testimony of the previous song. I'll say a bit more about handling contributions from the floor in a while, but I do believe it's worth taking the risk of allowing space for them. Not least, it helps people not to feel that the whole thing is so sewn up that there is nothing for them to do other than accompany the musicians.

As for the terminology, if you feel that 'PSH' is inappropriate, why not a 'God-Organised Spontaneous Happening' (GOSH), or even a 'Spirit-Led Organised Spontaneous Happening'? I'm sure your ingenuity would stretch to plenty more names for it. The only thing to beware of is that it doesn't become a 'Badly Organised Spontaneous Happening'. That doesn't bear thinking about!

I hope I have given a fair picture of what I mean by this model, and I also hope that some people have recognised it and are thinking, 'But that's what we do!' It's what I do too, and this book is intended to provide something of a leaders' manual on this model of worship. This type of worship is the most demanding to lead (apart perhaps from the sheer amount of physical energy needed by the singalong leader), and therefore requires the highest degree of Spirit-led planning and also of competence in potential leaders. The next three chapters will explore different aspects of some of the skills needed to lead musical worship efficiently. It would, of course, have been much easier for me to have written a book telling people how to say, 'Number 7,' more effectively, but then you might not have bought it!

So how might you actually lead a worship time which looks like this? The first question to ask is, 'Who is leading it?' Perhaps the most common scenario would be that of the *service* leader working with a group of musicians and singers which might contain the *group* leader and a *worship* leader. Obviously, there's one vital question to sort out right from the start: 'Who's in charge?' With so many leaders, you need to know clearly for any worship time who is to be given responsibility. If this is not clearly decided, and that decision communicated to all concerned, two opposite and equally unseemly disasters can occur.

The first is that no one leads. Awkward gaps and silences ensue, silences quite unlike those awesome times when the Lord is manifestly present and no one wants to do anything except to stand and enjoy him. Non-verbal gestures of the 'After you', 'No, after you' type fly backwards and forwards across the dais. Facial expressions lose their glow and become anxious, angry and resigned by turns, and the poor congregation open their eyes from their enraptured state to see what looks like a game of charades going on up front.

The other alternative is that everyone leads, and the worship takes on a form which combines highlights of both Wimbledon and the House of Commons with directions, encouragements, song announcements and so forth bouncing around the front of the church and leaving the congregation as a crowd of spectators with terminal neck ache. So appoint one leader, and make sure that everyone knows who he or she is. Rather than cramping people's style, this actually encourages participation since there is a safe and secure framework into which to add contributions.

If the worship is to be led from within the group of musicians, the service leader's role is easy. He simply has to hand over to the worship leader and know when to take leadership back again. But if the service leader is also the worship leader, a whole new problem rears its head—communication. How can the leader direct music if he is neither a singer nor a musician? It is not simply a case of his being able to thump out another chorus on the piano; he has to decide what he wants to do and then let someone else know in time for them to do it. And while in some of the more meditative choruses he may have time to wander over and place his order with the musicians, generally the whole process will have to be much more speedy.

The answer in my experience is twofold. The first part is to make sure you know your starting point for each song. I don't mean by this the note you come in on (although that does add a certain something if you can get it right), but rather the basic format you'll use. On my word processor you can set up for each document the details you want in terms of paper type, margin widths, print size, tabs and so on. But if you start a document without specifying any of these, the computer automatically puts in details it has chosen for you. This is called its 'default mode', and I find this a helpful concept for worship songs too.

When we first learn a new song, we make sure that we all agree and learn its 'default mode', in other words the way we will do it in the absence of any further indication from the leader. This may simply be straight through it just as it says in the book, it may be with one or two repeats of the chorus at the end, perhaps with the second slower and broader, it may be to do a two-part song in an AABABB form (this is shorthand for the first part twice followed by the second part, then the first part followed by the second part twice), or it may involve a key change half way through. Each song has its default mode, so if the worship leader asks for something and then gets slain in the Spirit everyone will know what to do at least until the end of the song.

But what next? That's all very well, and it does provide a good basis from which to work, but how do you communicate change as you go along, allowing for flexibility and response to what God is doing at any given moment? The second part of the answer is a set of hand signals. Since they are done silently, they don't disturb even the quietest of songs. Conversely, they can be understood during even the most rousing singing, clapping and dancing. When you get really good you can even do it with your eyes shut, thus not interrupting your own flow of worship, although you do need faith to believe that the musicians have interrupted their own sufficiently to have seen the signal. It needn't be as bad as it may seem initially; you simply need ways of communicating basic information. While it might be useful to have a universal sign language which worship groups across the globe could understand, a kind of manual Esperanto, it's probably best to develop your own within the church. You only need a dozen or so, just so that you can say, for example, 'Go round again', 'A bit faster'; 'Modulate up a tone'; 'Play through a verse quietly so I can do a voice-over'; 'Repeat verse two' (careful with this one); 'Stop'; 'Unaccompanied' and so on. We also have a very useful mouth signal, rather than hand signal, which we call the 'goldfish': an exaggerated open-mouthed gulp of air to show people at what point to begin singing. Practise these with your musicians until you can do a 'once-through-the-chorus-then-up-into-G♯-for-a-slow-voice-over-with-some-singing-in-tongues' with one hand tied behind your back. You can have great fun in rehearsals trying to catch one another out, but when you come into the Lord's presence for real in a service, you'll have such a trust and empathy that nothing you do will interrupt worship for God's people.

To whom do you signal? I'm not sure if it's possible to 'conduct' the group as a whole; even with a smallish group,

that in itself would be a full-time job, leaving little attention for the congregation or the Spirit. It's probably best,
therefore, to be in touch with the player of the most
dominant instrument, usually either the keyboards or a
guitar. This does, however, leave a major responsibility
with the group. First, the keyboard player or whoever
must actually be looking at you in order to see your
signals. Two sorts of pianists tend to have trouble with
this, the pretty bad and the pretty good. The pretty bad
pianist is the one who needs to keep his eyes glued firmly
on the music and can only lift them safely to see your by
now frantic 'back to verse five' signal as the last chord of
the final chorus fades into silence. The pretty good one is
the player who is able to put his fingers instinctively on the
right notes and for whom the keyboard becomes an exten-
sion of his worshipping being, such that he has his eyes
firmly shut while inwardly seeing a vision of several different angels and receiving a word of knowledge about
someone in the congregation with athlete's foot. Your, 'A
bit slower, please,' is clearly on an altogether more mun-
dane plane.

So, if they possibly can, musicians should learn to watch
carefully, especially towards the end of verses; the dominant one watching you, and the rest ready to follow him.
As you work together more and more as a team, the whole
business of signalling will become easier. It does of course
take years rather than months, but in time you'll be able to
predict what's likely to happen. And this, again, will set
free rather than restrict; you're far more comfortable listening to the promptings of God's Spirit if you think you'll
actually be able to obey them. If something more complicated feels right, don't panic; do a voice-over. Once, after
having sung 'Lord, you are so precious to me' we had a
prophecy about how God enjoyed our singing love songs
to him, but he also wanted to sing love songs to us. I felt it

would be good to respond to that by affirming God's word to us and articulating the fact that we are precious to him. Now, in my repertoire I haven't got a hand signal for that one, but it didn't matter. I signalled 'voice-over', and then said something like, 'Let's sing that again, but this time "Lord, we are so precious to you". The Lord's just told us that that's true, so let's enter into that truth as we acknowledge it before him. "Lord we are so precious to you. . ."' and off we went.

Hand signals only work, of course, if the group has some basic ground rules; they are not a substitute for lots of hard work on learning how to play songs. We can signal 'repeat the chorus' with the utmost clarity, but unless the musicians know how to do so, it won't work. How many beats, or bars, are there before it starts? This will need to be worked out for each song. In learning a song, it isn't enough simply to learn it straight through from the book; you then need to go on and learn how to get back smoothly into an extra chorus, a repeat of a verse, or whatever. There aren't really any hard-and-fast rules about this, but most musicians (and many non-musicians) can 'feel' what's right and what's awkward. Similarly, key changes need to be done smoothly, whether you're modulating up a key in the middle of a song to give it a bit of a lift, or changing keys between two songs. Extras like these need to be worked on and practised until you can be sure that all the musicians, on seeing a hand signal, will think, 'Oh, that's what he wants us to do,' rather than, 'Help, how on earth do we do that?'

In the planning stage (we'll talk about that in the next chapter) you need to work out which songs you think will flow uninterrupted together, and at which points you may want to insert some verbal material. We use six different terms for the way in which we flow from one song to the next.

Straight in vocally

This is where the next song comes in without an introduction or change in rhythm and tempo. So, for example, to get from 'I will build my church' to 'Hosanna' we'd go from the last line:

Jesus is Lord...is Lord! (2-3-4-1-2-3-4-) Hosanna, hosanna....

(The numbers represent the beats in the bar, not an interruption for some late football results.)

Similarly, a move from 'I just want to praise you' to 'For thou, O Lord' would go:

I exalt your holy name on high (2-3-4-1-2-) For thou, O Lord. . . .

This method requires a strong vocal lead and a very nifty OHP operator who is aware that this is what you intend to do. If you are using song-books, this one is best avoided except when moving to very well-known songs. Obviously there is little time to shout out the number between the two songs, but you can do so safely once the second one has started. If a key change is involved, it needs to be done swiftly by using the dominant (or fifth) chord of the key you are moving into. So if in the first example above you wanted to move to 'Hosanna' in A rather than G (which is the key of the first song) you would want to insert the dominant chord of A which is E or even better E7. So if we add chords to our diagram, it might look like this:

Jesus is Lord...is Lord! (2-3-4-1-2-3-4-) Hosanna, hosanna....
B7 Em Am7 D G   C G C G E7   A   E7

This isn't as complicated as it looks. You should be able to feel whether it is working or not even if you are not very musical.

Straight in with intro.

Here the rhythmic flow is maintained, but instead of singing the first line it (or the last line) is played as an introduction, allowing people to come in at the right place. This gives a less hurried feel, but introductions should be clear and not too prolonged if the flow is to be maintained. The same rules about modulation apply.

Voice-over

The musicians move straight into the next song and begin playing it quietly while the leader speaks, either to the people, encouraging them on or bringing something from the Lord to them, or to the Lord in prayer, wrapping up and articulating what the people might want to say in response to what they've just sung. Generally speaking, the deeper into adoration you get, the less you'll address the congregation and the more you'll address God. Voice-overs require something of the skill of the disc-jockey in getting the timing right so that the congregation are brought in at a convenient point. It's worth playing through a song beforehand and noting convenient places to stop talking and places where you must keep going at all costs. Again, all this sounds very difficult and contrived, but you'll know when it works. (The congregation will know when it doesn't work, because they'll be left hanging in the air wondering when to begin singing. If it flows properly it will be so natural and unobtrusive that it doesn't betray the fact that you spent two hours with the pianist practising it.)

Reverse voice-over

No, this doesn't mean that you are talking out of the back of your neck. It is exactly the same as a voice-over except that the musicians play through the last song instead of the next one. When you are ready to move on, they will pass smoothly to the introduction to the next song (and to the new key if necessary). A variation of this is to play the old song in the new key; there's a lovely example of this technique at its best on Graham Kendrick's *Make Way!* album. Listen to the link between 'O Lord, your tenderness' and 'Lord, have mercy on us'. This is slightly more difficult to achieve than the straight voice-over, but it is worth trying occasionally.

Tiny pause

Tiny because you want to break the flow and keep silence, perhaps for a change in mood, but you don't want people to be left wondering if you've fallen asleep or been struck with amnesia. If you want a more prolonged time of silence, that's fine, but you need to let people know that's what you're doing. The tiny pause is different. It's simply a way of getting from one song to the next without complete flow. It is best used sparingly if you want to avoid the stop-start feel of badly-led worship, but it can be effective now and then.

The PSH

This needs to be led in the sense that people need to know that this is what's happening, and they are expected, rather than just allowed, to contribute. I often come in with a short prayer after a song has ended, and then say something like, 'Let's all take some time to thank the Lord as we speak out our praises to him.'

In putting together a list, therefore, the leader will not just need to put down the songs but also the links. Just as we've developed our hand signals, we've also standardised a set of hieroglyphics which we put on the list to show what we think might happen. Added to this we put down the source of the music, using abbreviations for different song-books, the key or keys we're going to sing each one in, and some instruction about how many times through, and any creative repetition we might attempt. What's important is that you develop terminology and notation which is understood by all those involved with you, rather than that you learn ours, but just to illustrate what I mean, here's a sample list which we used recently. I'll be arguing in the next chapter for careful and fairly tight planning, so I make no apology that this list perhaps seems rather too sewn up and inflexible. It is my conviction that flexibility happens best within a framework. We may not stick to this list one hundred percent, but we will base what happens around it until God shows fairly clearly that we are to do something different. All the musicians would get a piece of paper which looks something like this:

Intro

G	We will magnify (SF2, 270)	2 extra Ch's, 2nd *rit*
	(A7) ↓ (intro.)	
D	God of glory (SF2, 197)	×2
	(D7) vo	
G	You laid aside (SF3, 527)	×2½
	(G7) ↓ voc.	
C/D	O Lord, your tenderness (NS, 23)	C×2 (A7) D×1½
	PSH	
	voc	
G/A	Lord, you are (NS, 17)	G×2 (E7) A×1½
	⌒	
	vo	
D	The Lord is my strength (SF3, 495)	→

The intelligent among you may have worked out the meaning of some of the symbols, but just in case you haven't here is a key.

The first column contains the key of the song. Two keys with a stroke represent the fact that we'll be bumping it up half way through. At the end of the line are details of how many times the song will be played through. So, for example, 'O Lord, your tenderness' will be sung through twice in C, and then be taken up via A7 (the dominant of the new key) into D and sung one and a half times (half a time through can mean either the first or the second half). In this example we'd go back to 'O Lord, I receive your love', but other songs would repeat and end with the first half, for example, 'Change my heart, O God'.

' ↓ ' means straight in from one song to the next, and it is qualified either by 'intro', or by 'voc'. If a modulation is involved, the pivot chord, always the fifth of the key you're heading to, is put in brackets.

'VO' means voice-over, and although 'rvo' doesn't feature in this list, this would signify a reverse voice-over.

We do occasionally use proper musical terms, and the *rit* on the second extra chorus of 'We will magnify' stands for something or other Italian which means slow down a bit. The '∩' symbol is the musical 'pause' sign.

'→' simply means that you go straight through the song in its default mode without any unaccustomed repeats, or choruses.

It is worth saying that we didn't all sit down one night at a rehearsal and work out how to write lists. This is a system which has evolved over a period of time, and which is no doubt still evolving. But in case it's helpful to you, I've shared where we are at the moment.

Another important point needs to be made here too. It's something I've recently discovered as a mistake I've been making, and at the moment I'm working on correcting it. It concerns air holes. Because I put a high value on smooth flow in a worship time, and because I'm always very nervous leading worship, I'd found great security and comfort in planning slick changes from song to song, like all those mentioned above. But I realised to my horror that people were feeling rushed along, almost without breathing space, and that they were finding it difficult to meet God between the songs and therefore in them. Around this time I went to a meeting where some of the real experts were in action, and I was struck by how much space they left, and how a very powerful worship time could be achieved with half the number of songs I'd have used. I'm not, of course, advocating a return to the 'spontaneous' worship model with its embarrassed silences, but with skilful musicians improvising between songs there can still be a sense of stillness and space—air holes for people to breathe in God's Spirit. I hope I'm getting better about this: beware lest your nerves tend to make you rush panting through a list.

Having worked out your list, all you have to do is to lead people in worship using it. Use hand signals either to confirm what you've already decided or to change it, listen to the Spirit, don't talk too much, don't be afraid to leave those air holes in the context of your smooth flow and worship the Lord yourself. Expect God to come and minister to his people, give him space to do so, and you can't go far wrong.

CHAPTER NINE

HANDLING THE PLANNING

AVING DECIDED WHICH MODEL we want our worship to look like most, we next need to work out how to achieve this. Unless you go for the spontaneous approach, the first stage is planning. This is in some ways the most difficult stage of all, and worship times can stand or fall on the work done before they ever begin, so I want to devote a whole chapter to it.

Who should plan the worship time? I don't think there are any set rules. Obviously planning is first and foremost a matter of prayer and listening to the Lord. So it may be helpful to talk to others involved in the service, the preacher and the worship group leader, if you have one. Try to discern together where the Lord is wanting to go with you. Some churches have a worship committee or something similar which meets weekly to pray and plan for the Sunday services. I'm sure this is ideal, but at times I feel this is a luxury which many busy churches can't afford. It depends how much emphasis you place on Sunday worship as opposed to the everyday work of the church: is the week to be used for making Sunday extra special for God's people, or is Sunday used for the equipping of the people for their work and witness during the rest of the week? This question 'Where is the real church?' will have to be answered, because it will affect the amount of time you give to preparation for worship.

In a previous chapter I talked a little about the process of putting together a service so that it has both integrity and direction. I'll now look at this in a bit more detail and from a dual point of view: planning a whole service and planning a worship time within that service. I find it useful to think of the planning process as one which has five distinct stages which need to be worked through methodically. I begin with the context, and then move through the feel, aim and flow, and only then on to the content. Let's examine these in turn.

1. Context

I find it helpful to subdivide this heading into three. We need to examine the thematic context, the liturgical context and the congregational context. First, we need to begin asking some of these questions: What is the theme of the service? What decides this: a preaching series, a lectionary, the church calendar, the leader's whim, or what? Where is the church at the moment? What sort of things does the Lord seem to be concentrating on with you?

Secondly, what is the liturgical context? Is it a Communion Service, an unstructured celebration event, or something in between? This will obviously affect the amount of space you have for your worship time, and its position within the overall framework.

Finally, who is likely to be there? How many might there be? Where will they be (if anywhere) in their Christian pilgrimage? Have there been any recent events which may be affecting the way people are feeling? What will be the corporate mood of those present?

All these questions can help to put your worship time into context, so that it feels like part of the whole service and fits in with where people are at. Experience will help you to answer at least some of them fairly easily, and the insights of others may be helpful too. When you think you've got a good understanding of this, move on to think about the next stage.

2. Feel

Having decided the context and theme of the service, spend some time getting inside it. Ask yourself particularly what the people will feel like being there. Take this a bit further by asking what they might feel like when they reach your worship time. If it comes after a sermon all about sin, hell and eternal punishment, they may not feel too keen on joining in vigorously with something like 'I love you, Lord'. Similarly, 'Who can sound the depths of sorrow' may not reflect exactly the mood of the congregation directly after a church family baptism. Think yourself into the situation, and try to get in touch with it on an emotional level too.

3. Aim

The feel is very much about where people will be starting from as they move into worship. The aim is about where you want them to be by the time you stop. It's one thing to give people permission to be where they are, but to do nothing about moving them on from there is quite another. If your desire in leading worship is to bring people into the presence of God, with the expectation that he in turn will manifest himself among them, it is clear that there certainly ought to be some change in the way people feel as a result. God may, of course, have other ideas entirely, but it never hurts to have an aim in mind, since it is a great help in actually getting somewhere rather than running on the spot. So, for example, people may feel very penitent and unworthy after the hellfire sermon, but it would be good if we could lead them towards a place of forgiveness, peace and security. Similarly, great excitement and exuberance are fine, but people may benefit from being led more deeply into the worship and adoration of their God.

4. Flow

Knowing where you're starting from and where you're hoping to get to are very useful prerequisites for any journey, but there is one more thing that you need: some idea of the route to be taken. That's what I mean by the flow of the worship. Returning to the five categories of worship I mentioned in Chapter 3, you need to decide how you're going to use those categories to put together a worship time which will move people from the feel they have now to the aim which we have for them. How are you actually going to move from putting the fear of God in people to helping them feel secure and accepted by him? Theologically we would answer that as follows. We'd need to move through an acknowledgement of our own sin, an affirmation of God's grace in forgiveness, penitence, reception of forgiveness, and celebration of freedom. But can we do all that in the context of worship? Yes, I believe we can.

I find it helpful to draw a graph of how I would expect a worship time might go, in order to get the flow right. The most useful way to do this is to plot exuberance against time, so that, for example, a move from noisy celebration towards quiet intimacy and adoration would look like this:

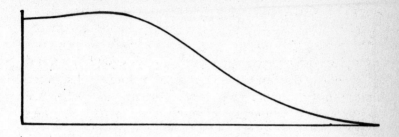

A worship time which built up from the quietness of, for example, the administration of Communion to an enthusiastic time of warfare might be represented like this:

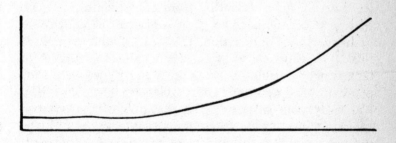

This sort of graph might describe celebration which quietened down into penitence and then moved into a declaration of God's forgiving power and his victory over sin:

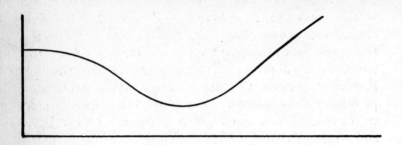

You might find all this rather theoretical and of little relevance to the art of worship, but I find that it helps me to see whether my expectations are too high and I am trying to cram too much into a worship time. If the graph changes direction more than twice, we may well lose the congregation around the next bend.

It's worth mentioning here that although the idea is that the worship flows smoothly from one phase to the next, there can occasionally be great impact in a sudden and dramatic change of direction. The most obvious example of this I've experienced was when, after a couple of increasingly rousing choruses of 'Majesty', we were suddenly dropped right into a very quiet arrangement of 'You laid aside your majesty'. The starkness of the contrast spoke volumes to me about Jesus' self-emptying. This is the very antithesis of flow, and can only be used very rarely. We call it 'contraflow'.

5. Content

Finally, having thought through the context, feel, aim and flow, you can begin to plan the contents. It's very tempting to begin here, but unless it is the culmination of the process outlined above, it may well be haphazard, to say the very least. But now that you know exactly where you're going, you can choose songs which will work together to take you there, by the route you've decided on. Find some songs which will pick people up from where they are, find some more which will reflect where you hope they'll get to and then, most importantly, find some more which will act as pivotal songs to help move from one to the other. Decide on the points where some spoken interjections might help, and where you might appropriately leave some air holes and open up for contributions from the congregation, prophetic words and so on.

It's worth saying that although my primary reference throughout this section so far has been planning a worship time within a service or meeting, this process also works in putting together a whole service. There still needs to be a direction, an aim, and a smooth way of getting there. The worship time may be just one small part of the overall flow of the event.

This may sound fine, but how do you actually do it? Perhaps it would be useful to end this section with a detailed look at two particular events which took place in our church and at the process used in planning for them.

The first was simply a normal Sunday service. I preached on Psalm 51 as part of a sermon series. It was the start of the series, so I introduced the whole subject and set the scene. I spent some time looking at what a psalm is, and then suggested a few ways in which we might use them to help us in our worship. In this way I had dealt with the thematic context.

What about the liturgical context? The service was Holy Communion, so the worship time would normally be during and after the administration of Communion and on to the end of the service, but since it was August the worship group was not on duty. Instead a pianist led for just one or two songs here and there, rather than for a full worship time. The congregational context was that of a normal crowd of our regular worshippers, with a mix of all ages but a considerable weighting towards young families.

What did it feel like to be there? The mood of Psalm 51 is penitence and sorrow for sin, and I told the congregation that we can enter into the experience of the psalmist and feel with him what he feels. As a result, people were quiet and contemplative as they gave space to the Spirit to prompt and convict them. The Communion part reminded people of Jesus' death for their sins, and so was also fairly quiet, but moving on from this towards the end of the service we were able to concentrate, as in fact the psalmist does, on the joy of being, and knowing oneself to be, forgiven.

My aim was that people should go out from the service cleansed by the Lord, filled again with his Spirit, and ready to serve and witness during the week ahead.

In considering the flow of the service, we needed to take into account the natural flow built into the Communion liturgy. What does it have to offer? (Free-church friends, bear with us for a while!) Obviously the Confession would be an important part of the service. Should we move it to the alternative position after the sermon? And could we give people a bit longer to meditate by separating the Confession from the Absolution a little? Why not put a song in between them? Sometimes there is the feel in the penitential section of the liturgy that it's all a bit too easy; one quick prayer and then the vicar tells you you're all right, so off we go to the next thing. A song between Confession and Absolution can spread this out a bit, and remind us of the need for a life lived in penitence, not just three minutes of contrition on Sunday morning. Yet we do need to hold together with that the very real sense of forgiveness being an emergence from sin and sorrow into new freedom and joy.

Where should we go next? Two different directions suggested themselves: a celebration of our forgiveness or, and I preferred this, a continuation along the theme of our individual sin and its effects. Reading through the Psalm again, it struck me particularly that there is a link between personal penitence and intercession (a link which we have already noticed in Chapter 3) where the psalmist prays for the restoration of Jerusalem (verse 18). Maybe we could do something with that. It would get us through the prayers and the Communion with a continued sense of the seriousness of sin, and if we held off from the celebration of our forgiveness until after we'd received the bread and wine, it would help to heighten the impact of the incredible grace of God in Jesus. We could have two or three songs after Communion which moved from quiet assurance to heartfelt praise, and end with a rousing hymn. A graph of this flow would look something like this, bearing in mind that we would need to begin the service in a slightly less subdued way:

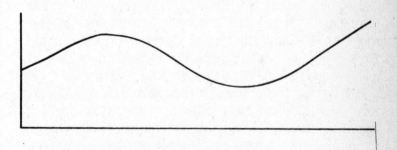

Now we were about ready to move on to the content. Already some songs were beginning to suggest themselves to me. But before making any choices, I looked specifically

at the readings, liturgy and so on to see if I could get any
more clues as to what might be appropriate. 'Create in me a
clean heart, O God' is a direct quotation from the Psalm, so I
thought that would be useful. The link between individual
sin and the state of the nation is made explicit in several
songs: 'Lord, have mercy on us', 'We are your people', and
'O Lord, the clouds are gathering'. We sang these after the
Confession and before the prayers. However, you need to
watch having songs which are too similar in sentiment to
prevent people from feeling that they are singing the same
thing but to three different tunes. There needed to be some
development of thought, so when we came to the end of the
administration of Communion we sang 'I'm accepted'. We
sang it twice through, beginning it as a quiet meditative
affirmation and then building up to an enthusiastic celebration. After that we sang 'I get so excited, Lord, every time I
realise'.

Finally, we looked at ways in which we could do something a bit more special and radical. To prevent breaking up
the flow of the music for the Absolution, we sang 'Lord,
have mercy on us' immediately after the Confession prayer,
and I pronounced the Absolution as a voice-over. The
pianist had to flow neatly into the key change and the next
song. At the administration of Communion the worship
group would normally have played, but since they were off
duty we had to do something else. Did we want music there
at all? Perhaps silence would make a helpful change. Otherwise we could have quiet organ or piano music, or even
taped music such as Allegri's *Miserere* (a beautiful setting of
Psalm 51 from the early seventeenth century). On several
occasions we have used taped music during our services for
meditation, and have found it very effective indeed. The tape
has all the strengths of a church choir, but with two important additional advantages over most church choirs I've ever
heard: they're as good as King's College Chapel choir (in

fact they are King's College Chapel choir), and you can switch them off whenever you like! After the tape and a couple of songs, we ended with the *Gloria* rather than having it at the beginning: it combines the celebration of God's glory with the continual need for his mercy in a way which concluded the service on exactly the right note. We used it in place of a final hymn.

Let's look at another very different example, just to hammer the point home. About 500 people from several different denominations all over the North of England attended a day conference for those involved in the 'signs and wonders' ministry. The subject for the day was 'Dealing with Demons'. There was no liturgy, just a worship time lasting about half an hour, followed by teaching and then ministry. Many of the people who came were from small struggling churches, and they looked forward to the day as a chance to participate in celebratory worship of a kind which they never experienced at home. They were raring to go, and entered into worship enthusiastically right from the start. Obviously this was a very different experience from a Sunday service based on Psalm 51. So where did we go with this one?

This time we were not planning a whole service, simply the worship time at the beginning of the day. I've already described the three contexts. Once again, we needed to begin by asking how it would feel. As I've mentioned, people arrived excited and eager to worship, yet many came discouraged and battle weary. We knew from past experience that the Lord often meets with people at the start of the day by refreshing and renewing them. We also realised that many of them would be feeling real trepidation about the subject matter of the day. There's nothing like studying the demonic to get people's worst fantasies going!

Our aim, then, was to move people on from discouragement and trepidation to a place of refreshment, renewal and security in the Lord's victory over the Enemy. This guided us in the flow and content of the worship.

Nobody needed much encouragement at all to begin by celebrating, so we sang two or three songs strung together without a break. These included: 'I will enter his gates', 'Hosanna' and 'O Lord our God, how majestic is your name'. Then we moved on into a deeper phase of adoration. Verbal encouragement, followed by some more meditative songs provided space for that to happen. Here the Vineyard music really came into its own. Songs included: 'Open your eyes, see the glory of the King', 'I give you all the honour' and 'I just want to praise you'. A time of silence and stillness followed, giving the Lord an opportunity to minister to people and speak to us prophetically. When it felt right to move on, we picked up on the theme of the day. Obviously we wanted to concentrate on Jesus' victory over the powers of darkness and to celebrate it, and perhaps to engage in some spiritual warfare as well to prepare for the ministry times later in the day. We declared God's victory with some songs like 'Let God arise', 'Christ is risen', 'For this purpose' and 'Victory is on our lips and in our lives'. In graph form the worship time looked like this:

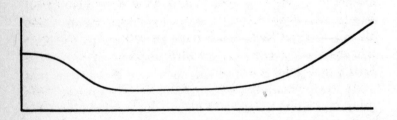

The next job, in both examples, was to go through the songs and look at them from a musical point of view. If you can't do this yourself, ask your chief musician to help you (and begin to teach you at the same time). Which songs are in the same key, and to which can you modulate easily? Your musician will know that it is easier to modulate up than down; that is, a move from E to F or from G to A will bring a sense of climax, whereas F sharp to E will have the opposite effect. All this will influence the order you put the songs in. This should not be the main consideration, of course, but it will need to be thought through if you are going for seamless music. If you are stuck with a really impossible key change between two songs which are otherwise perfectly appropriate, can you do it with just a tiny pause rather than a link between them? The pause needs to be long enough to establish the new key, but not so long that people wonder what's going on.

You then need to decide approximately when you might need to say something between the songs (if you work with a model which has verbal links), and think through what might be the best things to concentrate on. This will need to be kept very flexible, but there may be obvious times, such as the move from one phase of worship to another. If you want these spoken bits to be accompanied (voice-overs), you'll need to work out with the musicians where and for how long they need to be playing softly under your words, and where to move to once you've finished. When all this is sorted out, you'll have something resembling a list, and you'll begin to get excited about it as you imagine how it will feel if it all goes right.

At this point, some of you with a leaning towards the more spontaneous approach may be feeling that this whole thing seems so sewn up that it would be impossible for God to come and do anything. There is indeed a danger in this approach that having picked a list of songs we can do nothing but bash through them regardless of what's going on around us. Two things need to be said about this. The first is that there is no merit in flexibility for the sake of it. If we really have chosen our songs both thoughtfully and prayerfully, seeking to discern in advance what God is wanting to do, there should be no need to change things as we go along. If we find ourselves constantly being thrown by the Spirit during worship, and feeling the need to go off in completely unplanned directions, we may need to look again at the way in which we prepare. Having said that, however, we do need to be free to change if the need arises. How can we do that?

One possible answer is to have a list which begins with three or four songs and which then branches into several different strands. So after a general start with a few call-to-worship or celebratory songs, we might have three alternative lists, one based around adoration, one continuing the celebration, and one perhaps moving into penitence. It's up to the worship leader to choose the list which feels most appropriate when you all get there. This obviously requires a lot of preparation on the part of the musicians, and will involve the frustration of never using two-thirds of what you practise, but it is a good way of keeping built-in flexibility.

Perhaps a better way is to have several stock progressions of just two or three songs which work well together and which can be played at a moment's notice. For example, if you suddenly feel that the music needs to take a more adoration-orientated turn than you'd planned for, you can begin with 'I just want to praise you' and flow straight into the chorus of 'For thou O Lord', returning to sing it all the way through. This will move you in the right direction and give you the space to discern where to go next. Obviously the congregation will cotton on to this one if you do it too regularly, and will get the message, 'Oh dear, they're in trouble again.' But as we've said, changes of plan ought to be the exception rather than the rule if you've prepared properly. In the last analysis what really allows good flexibility is a firm grasp of the material with its default modes and variations, and good relationships. You really can get to the point where you know the musicians so well that you'll all spontaneously start the same song at the right time. You'll learn to know how others think, and they'll know how you're thinking, so you sort of feel your way through difficult moments. I'll say a bit more about flexibility and how to plan for it in the next chapter.

Let me end this section with two further points about planning. The first is that there are things to do to make the job easier. If you choose songs with any regularity at all, it is worth making a topical index of all the material you use and to update it as you gain and discard songs. A set and limited repertoire is essential if you are to keep your head above the flood of new songs constantly pouring out, and to classify them according to the five types mentioned in Chapter 3 can save a lot of time. Our repertoire consists of about 120 songs, and they are listed under the five headings along with their source book and key(s). We update this list about every six months, and try hard to lose some songs as well as to gain new ones. My high-tech friends tell me that this list is best kept on a computer. I must admit that's all a bit beyond me, but even a hand-written list of songs relating to different topics will be really useful, and will very quickly save the time it took to make it. Even if you don't do that, you can make good use of the topical and Scripture indexes increasingly being put in the back of song-books. It isn't a case of reading all the way through *Songs of Fellowship* 1, 2 and 3 every time, nor of sticking to the five songs you know will cover anything.

The second thing I need to say concerns the place of prayer. I've concentrated very heavily on the human side of the song-choosing process, but you mustn't take that to mean that it's the most important part. In the last analysis, we want to choose the songs which God knows will bless him and the congregation the most. I believe he longs to communicate with us and will give us some clues about how a meeting or service is going to go so that we can aid what he wants to do rather than get in the way. When I'm praying I often find myself suddenly singing in my head a song or progression of songs which would be just right for the service I'm planning, even if that isn't specifically what I'm praying about. So make prayer a priority, on your own and with the others involved.

The Enemy will do all he can to prevent prayer, and the sad fact is that the worship time can often go well without it. If that weren't true it would be easier. A strict correlation between prayer and success would mean that if we didn't pray the worship would be bound to flop. Since there's little in life more embarrassing than leading a flop, we'd make sure we did pray, at the very least to save ourselves that embarrassment. But it isn't like that. Things can go very well (or appear to) even when we haven't got round to praying, and so we feel the need for prayer less, not more. However, I believe this is false thinking, and sooner or later it is all bound to catch up with us as the spiritual poverty of the worship we're leading becomes apparent to us and probably to others too. So pray first, then plan. Either without the other is a recipe for disaster, but both together will mean that you have done your very best for the congregation and for the Lord.

CHAPTER TEN

THE WORSHIP GROUP

I ONCE LEARNED SOMETHING really fascinating from a lecture at theological college (well, all right, more than just once). Apparently in the good old days long ago, even before most of my lecturers were born, churches used to have orchestras to lead the singing during services. Then, in the eighth century, someone invented the organ. People caught on really quickly to the fact that you could still get lots of different sounds but would only have to pay one musician instead of several, so by the thirteenth century most parish churches in Europe had one. It was only fairly recently that groups of musicians began to become more popular, and now it seems to be something of a boom industry. Coupled with the developments in electronic technology, this means that once again there is much more flexibility and versatility available in church music. The popularity of the guitar, the advent of PA and synthesisers, and the change in musical styles have all contributed to the rise of worship groups in churches, either alongside or even instead of traditional choirs and organists. What exactly is a worship group, and what does it take to be a successful one?

I suppose it is worth saying what a worship group is not before trying to define it more clearly. Unlike the rash of 'Christian bands' which broke out in the sixties and early seventies the worship group's main task is not centred around performance or evangelism, noble and worth-while aims though these may be. It exists purely and simply to facilitate the worship of church congregations in services and other meetings. Although the musicians may occasionally 'perform' a piece for a special event, this is very much the exception. The vast majority of time will be spent in accompanying songs for worship.

This immediately sets the worship group apart from just about any other group of musicians. They are supremely in a servant role, and do nothing for their own glory or reputation. This will obviously have many implications for the way in which they function. This chapter is an attempt to discuss some of those implications in order to help those in or considering forming a worship group. Some of it may be rather technical, so please feel free to skip the bits you don't understand or which don't seem to apply to you.

Perhaps the first question to ask is: Who shoud be in the group? In many churches, of course, you simply have to make do with what you've got, but is there an ideal line-up you should aim for? I think it helps to consider the three main parts of music: melody, harmony and rhythm. Ideally a well-balanced group should be capable of handling all three. The melody, or the tune of the music, is most often provided by vocalists, but solo orchestral instruments are useful too, especially woodwind (such as the flute) or strings (such as the violin). The harmony consists of the underlying chord structure which fills the tune out and anchors it to its particular key. The guitar is the most obvious instrument to provide this, and a bass (usually electric, for ease of portability and amplification) can help considerably too. Finally the rhythm is contributed by drums or other percussion instruments, although the guitar is useful here too.

Obviously some instruments can function in more than just one way, and the biggest advantage of keyboards is that they can do all three fairly successfully. Therefore, in considering the line-up of your group, it is most helpful not to ask, 'What have we got?' but, 'What haven't we got?' Thus the usual five acoustic guitars will be great at keeping the rhythm and harmony going, but will do nothing at all for the melody, unless one of them is playing lead. Even then you won't hear him against the other four. So to add a clarinet and/or flute could revolutionise the whole sound of the group, especially if they were both able to improvise so that they could each carry the tune at different times while the other provided some sort of counter-melody. Similarly a string quartet would sound very good melodically and harmonically, but would be unlikely to cope well with the very rhythmic style of today's worship songs. Sympathetic drumming could change this dramatically.

So if I had endless resources and could customise my own perfect worship group, what would I have? I'd begin with the rhythm section, and have bass, drums and one guitar, and then add some solo instruments which work well together, like flute and oboe or violin and viola, or all four if I was going really mad. I might add a trumpet and trombone for some songs and, of course, some sort of keyboard, preferably a synthesiser or electric piano. Finally I'd get a few vocalists, and I'd have the whole thing led by someone with a good strong voice and an electrified guitar. Obviously this would be out of the question for most churches, but by looking at the melody, harmony and rhythm as I've explained above, some very effective ensembles can be put together. The actual line-up will be a matter of taste as well as a matter of resources, but what I've said will do as a general guide.

Of course, the higher the standard of musicianship the better, but you don't have to have Grade 8 with distinction to play most of the modern songs, so anyone who is reasonably competent can begin. While classical training is all very well, I would say that the ability to play from guitar chords and a lead line and to improvise is more important, the latter especially in orchestral instruments. It's possible to be a stunning orchestral player, and yet to be lost without a full musical score, play in a very wooden way, and have no feel for accompanying worship at all.

Let me say a brief word about one or two specific instruments. Guitars, in my opinion, should be capable of being amplified if they are to be of much use at all, or at the very least be steel-strung 'jumbo'-style instruments. To finger-pick a nylon-strung guitar in a group of more than about eight people will be a complete waste of time unless it is a very high quality instrument; it simply won't be heard. You can pick up a good electro-acoustic for under £200, or considerably less second-hand. This has the advantage over solid-body guitars that it can function perfectly well in smaller settings without any amplification, and the advantage over acoustics that it can not only be amplified but also used with effects pedals. I use a chorus pedal most of the time, which really helps to 'spread out' the sound, and a flanger occasionally, for the really dramatic songs. If you don't know what these do, your local music shop will be happy to demonstrate.

Amplifiers for electric guitars should hit the right balance between being easily portable and yet giving a good volume of sound before they distort. A decent bass guitar needn't cost you a fortune, but you should check the action and the tuning since some cheap ones go slightly out of tune as you go further up the neck. An adjustable bridge is a great advantage. Personally I prefer the sound and versatility of a fretless bass, but it does involve a bit more guess-work about where you should put your fingers. (When my fretless arrived, second-hand, the worship team found it tremendously amusing that the previous owner had very thriftily removed the strings before selling it to me. They now always refer to it as my 'stringless bass', and someone suggested that it would be just the thing for unaccompanied instrumentals. See what I have to put up with? I think they were most disappointed when I did buy some strings for it!)

I know less about synthesisers, but I'm basically very much in favour of them. When I think what some churches have paid for a pipe organ, I reckon they would have been much better off paying about a twentieth of the price and getting something which could make all the same sounds *and* grand piano, breaking glass and flying saucer noises as well. You do need to realise, though, that to play a synthesiser requires not just musicianship but a certain familiarity with the technical side as well. Some of them are so complicated that you need a physics degree to programme them, so it's better not to be too ambitious and go for one with plenty of pre-sets.

If you prefer a straightforward piano, make sure that it is tuned to concert pitch, especially if you're using it with orchestral instruments. It may be worth your while considering a digital piano if you are wanting to buy something. This is an update of the older electric pianos, but with touch sensitivity, much more accurate sounds, and often more of them. We use one which has three different acoustic piano sounds, two electric pianos and harpsichord, clavichord and vibes. There is also a built-in tremolo and chorus. As well as this range of sounds there is a MIDI facility. This stands for Musical Instrument Digital Interface, and it is a system whereby several different instruments can be controlled from one keyboard. So you can add some synthesiser sounds from the same set of keys, and fade them in and out over your piano by using foot pedals for volume. Since you don't really need a whole synthesiser, you can make do with a little box which has all the works and noises in it, but comes without a keyboard, and thus is considerably cheaper than a full synth. The digital piano has several other advantages over an acoustic one: it is more portable, can be easily tuned up or down slightly to fit in with your flat church organ, and the sound can be injected directly into your church PA system. The cost of a digital piano, synth box and amplifier would be approximately the same as that of a new modern upright acoustic piano, and considerably less than even the babiest of grands.

The church organ is the instrument with which most of us have to start, but it does have some disadvantages when used for modern worship songs. It is not primarily a very rhythmic instrument, at least not when played in the average church, so it can give the feel with some more lively songs that we are slithering along rather than bouncing. It is fine for filling in harmonies when used with other instruments, and for giving extra depth and power to more majestic songs, but as a lead instrument it has its problems. Worship songs also require a very different technique from that usually adopted by church organists. One of the worst worship times I have ever experienced was when the organist was playing songs as if they were hymns. The playing needs to be much more staccato so that the smooth feel which is excellent for hymns, is avoided in songs where it is not appropriate.

The whole way in which the congregation gets into a song is different from the approach to a hymn. The organist usually plays the first line of a hymn, stops, and then plays a chord during which people join in in their own time. Worship songs have much more rhythmic variety, so a firm idea of the rhythm needs to be communicated before the people start singing so that they can come in all at the same time without getting left behind. Worship group musicians will often play the introduction, or the first or last line, and keep strumming in time so that there is a clear lead in for the congregation. Organists for whom this approach will tend to go very much against the grain will need to adapt to this way of starting songs. Apart from that, though, the organ can be a very useful addition to the worship group, as long as its limitations are fully understood and the organist in question is adaptable and willing to learn new techniques.

So much for the instruments; what about the musicians? We've mentioned their musical standards, but there are other qualities which are important too. Most of what we said in Chapter 4 also applies to some degree to the members of the group as well as the worship leader, but the most vital thing is the spiritual maturity which enables people to feel happy with the servant role. The big test is how they react when asked not to play. If you suggest to your tuba player that he just sings for 'I love you Lord', how does he react? If he gets sulky and upset, he probably should not be playing at all. A true servant will understand and welcome the opportunity from time to time to worship without needing to play.

Beware of the 'artistic temperament' so common among musicians. While there is much to respect among those who have been specially gifted with creativity and intuition, there is often a fine line between temperament and sin. All of us need to know the difference between the two in our own personalities. While rejoicing in the first, we need to recognise the second and keep it firmly under control.

The most important quality in musicians, however, is that they should be worshippers themselves. We've said that this is true of the leader, but it is just as important for those standing behind him. The most effective way to help people in the congregation to worship is to offer them an example of worship. Because the leader has so much else on his plate, he may not always look as if he is worshipping, for example, when he is finding a new song in the music book or frantically giving the 'remember-all-that-stuff-we-rehearsed-on-Thursday?-Well-scrap-it!' hand signal to the pianist. But the group members can enter much more fully into worship, and should do so and be seen to be doing so.

If there is a time of singing in tongues, a spontaneous clap at the end of a song, a shout or whatever, they should give a good strong lead. They should also feel free to contribute either spoken or sung bits during the worship— they at least are more likely to do something appropriate and in a manageable key. Instrumentalists should learn to worship with their instruments, so that whether they are playing or singing they are equally offering something to the Lord as a love gift. Neighbours permitting, I think that a person should play his instrument during his own devotional time some days. (Just pray that you never get a flat above a charismatic bagpiper!)

I want to move on now to talk about practising. When the group meets together at some time before the service (by the way, this is a good idea), the most pressing task will appear to be practising the songs needed for the coming Sunday. Many groups never get further than this, and yet it is only one thing among many which a group needs to do. There are three main items on the agenda: the God-centred, the person-centred and the task-centred. Over a long period, an approximately equal amount of time needs to be given to each of these.

The *God-centred* part of your task is simply to ensure that each individual and the group as a whole opens up to God and keeps him right at the centre of things. Tell him you're glad he is present with you, and ask him if there's anything special he'd like you to do for him. It's amazing how many groups meet to plan worship without ever praying together. I should know, I've led some of them. The worship at the service may appear fine, but if God is almost left out of the practising, it is probably less useful than it could be. The Enemy has a vested interest in keeping you away from prayer, so be aware of that and ruthlessly timetable it in.

The *person-centred* part is about the way you relate together as a team, and, like prayer, is far too vital to be left out. The idea is to build up, over a period of time, a high degree of empathy between the members of the group so that they will be aware at any moment, especially at any moment of difficulty or unplanned activity, of what is going on in each other's minds and so respond as a team and not a crowd of individuals. You need to make sure that you programme in time for simply relating to one another. Praying together, sharing a bit about your latest joys or hassles, helping individuals in need, or simply listening to one another's records over a take-away—all these are good ways of making sure that you see one another as people and not just as worship-machines. You don't all have to be the best of friends, but it does help if some of you are.

One word of caution: beware of being, or of even appearing to be, élitist or cliquey. Many people in your church will regard the worship group as the highest form of life, and will view you as some kind of superstars—I was once asked to sign autographs. Others may react with jealousy rather than adoration, so you need to make sure that the growing friendship among members of the worship group, which means that you really do want to spend time with one another, is well balanced with time spent apart and given to other people.

It is very important that you take time to worship together; after all, that is what you're there for. Again, some groups never seem to be able to make time for this outside the actual services themselves. The best way to worship in a group is for just one or two musicians, who can do so with a minimum of fuss, to accompany the rest of the people so that they're not fumbling around for music between each song.

Finally, there is the *task-centred* part which basically involves the job you're there to do, although it is not quite as simple as that. It may help you to think of this in terms of two subdivisions: maintenance and development. By maintenance I simply mean going through the songs which you are expecting to use for the services between now and the next time you meet. You will need to make sure that everyone is familiar with them, that everyone is using the same arrangement and key (some songs appear in quite different versions in different books), that intros and outros are tight, that links between songs, modulations and repeats are clearly understood, and so on. In other words, to bash three times through all five verses of the song is not usually the best way to practise it; it's much better to do individual tricky bits five times so that you can put the whole thing together once at the end. As a general rule the verses are fine; it's the bits between them which cause trouble. You will also need to build flexibility into the whole thing so that if there is a change of direction you will be able to handle it.

Development, on the other hand, has nothing to do with what you will be expected to do this Sunday, nor for the next few Sundays. It is a bit like investing for the future, and will cover learning new material, deciding on and standardising default modes, working on new arrangements, perhaps having a workshop for someone who has written something themselves, and wants to hear how it could sound, or a master-class for particular instruments or styles of playing. Development includes anything, therefore, which will help the group to function more effectively in the future, although not straight away. After prayer, this is the most common item to be omitted entirely from the agenda of many groups, and yet it is so important to keep the group moving forward, with a new challenge always before them. It won't take you long to manage most of the songs likely to be thrown at you on a Sunday. Once you can do that adequately, where is the incentive to grow?

Staleness can easily creep in when no development time is built in for the group, and staleness in worship ought to be a contradiction in terms when you think who it is we're worshipping. Individuals and the group as a whole should always be stretching themselves—on their individual instruments, in their functioning together, and in their general musicianship. Not only is this likely to be the most enjoyable part of the rehearsal time, but it will prove long term to have been one of the most useful.

One final word on the way you practise: the word is discipline. If I had a penny for every minute I've wasted during rehearsals while we're all held up because the drummer is practising his paradiddles or the guitarist is twanging inanely away, I'd have £7.48. The leader should build into the group the rule that everyone stops playing when he says so, or when he is speaking, and stops *instantly*. Nobody likes this kind of firm discipline, but everyone likes finishing on time, and without one you'll never get the other. So concentration and hard work is the order of the day, and people can practise the clever bits in their own time, not the group's.

If the group has practised together and built up empathy and confidence, it should in time be able to handle prophetic worship. This seems to be a fairly new arrival on today's worship scene, although it has been going on since biblical times. Basically it is the ability to sing and play directly from the heart of the Lord, using words and music given by him. Just as in prophecy the person concerned will receive in his mind words from the Lord which he then speaks out, in prophetic worship the words will be put by the one who receives them to an improvised tune so that the prophecy can be sung and accompanied by the other musicians. The first time I heard of this concept I just couldn't believe it, and couldn't see at all how it could happen. But having now experienced it several times, I've seen how incredibly powerful it is. A singer and a group of musicians really can improvise spontaneously at the same time and communicate powerfully together what it is that is on the Lord's heart. It is usually based around a fairly simple chord progression which the musicians can lead into when someone begins to give a prophecy; the melody can be improvised over the top. Alternatively the singer can begin, with the other musicians drifting in when they have got hold of the key and structure of the tune.

Before a group can start to work on this type of worship, individuals within it need to begin on their own to build up confidence. One of the simplest ways of doing this is to lock yourself in somewhere soundproof with your guitar or whatever and a Bible, and simply turn to a Psalm at random and sing it. It doesn't matter what it sounds like, or whether the tune is well structured or takes off and never comes in to land. Just do it and keep doing it until you realise that it isn't half so impossible as you thought. You may feel that it is appropriate if your randomly chosen Psalm is one of those which begins, 'Make a joyful noise'. The first time I tried it I got a really miserable one, with the waters about to engulf me, enemies all around me, and my feet in miry clay and sinking fast. I started off feeling fine, but after a few verses of that kind of thing I virtually needed to go for counselling. Nevertheless, this is a good way to become confident about your own voice, particularly about improvising with it. Only when some of the group members feel OK about this can the group as a whole move into practising corporate improvisation.

If all this sounds a bit unspiritual, think of spoken prophecy. Unless a person can actually talk, and can do so out loud without dying of embarrassment, the Lord will never be able to communicate a prophecy to his people through that person. In the same way our practising the skills of improvisation can be seen as preparing ourselves in case God ever wants to use us. And, of course, as soon as we are able to be used in that way, we'll find that God does want to use us—frequently.

There is more to prophetic worship, though, than just 'singing a song the Lord's given me'. It can be anything which reflects the heart of the Lord during a worship time. Some of the most effective things I've heard have been 'accompanied pictures', in other words, someone describes a picture or vision they've received while the musicians paint the picture in sound with their instruments, adding to the overall effect considerably.

Sometimes the direction of the words can be from us to God rather than vice versa as our prayers take on a prophetic feel, 'breathing back the breathings of God', as John Wimber has put it. Sometimes the leader can encourage the congregation in this by setting up an 'echo', where he sings a line which is then repeated by the people. No doubt much of the liturgy in the Old Testament began in this way. And sometimes there are no words at all, simply playing which communicates non-verbally and touches people deeply with the touch of God's Spirit. Musicians should learn to play 'creatively', improvising together, drifting in and out of the limelight with all the skills of the best trad jazz bands, bouncing off one another and above all knowing when to stop. At times the Lord will anoint your creative worship and enable you to play 'prophetically', reflecting his heart and communicating deeply to his people.

The best thing I've seen written on prophetic worship is the section in Jo King's *Leading Worship* (Kingsway: Eastbourne, 1988). As well as looking at the spiritual qualities needed in the prophet, he gives some very practical musical ideas. The book ends with a series of exercises which can be used by the worship group to help them grow in different aspects of the prophetic and musical ministry. If you feel that you might be ready to begin exploring this area then this book is a must.

Finally, a lesson on how not to encourage people into prophetic worship. I remember one conference where we began a worship time at about 9.30 am. After one song the enthusiastic leader, who must have had a real gifting from the Lord to be that enthusiastic that early in the morning, told us that the Lord wanted us to form groups of three, face each other, and sing prophetic songs to one another in the groups; whatever the Lord was giving us for one another, or whatever was on our hearts, just sing it out. Imagine the scene! All around the room people fainted, suddenly needed to go to the loo, became instantly paralysed, and so on. Then, loud and clear above the chaos, a song rang out from one of our party, beautifully sung with a brilliantly improvised tune and the deeply touching words, 'O Lord, let the ground open up and consume me.' If you think that sounds embarrassing, you should have been there when we went back to the church and tried it at the PCC meeting.

I want to end this chapter with three more subjects. Two of them won't take very long since I am not an expert, and a more detailed discussion of them would be outside the scope of this book. But I would like to give some brief guidelines which I hope will be helpful. The first subject is PA. All I have to say on this is that it is vital, if you use it, to have decent equipment which is properly operated. The operator should almost be a member of the group, since he will have to work very closely with the musicians. There is nothing which destroys an atmosphere of worship quite like a screaming dose of feed-back, an over-amplified trombone with inaudible accompaniment from the rest of the group, or shouted instructions from the leader to 'go back to verse two' which are only heard by the front half of the congregation.

The PA operator has tremendous potential for wrecking the whole thing, and so must be very highly trained and, like the rest of the musicians, a sensitive worshipper himself—although not too much of one. I once watched a sound-man in a church standing behind the mixing desk thoroughly spaced out—eyes closed, arms in the air, really in touch with the Lord; in fact so in touch, that he was totally unaware of the fact that the system was feeding back something rotten. The screech went on for what seemed like about ten minutes before he finally came down to earth and noticed. I haven't got the first idea how you get a decent PA working, and I wouldn't know one end of an impedance from the other, but you need to find out from somewhere. Jo King's book has some helpful things to say here too, and you could also try talking to the aforementioned friendly neighbourhood music shop.

The second thing to mention briefly is the whole vexed question of copyright. Few Christians would disagree that unauthorised use of copyright materal, whether by photocopying, on OHP slides or whatever, is in fact theft. Everyone dislikes doing it really, but the trouble is that it is all so much of a hassle. Some churches say, 'We will get round to sorting it out one day, honestly, but for now we're sure it doesn't really matter.' I have some bad news and some good news for those in that position. The bad news is that it does really matter, because stealing is stealing, even when Christians do it in church, but the good news is that it is no longer a hassle, and can be done very simply and cheaply. The Christian Music Association runs a scheme whereby churches can buy a single copyright licence which covers almost anything they'd be likely to use. For the price of a stamp you can send to them for their explanatory leaflet which will tell you all you need to know about joining the scheme. After that there is one single fee, payable annually, which allows you to worship the Lord with a totally clear conscience. The sense of relief alone is worth the few pounds it'll cost you. If your church is not already in the scheme, write to CMA now (their address is in the appendix).

Finally, there is one more thing you need to know about worship groups: they are the single biggest target for the Enemy's attack in the entire life of the church. Spiritual warfare is very much on the agenda for those working with or considering forming a worship group, so you'd better realise that and get prepared. The Devil hates worship and will try his utmost to disrupt it in every way possible. He realises what a prime weapon it is against his kingdom, how upbuilding it can be for a church to get its worship right, what evangelistic potential there is in it, what power for healing, uniting, renewing and refreshing it holds—and he hates it with everything he's got.

His full armoury will be unleashed against those who try to make worship work. Some of his tactics include the inspiring of élitism and conflict with the rest of the church, interpersonal problems and arguments, dangerous sexual attractions between group members, 'artistic temperament' conflicts, prayer being squeezed out, unreliable members, spiritually unbalanced and over-the-top members, mutinies against leadership, sulks and shouting matches, backbiting, jealousy and competition, and a whole lot more. OK, I know that most church committees would be like that most of the time, but worship groups do seem to be singled out for extra satanic attack.

The role of leadership in such a group is an absolute front-line ministry, as all the above possibilities (and many, many more) are constantly monitored and dealt with at the first sign of trouble. Oppression, discouragement, despair and downright exhaustion are never far from the leadership, and the more effective the group becomes the greater the degree of attack you can expect. I'm sorry to have to say this, but it is true, and I've seen it time and time again. Worship is not flavour of the month for the Enemy, so he tries to destroy it, and if you look around the church today and back through history you may well agree with me that he's done a pretty reasonable job of it. How he must despise the renewal of worship which has been happening over the past few decades, and how he must fear for his kingdom as he sees worship taking root more and more deeply in churches as the Holy Spirit breathes new life into the dry bones which he has stripped of flesh. Above all, how he must tremble to see the church beginning to learn how to use worship as a weapon against him, and beginning to take praise out into his realm as we claim new ground in our cities and streets. Like a cornered animal, the Enemy is lashing out at musicians and worship groups, and we need to know it. Let me make three practical suggestions for those leading worship groups.

1. Put your armour on

Ephesians chapter six describes the equipment the Christian warrior needs in his battle against the demonic forces bent on destroying him. Meditate long and hard on this passage, and make sure you know what it means to have your armour on, not just for protection but in the offensive against the Enemy's kingdom. There are plenty of good commentaries on this passage, so I won't say any more here.

2. Learn some management skills

Since much of the conflict you'll be involved in will be to do with people, you have a responsibility to know how to handle them as effectively as possible, how to deal creatively with conflict, and how to step quickly on possible trouble without leaving the trouble-makers feeling crushed underfoot. Again, this whole area is outside the province of this book, but you do have a responsibility to grow in your interpersonal skills. It's no good bemoaning the fact that the Devil is attacking the group if it's your own ineptitude in handling it which is causing all the problems. The Devil probably isn't attacking your group in that case; he doesn't need to.

3. Get a friend

You need someone who will see it as their job to pray with you, to engage in spiritual warfare with you and on your behalf, and to listen to you as you unload the hassles and deal with your own uncertainties about how it is all going. Worship group leaders (at least ones worth their salt) tend to be in a position where they can easily be prone to self-doubt and discouragement, and someone who can come alongside as a friend and say things like, 'You're doing fine,' or, 'You do need to watch the relationship between Jack and Jill,' or, 'How much time is the group spending in prayer these days?' will be a tremendous asset for the leaders and through them to the group as a whole. This watch-dog/trouble-shooting/encouraging role is one you should be praying about. Ask the Lord to give you a friend who can act in these ways.

I don't want to give the impression that life in the worship group is one long war of attrition. It ought to be tremendously fulfilling and rewarding as well as being a great laugh, but to send you out to battle unprepared would be unfair of me. It won't be easy, but with the right care and protection, it ought to be worth it. There aren't many higher callings than leading worship, so get prepared, get praying and get in there! The church needs you.

CHAPTER ELEVEN

HANDLING THE CONGREGATION

I'VE CALLED THIS CHAPTER 'Handling the Congregation' because it fits in nicely with several other chapters about 'handling' this that or the other, but I don't want to give the impression for one moment that what we're trying to do is in any way manipulative. Apart from the Lord himself, those in the congregation are the most important people involved in worship, and as leaders we need to know how to honour and respect them, and to show that we do by the way we lead them. I want to consider first their needs, and secondly what they might do during a worship time, both helpfully and unhelpfully.

Before I discuss those things, though, we do need to remind ourselves of what it is that the Lord wants to do with them. First and foremost, I believe, he wants to come among them and do the sort of things he loves doing: healing, renewing, equipping—all the things we talked about in the first two chapters. Secondly, he simply wants to enjoy our worship. He wants to accept the gifts we are offering to him gladly and joyfully as they delight his heart, and he wants to enjoy watching us worship and getting pleasure out of it.

Those of us who are parents will understand a bit about this dual enjoyment. My oldest son is at the stage of learning to write, and of wanting to send me little cards and pictures for my study notice-board. My favourite is from his slightly earlier and more 'impressionist' period. It depicts a totally undifferentiated mess of green scribble, and bears at the bottom the very helpful explanatory title 'God help Joseph'. If he looks anything like his picture, he certainly needs all the help he can get. But I get the same twofold enjoyment from Steve's artwork that I believe God gets from our worship; I enjoy the gift, and the love and relationship which it represents, but I also enjoy watching him drawing and writing, because I can see from his face the fun he's having doing it and the sense of pride and achievement when it's finished. My wife has an important role in this process too. She's the one who clears the table, gets the paints or pens out, and restrains Steve's little brother in his attempts to help. She helps with spelling, and finally she clears up the mess afterwards.

The worship leader's role in all this is, I reckon, pretty similar to that of my wife in the art studio. Someone has to be there to offer resources to the congregation, to make sure there is space for them to worship, to help communication sometimes by having a slightly greater understanding of what's going on than the average member of the congregation, and then, with the ministry team, to clear up any mess created in the process. Leaders are simply the 'service department', keeping things running smoothly and effectively. Everything I say in this chapter should be understood in the light of this attempt not to manipulate or dominate, but simply to serve the worshipping people of God.

So what is it that they need? Above all else, I believe that the one thing they need is security. I would define security in this context as the certainty that everything is going to be OK. Whatever I do, whatever anyone else does, whatever God himself does, it'll be OK. Even if I do something wrong, it'll be OK. God is good, the leader knows what he's doing, everyone here loves me, so it's OK to be a part of it. It may even be OK to do something if I feel right about it; pray out loud, or jump up and down a bit, or something like that. What we're actually after as leaders is seeing everyone in the congregation involved and participating as individuals, and yet creating a corporate dimension which is much more than just the sum of its parts. Without security we won't be able to draw individuals in, and without individuals there'll be no corporate dimensions either, and the whole thing will feel like yesterday's Yorkshire pudding.

So security is vital, and we've talked a bit in Chapter 4 about how we can help provide it. But along with it come three other ingredients: *commitment*, *expectation* and *involvement* which are also pretty essential if our worship is going to rise regularly above the mediocre. The three are so closely tied in together that it is difficult to know where to start, but I think they involve respectively a decision of the will to be a worshipper, even if I have to do it in spite of the worship leader and everyone else, a belief that it will be worth while, since God will actually turn up and do something, and a decison to contribute something to the corporate nature of the worship experience rather than to keep it all nice and private between the Lord and me.

The staff of our church meet from time to time with a group of other church leaders from the area, including several house-church elders. When we begin to pray it's easy to tell the difference. They begin instantly with muttering, semi-audible tongues, shouts of 'Hallelujah!' and all the rest of it (one person said it reminded him of the old hymn 'Hoover around us while we pray'), while the Anglicans compose themselves silently for the time ahead and wonder if when they begin to say something they'll be interrupting a real prayer or only an interlude. I remember remarking to a fellow-Anglican the first time I heard this carry-on, 'They're so emotional, aren't they?' 'No,' he replied, 'we're emotional; they're committed.' I realised he was right. We were sitting there wondering how we felt, and deciding whether it was going to be a sufficiently good prayer-time for us to get into it and get excited about things, while they were just getting on and making it a good prayer-time, totally unconcerned about what they may have been like emotionally. I think that attitude to worship is what I mean by *commitment*. The obvious expectancy revealed in their prayers, and their desire to be involved publicly with others reflect a commitment within the Pentecostal and Restorationist traditions which other churches would do well to learn from, even if they did it a bit more quietly. It certainly is a joy occasionally to lead worship when there is a large house church contingent present; they're always raring to go right from the very first chord, and it makes the leader's job considerably easier when you have a congregation that committed. It's very different from usual when the first few songs can be spent attempting to bump-start the people in a way which feels reminiscent of trying to stir cold tarmac.

What I'm talking about is not, of course, a denial of our true emotions. There will be times when circumstances and the way we feel about them will cause us to come to the Lord expressing anger, heartbreak, doubt and so on, and this is totally biblical as well as profoundly realistic. But whether we come joyfully or with agony into God's presence, the point is that we do come, and we set our wills to do so either because of or in spite of our emotions. At times it will involve the sacrifice of praise we referred to in the first chapter, but to offer that sacrifice shows the commitment which is an essential for true worship.

Expectancy is something we bring to worship with us, whether we're conscious of it or not. The problem is that it may be either positive or negative. If we arrive to find out that it's 'him' on duty to lead worship tonight, our expectancy level may soar into the positive or plummet into the negative depending on our past experience of 'him'. Since all expectancy tends to fulfil itself, the view of 'him' which we have will be reinforced even further. Our moods, as well as the personnel, can affect the way a worship time goes, as can many other factors. Obviously a good dose of commitment will help in the expectancy department, but the fundamental way of raising the level is to concentrate first and foremost on the Lord and not on ourselves or anyone else around. The more we expect him to do, the more he actually will do; the more he did last time, the more we'll expect him to do this time, and so it goes on. This is honestly not an attempt to psych ourselves up or to kid ourselves with some kind of 'double-think'; it genuinely does work like that.

One of my major responsibilities at the moment is to lead teams which go out to other parishes to run evenings or weekends for them. I always tell clergy at the churches I will visit that the single best thing they can do in preparing people for the weekend is to work on their expectancy. The whole thing is a bit of a vicious circle, so it's better to have a positive vicious circle (if you can have such a thing) which spirals upwards than a negative one which goes the other way.

Involvement, thirdly, is important if the worship is to be more than a performance by the person at the front. It is a conscious decision to be a part of what is going on, to look a part of what is going on, and even at times to do something which may affect what is going on. Whether it means contributing a prayer, a prophetic word, a picture, or just joining in fully in the worship of the whole congregation, it is essential to the flow of good worship. Depending on the size of the gathering, it may be more or less easy for someone to contribute in some kind of a publicly vocal way, and a church should, of course, have some kind of small group where people can learn gradually to contribute out loud in a less threatening atmosphere. But it is still necessary for the worship leader to get some kind of sense of the people's willingness to be involved in worship.

It can make all the difference if your congregation is good at this, and a good way to tell how good they are is to watch what happens between songs rather than during. If people switch out of 'worship' mode and into 'looking around to see what's going to happen next' mode, the chances are they're not very good in the involvement stakes. But if they remain engaged with the Lord and very obviously still worshipping even when the music stops, they're the sort of worshippers it'll be a joy to lead. This is once again where the house-church style of worship comes into its own, where every spare moment is filled with praise, uttered enthusiastically and semi-audibly. It really does help the leader to feel that it is not, after all, up to him alone.

What makes the difference? Essentially it has to do with whether or not people are used to being worshippers on their own. Those who regularly come before the Lord in praise and adoration in their own devotional times will feel happy with doing so publicly, and won't mind too much whether or not a song happens to be going on at the time. But the insecure people, who feel a bit lost when things aren't happening up front, are often those who find solo worship difficult. Leading worship in a large gathering with a high proportion of such people is very hard work; trying to do it in a fellowship group is disastrous. Above all, leaders need to work on equipping people for their own individual   worship.   Strong,   committed,   expectant, involved worshippers, when put together in a crowd, will make for exciting and moving worship.

What sort of things, then, might people from the congregation do during a time of worship? It is worth saying right from the start that a worship leader is dealing with a very varied collection of people in any congregation, and their contributions will vary considerably. Careful handling will be needed to make the best of them, and it is a very skilled job indeed to do this well. So let's look at some possibilities.

1. Sentences of praise

Sometimes it's helpful to give people the space to respond in a personal but public way to what's going on musically. For example, after singing something like 'God is good', you might encourage people to speak out particular aspects of God's goodness which have struck them especially over the last week. People might respond with one-sentence prayers like, 'Thank you, Lord, for your provision for our needs,' 'Thank you, Father, for your healing power,' and so on. Not only is this good because it is a way of encouraging one another, but also because it gives people the chance to express personal thanksgiving in the context of the whole congregation in a way which is honouring to God. And also, if we're honest, it probably gives some of us a prod to thank God for our blessings when we may well have taken them for granted. The same principle is effective further on in worship when, in the middle of a phase of intimate adoration, people are encouraged to speak out their words of love and devotion to the Lord. It can be an awesome experience to share with one another that deeply.

Training a congregation to speak out sentences of praise may take a bit of time, since it may be a new way of praying which requires one of two equal and opposite new skills. The first is to be able to pray out loud in that way at all. This will be difficult in churches where everything has been led very much from the front before now. Praying in small groups could help here, as could your own example and that of one or two 'plants' in the congregation whom you have previously warned. The shorter the prayer, the easier it should be, and to encourage people to 'break the sound barrier' and do it for the first time can be a great help to them—something which will be important in lots of different areas of their Christian experience.

Some people, though, will have the opposite problem, and will not need asking twice to get going with their long, theologically exact prayers, which cover everything from the needs of their Aunty Gladys and her varicose veins to the plight of the church in Papua New Guinea and back again. Not only does this distract from the real task in hand, which is to give praise to the Lord, but it also alienates other people and makes it impossible to draw the less confident into praying, since they may easily feel that they need at least to match the verbosity of the previous prayer, and that the 'thank you Lord for your love to me' which they had up their sleeve is nowhere near stunning enough.

I'm not implying at all that the more prolix pray-ers are in any way insincere, just a bit unhelpful in this context. The leader of worship may need to do something to restrain people gently. First, he could give an example by saying brief prayers, and then, if necessary, gently insist on 'one-sentence' prayers. He needs to give clear instructions as to what he is inviting the congregation to do, without intruding on the sense of worship which has been reached. In extreme cases someone in authority may even need to have a quiet word afterwards with the offending party to explain that their contributions, although ideal in another setting, may not have been the most helpful thing for that particular time. There are dangers here, but used properly such verbal interjections can boost the worship.

2. Spiritual gifts

One of the more positive aspects of renewal is the rediscovery of the body of Christ in worship, and the possibility of God using any individual within that body to speak to the body as a whole. In the past, the scenario has been that the word of God has been mediated almost exclusively from the front, with the congregation simply present as those who responded and joined in the liturgy and hymns when told to do so. Nowadays, however, we are used to the Lord speaking through anyone in the congregation by means of prophecy, tongues and interpretation, pictures and so on. This has got to be a positive step forward, but it is not without its dangers. It seems to me that we can often fall down in one of two ways, and great skill is needed in testing and in responding. Let's have a look at each of these.

The Bible is very clear that any so-called manifestation of the Spirit should be weighed up in order that the congregation is not led astray by something which appears to be from the Spirit but actually is not. There are enough accounts of false prophecy in Scripture to make us all aware of the dangers inherent if it is not checked out properly. I find it helpful to think of the testing process as having two main stages. First of all, the person who thinks he is 'getting' something should test it out himself. Commonly what happens is that he will begin to feel physical sensations in his body (heat, thumping heart, hair on end, etc) followed by the impression of a few words on his mind which, if spoken out, will be replaced by a flow of words given a bit at a time. His first task, therefore, if he thinks that what he is experiencing is the Lord and not just the gorgonzola he had for lunch, is to pray silently something like, 'Lord, if this is not from you, please take it away.'

Sometimes exactly that will happen. His mind will go blank and he won't even remember what he was going to say. But more commonly the words will return with even more force. The more timorous charismatic may like to repeat the process to be absolutely sure: 'Lord, I really mean it. Please take this away if it's not right for me to say it!' Doing this much more than twice will usually be counterproductive, so after that it's best to go for it anyway.

Then there is the second part of the testing process. This involves the weighing up of the word by the church. Different churches will handle this in different ways. Sometimes it is insisted that anyone who feels he is getting a word or picture should share it first with an individual or group in leadership. Sometimes all contributions have to be expressed through the vicar or minister, and in places contributions are dealt with as they come, so that they are weighed after everyone has heard them and not before. I feel that there is a lot of truth in the view that the congregation itself is the best judge, since they can't help but respond to God when he really speaks powerfully, whereas less worthy contributions will be forgotten in no time, and probably won't do anyone much harm. However, there may still be the need for some kind of public assessment of what's been said; whether this is done by the church leader, a group of leaders, or the worship leader, these four questions will have to be asked before any decision or public statement is made.

Is it scriptural?

Does it tie in with what the Bible reveals about God's character and his dealings with men? Is it the sort of thing which the God whom he knows and loves would say? If not, it must be suspected of being wrong. Some of you may have been at the famous Fountain Trust meeting several years ago when someone said, as from the Lord, that Roman Catholics and women who wore trousers were an abomination. Not only was this suspect because neither trousers nor Roman Catholics are mentioned in the Bible, but more importantly because our God just wouldn't say things like that. At least, that's what the leadership at the time thought. I'm inclined to agree with them.

Is it positive?

It seems to be a characteristic of biblical prophecy that it always leaves what has been called 'a door of hope'. Satan wants to force us into a corner from which there is no escape, while God, on the other hand, wants to lead us out into freedom. Therefore a 'prophecy' which is all about our sin, wickedness and degradation is to be suspected if it doesn't go on to say something like, 'Therefore repent and turn back to me, and I will wash you clean from your sin.' A totally negative word is not from the Lord. God may indeed have to say hard things to his church at times; that of itself does not make a prophecy false, but if it simply leaves people feeling guilty and battered, it is definitely out of order.

Is it right?

Does it fit in with what God seems to be doing at the time? If not, it's probably right to forget it. I was leading a worship workshop recently, and during an open praise session between two songs someone piped up about how we should not be singing praise just in church, but should be doing it outside in the streets as a witness to the unsaved. While this was no doubt true, I didn't feel too good about it, but left it without saying anything. But when the same person spoke out again much more vehemently about what was the good of this noise if only the saved could hear it, I felt it right to step in and stop him on the grounds that God was not challenging us to evangelism right now, but was teaching us to worship. What God was leading us into was not 'noise', but praise which he really valued from his children. My point is that in another context that word may have been exactly right, but not just then.

Is it anointed?

Sometimes you can tell after a word has been given that there was great power in it. You can see from the faces of people in the congregation that it has 'cut them to the heart', and the almost stunned silence which follows speaks clearly of the effect which the Spirit is having on the lives of those who heard. But at other times a word can be very scriptural, positive and contextually correct, but still gives you the impression of having left the person's mouth and trickled down their chin and into their top pocket. Somehow the words seem to lack power. This is not because they were spoken vehemently or otherwise, but because they lacked the Spirit's authority.

What do you do, then, if a 'prophecy' fails one or more of these tests? I think you have to ask where the word did come from, if not from God. In most cases it will have come from misguided human enthusiasm, linked sometimes with a slightly unstable personality. An article by Cecil Robeck in *Theological Renewal* (July 1983) identified three types of 'false prophet': the 'Demagogue', who is obsessed by power and considers himself untouchable and beyond any testing; the 'Railer', who works very much from his own emotional agenda, and the 'Deceiver', who attempts to spread wrong doctrine and confusion. In his editorial Tom Smail added to these three a fourth category, the 'Prattler of Pious Plati-tudes, in whose hands the two-edged sword of the word is blunted and turned into a butter knife or a jam-spreader'.

When, in one of our services, someone told us that the

Lord said we were a load of hypocrites, we were able to discern very quickly that it was purely the girl in question reflecting her opinion of the church, an opinion which was no secret to anyone. She was acting as a 'Railer'. The other categories are similarly easy to spot. Unless the person is being a nuisance or articulating wrong doctrine which needs to be corrected, these types of words are best left uncommented upon, perhaps with a private chat afterwards if they do it repeatedly. Most often the congregation themselves will be the best judge of such words, since they will have forgotten them within about three minutes. The same applies to what I can only refer to as 'low-grade' words, the kind of thing which is very nice but has little effect on things. 'My children, I love you,' may be just what the congregation needs to hear at that time, but often simply leaves people feeling, 'Yes, that's nice.'

If you do need to say anything negative about a word, remember that the idea is to shut the person up and protect the congregation from possible error, but to do so in a way which is loving to the person and which does not freeze any other potential prophets with terror in case they blow it too. Such phrases as, 'I'm sure that's right, but I'm not sure that's what the Lord is doing right now,' or, 'I think the Lord would want to be a bit more positive than that towards us,' are probably more effective than outright confrontation, and can leave the person feeling, 'Good try, nearly got it right' instead of, 'Oh no! I'm a false prophet possessed by an unclean spirit!' At times you may run into what you consider to be a deliberate satanic counterfeit of prophecy, and this will need praying against specifically and the person rebuking more strongly (and not uncommonly being ministered to for deliverance) but this is pretty rare. Most times it is simply human nature, not the Enemy. The gift of discernment is obviously vital here, and as you get more experienced you will rely less on these four questions (although they still form a useful framework) and much more on how you feel about the word and about the 'prophet'.

If, however, as is far more likely, the word does feel OK, you then have another problem – what do you do with it? The area of responding to the word requires a similar amount of skill on the part of the leader. We have all experienced times when a word has really got to us, but we are then rushed into the next song with no chance to take it on board. Often what is needed is simply some space to respond personally, so an invitation to keep silent for a few minutes and allow time for the Lord to apply the word to our hearts is appropriate. At other times we may need to act in response to what the Lord has said, and our worship may need to change dramatically and go off in a new direction, for example, penitence.

This is where the skilful worship group comes into its own, as musicians are able at a moment's notice to begin a song which is not on the list but which leads people in the direction which is appropriate. By the time the leader has said, 'Let's respond to the Lord's call to humble ourselves before him,' the musicians will already be playing the introduction to 'Lord, have mercy on us' or something similar. Thus the flow is not broken, even though the direction may have changed suddenly. Perhaps the word will have spoken to individuals rather than the congregation as a whole, and there may be the need to invite people to receive ministry, either then or at the end of the service. There may be several options, but the leader will have to ensure that some response is made, otherwise the effect of the word will be lost. When the Lord really speaks, pressing on regardless is not an option.

3. Spontaneous songs

Sometimes, even in the most well-planned worship time,

someone from the congregation will want to take over, and may suggest or even start up a song. How do you handle that? It is worth remembering that basically this is a good thing, even though it may inconvenience you at times. You are there, after all, to help people worship, so if they do actually start worshipping in this way, it is to be welcomed since it shows that you are doing your job properly. However, you do need a bit of discernment here. Does the song fit with the flow of where you are going? If it does, fine—go for it.

There is one law here which I have found to be almost universally true; I am even tempted to call it 'Leach's Law'. It states that a worship song started from the congregation will always be started in a key with the highest possible number of sharps or flats. At times really skilful people can excel themselves and go for quarter-tones. I remember our pianist once shrugging and pointing despairingly at the little crack on the keyboard between B and B flat while the congregation were lustily singing 'I love you, Lord'—but unaccompanied. Even with a tunable synthesiser it's next to impossible to help them out on that one. So what can you do? You need brilliant timing to be able to wait until the gap between the first and the second time through, and then to thump out the dominant chord of the key you should be in to lead them to the right place for the repeat of the song. If you can play in A sharp minor, fine, but if you do need to modulate, that's a helpful way to do it without breaking the flow.

But what if the song is totally inappropriate? If, during the gap between 'Lord, you are so precious to me' and 'I just want to praise you', someone shouts out, 'Can we sing "You shall go out with joy"?' a good stock answer is, 'Yes, but not now!' (If you can actually remember to fit it in later on that's OK, but don't feel you have to.) But if they are even braver and just start singing it, there's not a lot you can do, except make no attempt to accompany them and let it die after the first verse. Then you can get back to what you were doing before you were interrupted. The chances are that everyone else in the congregation felt the inappropriateness of it as much as you did, and will very quickly settle back into the direction they were going in beforehand. Let me emphasise again that basically participation is a positive thing, but it does have to be handled properly if it is to be as effective as possible.

4. Clapping

And why not? If the song demands it, people may begin to clap along in time. You just need to watch the dramatic tempo changes you rehearsed so carefully, like the last verse of 'He that is in us'. Unless you give a clear indication of what you're going to do, you may have a burst of what sounds like machine-gun fire from the congregation. And something which speeds up, like 'Jesus put this song into our hearts', is liable to go completely over the top if the congregation is given too free a hand (or should I say pair of hands?). The musicians, and not the congregation, need to be in control of the tempo. But apart from those obvious difficulties, clapping can be really exhilarating. It can also be good at the end of a particularly rousing song of celebration when a spontaneous burst of applause breaks out. It's so obviously the Lord who is being clapped that I don't see any danger in removing the spotlight, as it were, from him.

5. Shouts

Graham Kendrick's *Make Way!* has popularised what many churches have been doing for years—shouting in worship. Like clapping this can be an exhilarating experience, particularly suitable for those times when you are concentrating on warfare or proclamation. You just need to make sure that the people know what it is they're supposed to be shouting (usually by getting them to repeat words after you) and that they are given a strong lead from the rest of the worship group which encourages them to bellow out with all their gusto. There is nothing more uninspiring than a 'festal murmur'.

6. Singing in tongues

This will often happen almost spontaneously after a song has ended, most commonly a song which is about intimate adoration but has a bit more power to it than some of the quieter ones. 'For thou O Lord' is particularly good, especially since it does not end on the tonic note, thus giving people a slightly unfinished feel. There is a strange dynamic about singing in tongues whereby you usually either make it or you don't. There seems to be a sort of threshold sound level above which people cannot hear themselves singing. This makes them feel unembarrassed about joining in loudly which, of course, raises the sound level even more. But if the threshold is never reached, the overall sound is thin and weedy, which in turn makes people sing more quietly lest their contribution actually gets heard. So a good strong lead from the worship group and others who have got over their self-consciousness is important if it is to take off. When it does work, however, there is real power in a time of free praise. It is a time when people are often healed or touched by the Spirit, and it is also helpful for people who would like to receive the gift of tongues—many of them receive the gift at this time. It can either be unaccompanied, or the musicians can improvise quietly and sensitively around the tonic chord. Sometimes it can be more structured, as when the leader suggests that people sing their own words for one verse or chorus of a song. You need to make sure that you do not exclude people who don't speak in tongues by saying something like, 'in tongues or in English,' when you are giving instructions for free praise.

7. Dance

I have to admit to being somewhat ambivalent here. I'm never quite sure whether the charismatic movement has done something important in rediscovering the physical nature of Old Testament worship and reintroducing dance, or whether, like the old sacrificial system, dance is something rather messy from the old dispensation from which we've been redeemed now that we live under grace. When done well, liturgical dance can be profoundly moving and say things which mere words can only hint at. But quite honestly the sight of 400 people jumping up and down on the spot does nothing for me at all. I suppose I find it most effective when choreographed to fit a particular piece of music (I remember particularly a dance my wife produced one Easter to taped music of Elton John's 'Funeral for a Friend' which had me in tears), but much less helpful in the context of what this book would call 'worship'. Still, if people want to do it they're welcome. I find it a healthy trend that it is increasingly going on at the back rather than at the front of the church, which speaks much more of people's physical offering of praise to the Lord than of exhibitionism.

I would certainly want to encourage people to use their bodies much more in their private devotional lives, and it is therefore natural that this should overflow into public praise. As a worship leader you should be prepared for it (I was once nearly put off my stroke on the guitar when a very dapper little man in a smart suit suddenly leaped over three seats and began to stalk and gyrate across the front of the church at high speed like a clockwork toy with an overwound spring), but I can't imagine myself ever wanting to put pressure on anybody to do it. Maybe I have yet to be 'released' into dance; I don't know, but I'm neither in a hurry for that to happen, nor would I want to stop anyone else.

8. The demonic in worship

I put this here, not because I feel it has any connection with point seven above, but because it is something which people in the congregation 'do' from time to time which needs handling by the person up front. In Chapter 2 we mentioned that God comes among us as we worship, and that at times his presence will provoke demonic spirits to manifest themselves. This may happen in various ways, as it did in Jesus' time, with the sudden shouting out perhaps of obscenities, screaming, animal noises, or physical contortions, occasionally of a quite violent nature. The first time this happens it can be quite a shock. If you're leading you need to get over the first impression that it's somehow personal—no, it's not your guitar playing that's making them scream—it's the Lord. The great sense of relief which comes over you when you realise this should help you to cope.

A fundamental rule is that the one person who should never get involved in dealing with the demonised person is the one leading worship. Your role is at the front, providing security for the congregation, reassuring them that this is perfectly OK, that you've seen it hundreds of times before and that we can handle it fine. Never mind that you're absolutely terrified; just keep smiling and announce the next song. Meanwhile some of the congregation experienced in the healing ministry should take the person out of the main body of the church and pray for him. I find it tremendously helpful to remember that when a demon manifests itself it is good news not bad, because it can then be dealt with. I'll never forget John Wimber, at a particularly noisy ministry session during a conference, stalking around the stage beaming and saying, 'I love it when demons scream—it's music to my ears!' People were being set free, and that's what matters. (By the way, don't think that being a worship leader lets you off the hook entirely in the deliverance ministry. You should still know how to handle it, but not when you're supposed to be at the front.)

I hope this chapter hasn't sounded too negative. At times the congregation can be a real nuisance in worship, but we need to remember that they are the most important, and not us. We're just there to help them, not the other way round. It's another valuable and sadly true insight of John Wimber's that the average pastor basically dislikes and resents his flock since they get in the way of what he is trying to do. It would be tragic if worship leaders fell into the same trap. We would do well to listen to Paul's advice to his Philippian friends: 'In humility consider others better than yourselves. Each of you should look not only to your own interests, but also to the interests of others' (Phil 2:3–4). We need to put that into practice in the way we lead them into God's presence in worship.

CHAPTER TWELVE

CHILDREN AND WORSHIP

WHEN I WAS FIVE YEARS OLD my father had a conversion experience which was, for him, quite a dramatic turn around. As a family we began to attend the Baptist church with which my mother already had links, and of which both my parents are still pillars. It was not until seventeen years later that I left the Baptist church and joined the Church of England, in which I was subsequently ordained. As you might imagine, the whole question of baptism was for me a crucial one. It has only really been during the past two or three years that I have become convinced that infant baptism is right. Before that, even though I would perform the ceremony frequently as part of my ministry, I did so with many uncertainties and misgivings. I mention this because it seems to me that before considering the place of children in worship, one has to have a pretty clear idea of just who children are and where they stand in relation to God. 'Baptist' and 'Anglican' theologies of children (and I use the terms in inverted commas, not wishing to imply that every single Baptist or Anglican would subscribe wholeheartedly to those particular viewpoints) are very different, and need to be faced and considered if worship praxis is to have integrity.

Baptists quite rightly stress the need for a personal response to God, and would see baptism as following such a response, which can only be made by someone who has come to a conscious and informed decision to do so. Anglicans, however, would want to add to that the possibility of the biblical idea of 'family faith', where someone brought up within a family relationship to God is included within the covenant until such time as they consciously rebel against it and place themselves outside it. Thus, in practice, 'Baptist' parents long for the time when their children will 'make a decision', 'accept Jesus into their hearts' or whatever they call it, while 'Anglican' parents desire rather to see their children grow in the relationship with the Lord which they already have, so that a family faith gradually becomes more and more of a personal faith. This theology only really became convincing for my wife and myself as we had children of our own and began the process of bringing them up.

Our boys, now four and five years old, pray regularly, read the Bible with us (at least some of the easy words), love to go to church, enjoy singing worship songs, experience spiritual gifts, pray for healing for one another, and bring Jesus into most of the conversations they have, not as a remote abstract figure but as a powerful personal friend. We often wake up in the morning and find them already in the bathroom praying together, or are woken up by them going on a 'praise march' round the house. (I hope God enjoys it more than we do at that time in the morning!) I mention this not to claim any credit for the way we handle our children (far from it—we consider ourselves to be beginners, and would not want to claim infallibility at all), but to explain that Chris and I cannot cope with a theology which says that until they have 'made a commitment' they are not really Christians. At times their faith and love for the Lord put us to shame, and having them in the family has really brought to life the words of Jesus that anyone who will not receive the kingdom of God like a little child will never enter it (Lk 18:17). Jesus said that in children there is a model of the kingdom; how can those of us who are within the kingdom exclude those in our families who are able to show us what it is really all about?

I say all this not to enter into polemic against the 'Baptist' position, but to help explain some of what I have to say on children and worship. My conviction is that the children of believing parents are, unless they have specifically decided to the contrary, Christians, and are therefore capable of being included fully in worship. In fact, they often have much to teach us about it.

I want to tackle this subject under two main headings: first I want to consider worship in church services, and then I'll move on to look at worship within the family at home. There will be links between the two, but I want to tackle them separately because different things will be appropriate in each case.

In evangelical circles, where a high value is put on understanding with our minds, there is an abundance of Family Services where everything is geared to being comprehensible by the youngest member. Yet, as Maggie Durran has pointed out, this can be a false path:

> Many of the difficulties with children are the result of thinking that faith in God is based on understanding, an aspect of the intellect. In fact faith in God is based first on God's action in redemption. We are saved not by our efforts or our thinking, but by grace, a free gift of God. . .We become confused because we have unconsciously learned that the way we are able to behave or think affects God's redemption.[1]

She discusses the different stages that the developing

child goes through, and the different relationships he has with the worshipping church family in each of these stages. The under-three needs to receive from the church unconditional love and a sense of belonging—adults need to be patient with him and encourage him to participate. The three to six year old will need above all to join in with what is going on. The six to twelve year old will be able to offer much in terms of service. The teenager will need to begin to assert himself and work out his own adult faith and praxis. Some of this is based on intellectual growth and understanding, but much of it is not. Church services should, therefore, seek not to communicate intelligible truth to children all the time so much as a loving atmosphere in which they can experience, either directly or through other Christians, the fulfilment of their particular needs at their stage of growth.

Our church has recently made a conscious decision to go at least partly for a less 'Evangelical' and more 'Catholic' approach to involving children, with an acknowledgement that they learn as much from the 'atmosphere' and what they take on unconsciously as they do from that which is directly intelligible to them. Thus it isn't as important for them to be able to understand every word of the service as it is for them to experience being in and feeling a part of a worshipping community and seeing that community worshipping as adults whether through liturgy or in the liberty of the Spirit—hopefully both.

These twin themes of involvement through atmosphere and participation will affect the content as well as the form of our services. It is not necessary to edit out all words, songs or bits of liturgy which are beyond the comprehension of children. What is important is that they see adults meeting God through the words, and are able in some way to join in with that meeting. Very simple things like issuing service books to children (or even better encouraging them to bring their own copies) can include them, and it is amazing how much they can learn without actually understanding fully. In our family Steve, who's five, and isn't very good yet at reading words like 'troll' and 'porridge', can handle the Rite A confession with no trouble; 'negligence', 'weakness' and 'deliberate fault' included. And his little brother Paul, when he was three, not only learned the entire *Gloria* off by heart, but could also sing it to the setting we use on Sundays. He has his own children's Communion book, of which he is very proud, and even though he can as yet only recognise words like 'look', 'and', 'the' and 'doggy' (the latter of which features only minimally in the text of Rite A), he 'reads' it intently as he sings his little heart out, sometimes even managing to have the book the right way up. They may not understand every last theological nuance of the words, but then neither do their mum and dad. We're all learning together.

This principle applies equally to the worship songs we use in church. From time to time it may be appropriate to sing 'Two little eyes to look to God' or 'Have you got the sunshine S-M-I-L-E?', but children will probably take much more lasting spiritual value on board by joining in with adults singing something like 'Father God I wonder'. Some more deeply theological songs may genuinely be beyond them (Paul thinks for some inexplicable reason that 'Meekness and majesty' is really called 'Dip dip dip dammamy'), but they can cope perfectly well with things like 'I just want to praise you' or 'Fling wide your doors'. In planning worship times with children in mind you can still use the 'graph' method of Chapter 9, as long as you remember to move much more quickly in order not to lose the concentration of younger children. If they can join in with adults who begin to dance in some of the more exuberant songs, there will be an added bonus and point of interest and involvement for children.

Just as there is less need than one might expect to change the content of worship times, there is also little need to change one's theology of worship. The worship cycle works perfectly well with even the youngest children; you just have to pedal a lot faster. Adults may enjoy the luxury of a long drawn-out time of worship which leads to the powerful presence of God among them, but with children you will have to get there in the space of three or four songs. But expectancy is what counts, and if they can be helped to expect the presence of God in a short time, he won't let them down by not turning up until the regulation twenty minutes of singing have elapsed. At our church we sometimes see children involved in ministry to one another as the Spirit comes upon them during worship, and this is something which we long to encourage more and more.

Our services, therefore, need to get the right balance between involving children in ways appropriate to their ages and needs, and yet allowing them to take on truth experientially as well as intellectually. We obviously need to take into account their limited concentration span, and move things along faster to keep the interest level high, but apart from that there is little need to change either the content or theology of our worship. Again, Maggie Durran says:

> Those who lead worship for all ages, with a concern for the nurture of all members, will then look for structures, forms and liturgies which facilitate the worship of *everyone* present . . . the church's gift to children is in making a way open for children to give their response to God along with the rest of the congregation. The child will not be satisfied with a *children's slot* in the service, for that implies first that the child is there to receive when really he is nurtured most through giving. Secondly it says that his presence throughout the remainder of the service is not relevant to God.[2]

The last word on this comes from Ishmael, a singer and

musician who has become one of the country's most effective children's worship leaders. He cries out from his heart on behalf of undervalued and undertrained children everywhere in a song called 'Little Troopers':

I'm fed up with silly stories—and modelling plasticine.
And being told I'm too young to talk—in church be even seen.
Though I'm just a child—I'm still a spiritual being
But this soldier's got a lot to learn,
But who's going to teach me?[3]

But what about worship in the family? Do the same rules still apply? And how do the two link together? An important concept here is what I call the 'priesthood of parents'. In the Old Testament the priests had a dual function: to represent the people to God, and to represent God to the people. I believe it to be true that parents *ought* to do the first, and indisputably *do* do the second.

First, we ought to be praying for our children, quite apart from whether or not we pray with them. In an age of increasing child abuse both within and outside the family, of occultism rife in schools, of lack of love and discipline in families (even within Christian families), and of ever-increasing numbers of children living in one-parent families, we cannot doubt that spiritual warfare is being waged by the Enemy against our children. We need to pray to protect them from all sorts of influences which would seek to harm them. Although this ought to be the job of the whole church family, we live in times when the nuclear family is where it is at, and so the main responsibility for prayer and care for our children rests with parents. We pray every day with our children for their protection (in terms, of course, which don't give them juvenile paranoia), and we often pray over them as they sleep as well. Our worship together takes this spiritual warfare seriously, while all the time stressing the victory of Jesus over the Enemy.

But as much harm, or perhaps even more, can be done if we fail to take the other half of our priestly function seriously—representing God to our children. Not only is it a fact that we show our children what God is like; for the very young it goes even further than that, and it is true to say that to them we *are* God. Let me explain what I mean. I don't know how many people I've talked to who are screwed up one way or another in their Christian life because they think that God is somehow like their human father was. We have literally thousands of Christians in this country who have given over their lives to a God who gets impatient with them, who will only forgive them if they do the same sin no more than once, who will only heal them if they can manage to deserve it, who sends punishments and disasters on them for minor violations of what they consider to be his law—the list is endless. People are living in the grip of lies which they have been fed simply because we all have a built-in tendency to think that one father is very much like another, whether earthly or heavenly. The job of parents, therefore, is to act as much as possible towards their children as God would, so that their whole relationship becomes a picture and a revelation of the character of God. This means first of all, of course, that we have to get our own picture of God sorted out and cut free from any negative effects from our own parents, but after that we need to act always towards them as God would.

Not only is this true for us as parents; it is also true for those in leadership in the church. This came home to me most graphically one day when a young child in church, whose mother normally received Communion from one of our team of lay administants, saw me approaching with the chalice. In the sort of stage whisper that only children can manage, and usually only at times when their parents think they ought to be quiet, he exclaimed, 'Ooh look, Mum. God's bringing ours today!' He really did think that those who spent most of the service down at the pointed end all dressed up in funny clothes were divine. This realisation changed my behaviour considerably, as I suddenly grasped the responsibility that was mine to reveal God to little children. I thought about the way we administered the blessing to youngsters at the Communion rail; usually we swept past, brushing them with the edge of our gold vestments, momentarily pausing to put a hand on their heads and mumble something which might as well have been in Latin for all they knew. Whatever sort of a God did they think I was? So I began to slow down, to look the kids in the eye, to smile at them, to pray for them in a way which they could relate to, and occasionally to give them a playful little tweak on the nose as I finished. One day, when a litte girl hopefully held out her dolly, I thought, 'Why not?' and blessed it too. This action, observed by several adjacent children, opened the floodgates, and next week I was blessing a whole menagerie of doggies, teddies, bunnies, gollies and even, I seem to remember, an emu. Then came the craze for wearing those little springy antennae on your head. Each child expected not just a blessing but a quick ping of their boppers too.

Now, although I don't know any theological justification whatsoever for this sort of behaviour at the rail, I do know this: if those children thought I was God, then they definitely thought I was a nice God. Since I believe God is nice (you really learn profound theology through reading books like this, don't you?) I wanted to reveal this to those children who were in my pastoral care. (It was good later on to see our children exercising a similar priestly role to their toys, when one day they 'played Communions' and lined up doggy, wombat and various other furry creatures and went along the line giving each in turn a bit of pretend bread with the words, 'A piece of the Lord . . . a piece of the Lord.'

I say all this because it has implications for the way we worship in families. It seems to me that one of the most powerful ways in which we get in touch with objective truth about God is through worshipping him in spirit and in truth. As we read of God's revelation of himself in the Bible, as we sing truths about him together, as we celebrate and affirm that truth in liturgy, the subjective and warped God we are tempted to take on board is replaced more and more with the true and living God who has revealed himself to us in Jesus. This is important not just to the children but to us as parents as well, because our priestly role becomes more and more accurate, and we reveal more and more clearly the true nature of God. Thus family worship is a dynamic process which leads us into more and more of the truth. While this is true in public worship to some degree, it is in the closer relationships of the immediate family that it becomes vitally important.

So how might we organise our worship times in the family? First of all we need to make sure that we know and understand the constraints on us. The ages of our children will affect both the length of time we take and also its content.

Even at the same age, different children have very different characters, with different levels of understanding and concentration. Some will enjoy bouncing around and can't keep still for any length of time at all, while some will be content to sit quietly for longer periods. Knowing their temperaments will help us considerably in getting our expectation of our children right. Go with them, and don't force them to do something which it is just not in their make-up to do.

Secondly, we need to make sure that there is an in-built balance in our worship times. The primary balance should be between the intellectual and the experiential so that children don't just learn about God, but experience him too. There should also be a balance between the different elements of worship. I find it helpful to think in terms of public worship, and to attempt to have most of the same elements in our family times—not all of them every day, but with a good balance over a period of a week or month.

Regularity

Just as time is set aside in the week for public worship, so time should be set aside during the day for family worship. Everyone should know this, and it should be part of the routine; in fact, it should be such fun that it is a part of the routine which everyone welcomes and anticipates eagerly. People often say that they don't feel the need for a regular devotional time in the day because they can pray any time. This is no doubt true, but my own experience is that it is much easier to pray 'any time' if I have first prayed 'some time'. This is likely to be especially true with children.

Worship

Both spoken and sung worship form an important part of our church services, and so should also be present in our family times. Singing together is natural for children, even if it is sometimes slightly embarrassing for teenagers and adults. Very young children have a tremendous capacity for remembering words, and you should have a repertoire of about a dozen or so songs which everybody knows. You may not get into a fully fledged worship cycle, with the *shekinah* of the Lord descending into the bedroom on every occasion, but singing should still go somewhere, and lead you deeper into God's presence. We have found worship tapes very helpful, both to join in with and to have on as background music, for example with meals. They can help tremendously in teaching words to children (although at times you may have to correct them if your cassette player is not of a very high quality. A friend's young daughter used to love singing 'I get so excited Lord every time I realise—I'm a gibbon'!).

The ministry of the word

In church this would consist of Bible reading with some sort of an exposition or explanation. Both these elements can be included in family times, with a reading of appropriate length and complexity followed by a discussion which draws out an application for the children, and sometimes corrects misunderstandings. Our children, having read about Jesus raising someone from the dead, were most concerned about how he did it when they were 'stone'. They had often seen the gravestones around our church (or 'gravy stones' as they called them), and knew that they were in some way connected with dead people, so what was more logical than to think that dead people turned into large slabs of stone with writing on? (On one occasion Steve and I were walking in the grounds of our local cathedral, where some of the old gravestones have been laid down as paving flags, when he suddenly noticed the carved words on one of them. Being more used to them in the upright position he asked me, 'Who died flat down like that?') It turned out to be the case that raising from the dead presented no problem in theory, but the practicalities of the defossilisation process were totally beyond their understanding. This led onto a helpful discussion about souls, life after death, and so on.

A suitable version of the Bible is important. The best one for younger children is the Good News Bible, which ought to be appropriate for anyone with a reading age of nine or above, but some of the children's Bibles are even more helpful. They have lots of pictures and a selection of the narrative portions of the text, but they omit genealogies, lengthy liturgical sections dealing with the cutting up of animals, and some of the more gross sexual misdemeanours. We use *The Lion's Children's Bible* (Tring: Lion, 1981). Whichever one you use, it should become a treasured book, in the same way that the old family AVs used to be in previous generations. You may like to use Bible notes (there are some available for everyone from very young children up to teenagers), and supplement the reading with other activities such as drawing, colouring, glueing and so on. One family we know keeps a scrapbook which illustrates the words of songs or Bible passages with pictures which are cut out and pasted in. There is plenty of scope for creativity here.

Confession and forgiveness

These are important in church worship, and should be present in family times too. It is important not just for children to repent of their iniquities, but for them to see you doing so too. This can also provide an important time when you say sorry to one another, again both ways. We have a piece of family liturgy which means that whenever you say, 'Sorry,' the response is always, 'I forgive you.' The wrong is not ignored by leaving no response, nor undervalued by saying, 'It doesn't matter.' Sin does matter, always, so it is faced fully and then forgiven. After that, it is never to be mentioned again. This is vitally important because in the family we are demonstrating God's way of dealing with sin and forgiveness.

I find Isaiah chapter 6 helpful here. In verse 7 the seraph declares Isaiah's forgiveness with the words, 'Your guilt is taken away and your sin atoned for.' Very often Christians get these two things totally the wrong way round. We try to take away sin by pretending it never happened or that it didn't really matter, and then we need to atone for the guilt which remains by working harder to be better. That is not God's way. He confronts us with our sin—its full horror and terrible effects—by showing us Jesus and the agony he suffered so that it might be atoned for. He then takes away our guilt by showing us Jesus' love, grace and perfect acceptance. By the way we confess to and forgive each other (we to them as much as they to us), we are showing our children an important spiritual principle and giving them a glimpse of God's ways, the correct understanding of which will prove vital to them in times to come.

Prayer

This is obviously central. We should not pray on behalf of young children since they are perfectly capable of doing it well for themselves. You need to set an example for them by keeping your prayers brief and simple. I find the Anglican method of praying for one thing and then saying 'Amen' before moving on to pray for the next thing, as it were in a separate prayer, preferable to the non-conformist pattern of putting everything together in one long prayer. We have another rule that everyone prays on every occasion, in order that both a pattern and a habit are established. This caused a few ructions at the beginning, but is now firmly established and causes no problems.

Subject matter for prayer should be kept topical, and there should be a balance between praying for our own needs as a family and for those outside. If Daddy has an important meeting or a particularly difficult day ahead, everyone can join in praying for him, and if a church family member or a relative is ill, this too can capture the imagination of young children. Imagination is important, as they are encouraged to get in touch with how Sally feels stuck in bed with chickenpox. How did you feel when you had it?

Itchy? Then what do we want to pray for Sally? This can add much more to the prayer than simply saying, 'Please make Sally better, Amen.'

Never underestimate the power of imagination and emotion even for very young children. We happened to be driving back from holiday on the day of the Nelson Mandela Birthday Concert, so we explained to the boys that instead of following our normal practice of taking it in turns to choose tapes to listen to, Mummy and Daddy wanted to listen to the radio all the way. Of course, they wanted to know what was on, so we explained (rather simplistically) that Nelson Mandela was a man with a brown face who lived in a country where the people with white faces didn't like people with brown faces, and he had been in prison for twenty-six years, which was ever since Mummy and Daddy were little, and ever since our friend Helena was born. About half an hour later we stopped in a little town for lunch, and had just got out of the car when Steve suddenly began to howl, just as if he'd fallen over or banged his head. He was inconsolable for a few minutes, but when he calmed down we discovered that he hadn't hurt himself at all, but was crying 'because of the man being in prison for twenty-six years'. Something about that situation had touched his little heart, and all four of us sat on the wall of the car park and cried and prayed together for a world where such evil can happen. As adults we would have just enjoyed the music of the concert, but it took a child to melt our hearts and show us something of the grief of God for his world. Nelson Mandela and South Africa have stayed on Steve's prayer agenda ever since.

At times you will have to bear with the children in praying over their concerns. If they tell you that Wayne is having a lot of fights at school and is very unhappy, you may feel that he is a worthy subject for your intercession, but when you are asked to lay hands on Kangaroo for his sore throat, the temptation is to tell them not to be so silly and to think of something proper to pray about. This would probably be unhelpful, however, and it is worth going along with it. At times like these there is almost always full and immediate healing, as they declare joyfully, 'Kangaroo's better now!' (Personally I value anything which helps me feel more successful in the healing ministry!) It is also helpful to bring something to bear from the Bible reading you've used when you come to prayer. If you've read about Daniel and the lions, you might introduce the idea of persecuted Christians in other countries and pray for them, or even better about one particular person on whom you have some details.

Listening in prayer is important, and very young children can hear God speaking to them once you've explained in terms they can understand how he actually speaks. We have some friends whose three year old heard the Lord saying to her, 'Daddy is not to play squash tomorrow as he will get locked in.' She had no idea that he had a game booked, and had never seen a squash court and so knew nothing of the possibility of getting locked in. Daddy cancelled his game, believing that he had to give his daughter credibility. If she was wrong and had made it up, it at least left her free to try again.

Ministry

Ministering to each other is one stage further on from just praying about each other's problems. Our boys are familiar with John Wimber's method of healing, and we will often minister to a member of the family who needs prayer for healing or something similar. Spiritual gifts will be used, here and in worship, and we have seen some quite dramatic answers to prayer within the family. Having said that, however, it seems to be the case that healing is at its least effective in the family, so don't be too discouraged if it doesn't work. It'll give you a good opportunity to explain to your under-fives your theology of suffering and failure. I'm serious: they'll need to face it sooner or later, so why not right from the start? A lot of disillusionment can be avoided later.

Liturgy

I've already made the point that children can cope very well with liturgy, and it can be incorporated very successfully into family worship. I've mentioned singing the *Gloria* or the *Sanctus* together, but how about learning the Lord's Prayer (using the same version you'd use in church), or using daily the Collect for the week? Children should be getting something from it by the time you've repeated it every day, and you can use it to introduce the idea of the church's calendar and year. As with all liturgy, it can be a good talking point to explain what it all means and to pick up on any hard words or phrases. Older children might be able to cope with a liturgical framework to the worship time, for example a very simplified form of Morning Prayer, but you'll need to watch out for the first signs of staleness and be prepared to make some changes.

Ceremonial

As I've explained in a previous chapter, this isn't about whether it's Steve's or Paul's turn to hold the monstrance this morning, but rather about everything you *do* as opposed to what you say or sing. Vigorous bouncing children will endure worship times if they are told to sit still and listen, but will enjoy them if they are allowed to bounce around or dance. If you are 'released' enough (or more to the point if you are awake enough), you may even like to bounce with them. If you want to raise your arms, do action songs, or otherwise express yourselves physically, go ahead. It is the most natural thing in the world for children.

I also feel strongly that the worship time should be a time of physical closeness in the family. We have ours in bed together in the morning, and I'm sure our kids will grow up subconsciously associating worship with warmth, comfort and closeness. I remember as a very young child sitting with my mum through many interminable Baptist sermons. Their content naturally enough meant nothing at all to me, but I can recall feeling warm and secure as I snuggled up to her for half an hour. If the family are all sitting around a table, there will be a much less intimate feel to the whole proceeding.

This only really leaves the notices and the collection, which you may feel are inappropriate for this setting, although you could take some time to share what each of you has on the agenda for the day ahead (especially important for older children) or to pray about a particular person or project to which you have decided to give as a family. I'm not suggesting that you turn each morning's session into a church service, but that over a period of time your family worship has a balanced combination of most of the above ingredients. Let me end with three keys which can unlock a successful devotional life for your family:

1. Make it fun

Nothing is more designed to kill children's spirituality stone dead than having to endure a numbingly boring 'quiet time' every morning of their lives. If it is not a time to which they look forward eagerly, and if you detect a build up of resentment, boredom and withdrawal, do something quickly before it's too late.

2. Keep it varied

If you've hit on the right formula which works perfectly for you, praise the Lord and prepare to change it, because it won't work for very long with most children. Keep things under constant review, and never allow staleness to creep in.

3. Don't give up

Like just about everything else in both the Christian life and family life, your worship times will tend to go in fits and starts. Perseverance is a useful virtue, and you will need plenty of it. But keep trying, because you will be doing for your family and for your children something of immeasurable value. It'll prove to be well worth the hassle.

Notes

1. Maggie Durran, *All Age Worship* (Angel Press: Chichester, 1987), p. 3.
2. *Ibid.*, p. 7.
3. Ishmael, *Training up the Troops* (Kingsway: Eastbourne, 1988).

CHAPTER THIRTEEN

HANDLING CHANGE

I. For Leaders

IN MANY WAYS this book has been setting out an ideal. I've tried to describe some of the ways worship ought to work in both theology and practice, and I hope that I've been fairly practical in showing how it might just be made to work. I may, during the course of the book, have convinced you that some of the things I've described are not only right but even desirable. You may be feeling that you'd like your church to take some of them on board. But now you realise that there is something in the way—the people.

It's been said that the single biggest obstacle to church growth is people, and the same applies to just about any area of change in the life of the church. So if we're going to change something as deep-rooted and emotionally charged as our worship, we're very likely to experience opposition, and at times very ruthless and bitter opposition. The very fact that you are reading a book like this may mean that you already want change and are even experimenting with it, so the chances are that you know from experience what you are up against. How can we get anywhere at all in introducing renewed worship without starting World War Three?

In discussing change and its difficulties, I'm aware that I'm addressing two completely opposite groups of people. First, there are clergy and church leaders who are trying to drag reluctant congregations into the twentieth century, and even into the charismatic bits of it. Secondly, there are congregational members who are trying to do the same with their leadership. I want to say some things which may be helpful for both groups, and I would encourage everyone not just to read the chapter which applies to them, but also to the other person or people since there may well be insights for you there. (It will also help you to spot whether any of your congregation/leadership have read this book and are trying it out on you!)

So first, church leaders. I want to give four major pieces of advice, and talk a little about each of them.

1. Understand the situation

There are different ways of describing what it is that you are trying to do. You may call it 'developing the church's worship life', 'renewing the liturgy', 'updating the services' or whatever you like, but you need to understand one thing very clearly: you are trying to introduce change. Once you come right out and say that, it helps to explain why you have such a job on your hands. 'Developing worship' sounds as if anyone ought to be able to do it with one hand tied behind their back, but everyone knows that introducing change to a church is only marginally easier than doing the totally impossible. That immediately makes all the heartache, opposition and failure you've experienced so far understandable. What else would you expect from trying to change things?

Not only is it change you're involved in, however, but it is change of the most radical sort. There is something about worship, as we've already said, which gets right to people's hearts. To many the Sunday services are 'church', and to mess around with them is to challenge the whole identity of their faith and its expression. For many the patterns of service which you now have, provide (incredible though it seems to you) a form of worship which is dearly loved and which really does get them in touch with God in ways which are real and profound to them, and which, in many cases, has done so for a large number of years. They see no reason for any change at all, and so change will always be perceived not as improvement but as loss. In trying to help them through their bereavement process, you need to realise that to them it is you who seem to be the murderer.

You need to remember as well that there are different forces involved in resistance to change. In a previous church we experienced a period of particularly bitter personal opposition over an issue which had nothing at all to do with worship, from one person whom I shall call Alan. This really wore us down over a period of time in a way which many of you will understand only too well from personal experience. We became obsessed by him, stayed awake at night worrying about him, spoke despairingly about him when we sat at home and walked along the road, when we lay down and when we got up. We dreaded meeting him, and dreaded even more meeting him in church services, having to give communion to him, and so on.

One day a friend from outside the patch was visiting, and got the whole story in every anguished detail. I remember the profound sense of relief which gradually spread over me when he said, 'Well, of course you know that it's really a spiritual battle you're fighting, not a human one.' Immediately it all fell into place. Why hadn't we twigged before? This was not about Alan at all; it was about Satan, who felt nowhere near as hostile in comparison. It was nothing personal. What a relief! After that it all took on a new perspective. Instead of facing Alan with dread, we were able to look him in the eye with the knowledge that he was, sadly, a tool in the hands of the Enemy sent to obstruct us. He could still do that just as effectively, of course, but our whole attitude to him was different, and we could even begin to conceive of loving him, as we knew we were supposed to, rather than wanting to disembowel him on sight, which we actually felt like but thought wasn't very sanctified.

It came as a tremendous liberation to take seriously the fact that we were struggling against the spiritual forces of evil in the heavenly realms, and not just against flesh and blood. We need to grasp the vested interest the Enemy has in keeping our church life, and perhaps particularly our worship, free from improvement. Not all change is improvement, of course, and the Enemy will fight hard to introduce as smoothly as possible the sort which isn't, but it is true to say that his motto is very often, 'As it was in the beginning, is now and ever shall be, world without end.' Heavenly battles need fighting with heavenly weapons, and the place of prayer in change management cannot be emphasised too much. I've found fasting vital too, and it seems to be true biblically that it is commended for and practised by those seeking to break some sort of new ground for the kingdom.

But I gained a further insight when discussing Alan and his atrocities with another friend at a later stage, and recounting the liberation I'd received from the previous insight. 'Yes it is a spiritual battle,' he said, 'but it's a human battle too. Alan doesn't like what you're trying to do!' I hadn't thought of that, either, and once again I had to begin to see Alan through new eyes, not just as an arch-villain trying to oppress me at every turn, not even just as an innocent pawn in the game of dark forces about which he knew nothing, but also as a human being with prefer-ences and sensibilities which I had offended.

In handling change and opposition we need to hold these two forces in balance. Our struggle is, in fact, against flesh and blood *and* against spiritual forces of evil, and we need to know how to fight both battles in an appropriate manner. People need to be loved, listened to, argued with, resisted and confronted at times, but above all respected, while the Enemy needs to be rebuked and fought at every turn with the spiritual weapons appropriate for the job. We want to introduce positive change in spite of the Enemy, but wherever possible with the agreement of people. Whenever we get those two the wrong way round, we're in serious trouble.

2. Understand the people

I find this diagram extremely helpful in making sense of the dynamics of change in church life

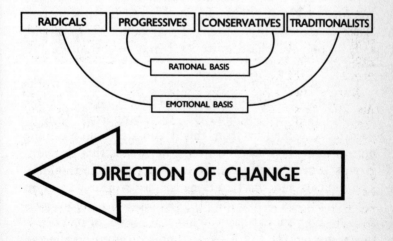

What it means is that in any group of people contemplating any change there will be four sub-groups, each with a different attitude to change itself. The radicals are those who find you overcautious and conservative. Why can't we just get on and do it, and why stop there? And why don't we change x, y and z while we're at it? There's no point in pussy-footing around wasting time. The progressives would agree broadly with this, and would very much like to see the change come about, but would want to work carefully through it and make sure that it was achieved properly and that people would mostly be carried along with it. The conservatives, on the other hand, would not be so kindly disposed towards it. 'After all, have we really thought through the implications fully? And what about the point made by so-and-so? We never really dealt with that satisfactorily, did we? Generally speaking, we should wait before doing anything. Time will tell.' Finally, the traditionalists are those whose response to most things is, 'Over my dead body!' (You may like to try replying breezily, 'Oh, I hope it won't come to that,' next time you get one of those.) 'No change is ever for the better'. 'They're spoiling my church', 'I shall be forced to resign', and so on. All these attitudes betray the traditionalist outlook.

You will no doubt be able to see already how this works out in your church, and may have begun to engage in some preliminary pigeon-holing. But three important insights need to be picked up from this if you are to do anything more useful than classification. The first is that different groups function with a different basis to their thinking. The radicals and the traditionalists are working from an emotional basis, while the progressives and the conservatives have a rational basis. What that means in practice is that some people will listen to, and may even be affected by, discussion and argument, while others will not because they are looking at things from a completely different angle. It is much more to do with the way they feel about the change than about the objective value or otherwise of making it. Much time has been wasted in trying to talk people into things, setting out logical pros and cons, building up decisive arguments, and so on, when really they need listening to at a much deeper level, so that their frustrations can be expressed and heard. You may need to override them in the end, but at least you will have done so with a clear understanding of where they are coming from.

Secondly, you need to be aware of the demands of your role in dealing with these four groups of people. The temptation is always to gravitate towards those who are like-minded, and draw around ourselves a little company of people who agree with us. While this is important, as I'll show later, it is also vital that we give care and attention to those who are anything but like-minded. We need to develop the ability to be all things to all men.

It is fascinating to note how Jesus manages this in the Gospels, but even more so to see how he often turns it around and becomes to all men just the opposite of what they seem to demand. So, for example, he confronts the heavily-traditionalist scribes and Pharisees on many occasions with such radical comments as, 'The Sabbath was made for man, not man for the Sabbath' (Mk 2:27), and, 'Nothing outside a man can make him "unclean" by going into him' (Mk 7:15). Yet when he is with his closest followers, those who are the most radical and are at the forefront of the advance of the kingdom, he says, 'It is easier for heaven and earth to disappear than for the least stroke of a pen to drop out of the Law' (Lk 16:17), a fairly conservative statement by any standards. (All those essays theological students have had to write on 'Jesus' attitude to the Law'—nobody ever saw it as a pastoral rather than a theological problem!) Jesus' ability to deal with people according to their rational or emotional positions, and even to challenge them in those positions, is something we would do well to develop in our own ministries.

The third thing to understand is that if you do in fact manage to move people anywhere, they will move *en masse* according to the diagram above. In other words, radicals will always be radicals, and however much you go along with what they want, they will still keep wanting more. Similarly, if you can get the traditionalists to move without leaving the church, it will only be a matter of time before they are being traditional about the things which they were until recently fighting against. This is both highly amusing and highly frustrating, depending on the day of the week, but it is fact, and needs to be recognised as such.

It ought to go without saying that any dealing with people must be done with love, yet that is often very difficult, as it was difficult for me to love Alan. I like the saying of Bishop John Taylor of Winchester: 'Look upon your congregation believingly and with compassion.' John Wimber has described church leaders as 'loving change agents'. The moment we start hating and resenting the people of whom we have been given pastoral charge, we need to stop short and get God's perspective on things, and repent before him. Jesus was often angry and frustrated by the blindness and obstinacy of the people among whom he worked, but he never for one second stopped loving them with all his heart. At times that love involved anger and hard words, but we need to make sure that any hard words we speak and any anger we show come from the heart of the Father and not from our own frustration and impatience.

I find it helpful to think of people as responding: to their own backgrounds, to the way they have been taught in the past, perhaps by other church leaders, to their own emotional conditioning and, yes, even at times to the Enemy who longs to frustrate progress (just as at times I respond to him and get in the way of others' ideas of progress).

When, in a parish situation, I used to get frustrated because everyone thought that what I was trying to do was wrong, I often pondered over what caused everyone to be so misguided. It came as a stunning revelation to realise that I was wrong because clergy whom they respected and admired had in the past taught them certain things which I was now contradicting. It wasn't their fault if they thought, for example, that spiritual gifts had died out at the end of the apostolic era. They'd been taught to believe that, and it was a belief which suited them and made them feel comfortable. Now here I was saying that they'd been taught wrongly. No wonder I got a cool reception. That way of looking at things helps me to keep a better perspective on people and the way in which I treat them.

3. Understand your role

Someone at a recent training day for church leaders put this very clearly when he said that some leaders spend their time acting as referees rather than as captains. Much clergy time is spent in keeping the peace, holding different warring factions in the church apart, trying to get a balance, and trying to respond to different pressure groups without treading on anyone's toes. I think it was Eddie Gibbs who described the Church of England as 'a genteel state of anarchy', and that description will ring bells for many people. And yet surely the role of a leader should be to lead.

Fashions change, in leadership as in every other area, and we have been through a phase in which it was far more easy to define what leaders weren't than what they were. Facilitative, enabling, collegiate leadership was all the rage; you didn't manipulate, dictate, direct or do very much at all which looked like leading. In some ways this was positive, and provided a much-needed corrective to the 'benign dictatorship' run by so many clergy. Yet I believe we are now coming to see the poverty of a leadership style which relies solely on facilitation, and the pendulum is beginning to swing back in some circles to a more positive and definite role. What looked like non-directive leadership has been recognised in many cases as an avoidance of any leadership at all. What we need is not another pendulum swing in reaction to this model, but for the pendulum to reach equilibrium at a point where our leadership, like that of Jesus, is clear and definite, can inspire others to follow, and yet at the same time teaches, and includes and enables others in teamwork.

The captain of a team is the one who sees the objectives clearly, and is the first in going out to achieve them. He needs to inspire confidence in those he is leading, and to make sure they agree on policy and tactics. At times he may need to exercise a strong leadership and deal with those not wanting to go his way, but in the end a team will only be as good as the leadership it gets from its captain. Of course the church is not to be run as a dictatorship, but I am becoming increasingly convinced that unless leaders take a more actively aggressive role and stop spending their time simply trying to keep the peace, the church will continue sliding downhill towards a constant state of confusion and in-fighting.

In an ideal world change should take everyone concerned along with it, but that will almost never happen this side of eternity. Unless we can free ourselves from the terminal fear of people leaving our churches, we will be doomed to mediocrity. We need to be free to say to people, 'I'm really sorry we can't agree, and yes, perhaps it is right for you to move to another church more in line with your faith and spirituality. Go with my blessing, and I hope we can still be friends.' Even if this decimates your congregation, leaving you with only two old ladies, one teenager and the church mouse, at least you'll be able to begin to move forward from there, without needing to spend all your time and energy fighting the opposition.

If this is a call for more authority in our churches, it needs to go hand in hand with a greater understanding of our responsibility. Authority is not a licence to go round bulldozing people into our way of looking at things, and a continual sense of responsibility to our flock helps us to remember that. Peter describes Jesus as 'a stone that causes men to stumble'; we need to be absolutely sure that if any of our people stumble it is over Jesus himself, and not us as leaders.

In fact we have a double responsibility, and it is the holding of these two in tension which causes problems. First, we have a God-given responsibility towards those for whom we have pastoral care in the congregation, even the awkward ones. We have to love them and strive with the Spirit to present them mature and spotless to the Father. But we also have a responsibility to those outside the church, to win them to faith in the Lord. Sometimes these two responsibilities conflict when those in the church seem determined, by their conservatism and intransigence, to keep the outsiders outside by maintaining the church in a state of terminal irrelevance. It is our job as leaders to work out these two areas of responsibility, but if at times we leave behind those inside, that may be a necessary evil in order to fulfil our responsibility to those outside.

4. Understand the principles

Bearing in mind all that we've said so far, how can we actually effect change? Here are three brief principles which may be helpful.

(i) Do it gently

It is always better to add things than to change them, thus giving people who don't like the change the chance to continue, at least for a while, in the old way. The new evening service to which I've referred was an example of this. No way were we going to get any 'charismatic' worship going in our 8 am Prayer Book Communion service or in Solemn Choral Evensong, so we didn't waste any time trying. In starting a brand-new service we had complete freedom to make our own rules, so we could begin from week one working out our vision in an uncluttered way. It's also much easier politically getting something completely new through church councils and other such bodies, since those who don't like the idea won't feel so totally committed to voting against if they don't think they'll ever have to go. The hope is that in time people will become firmly convinced of the value of the new, but if they don't, the old is still there for them.

So perhaps you need to realise that you are fighting a losing battle in trying to renew the worship at some of your services at least, and begin instead to see where you could start with a clean sheet, either with a new Sunday service or possibly a weeknight home group or Saturday celebration.

There is, however, one danger which needs to be guarded against in this approach: it must never appear that you are denying people's past, but rather that you are trying to grow from it. In attempting to bring about change, it can easily seem that you are writing off people's previous experience, teaching and spirituality. You may appear to be saying, in effect, that everything they've been brought up to believe and do has been wrong, but that you now have the real answers and they'd better discard all the wrong ones quickly. A much more positive approach is to teach people that the new things you are trying to bring about are a natural next step from where they've been before, and that they can be helped to grow into them as an integral part of their pilgrimage. This policy can be implemented especially in your preaching and teaching, but it also has an important place in the pastoral care of individuals who are finding change difficult. In this way the past is reinforced, not written off, and this in turn gives people greater freedom to leave the past behind in a positive way.

In Isaiah 43 the prophet uses the oft-quoted words, 'Forget the former things; do not dwell on the past,' (v.18), but only after he has reviewed the past:

> This is what the Lord says-
> he who made a way through the sea,
> a path through the mighty waters,
> who drew out the chariots and horses,
> the army and reinforcements together,
> and they lay there, never to rise again,
> extinguished, snuffed out like a wick.
> (Is 43:16–17)

He acknowledges the past, but then, in the light of that, urges the people to move on: 'Forget the former things; do not dwell on the past. See, I am doing a new thing!' (vv 18–19). It seems to me that this is a very positive approach to follow in all our management of change.

Another important thing to remember in bringing about change gently is that you can make people feel very insecure and threatened if you change too many different things at once. I have never been rock-climbing. It seems to me that there are many more attractive suicide methods which don't involve buying such expensive equipment. But enthusiasts assure me that an important principle is involved which can teach us a lot about change management. Normally you would have with your hands and feet four points of contact with the rock-face (or five if you include your teeth). The art, so I'm told, is to move only one thing at a time, so that you retain as many points of contact as possible. Only when both feet and your left hand have a secure grip do you venture to let go with your right hand to search for a new handhold, and only when you are convinced of its security do you go on to move a foot.

Similarly in church life, it can add greatly to people's security if you only change one thing at a time, and allow people to get thoroughly used to that change before moving on to the next. If, however, they turn up one Sunday to find all the pews moved, the hymn-books replaced with an overhead projector, the choirmaster playing a DX7, dance instead of the notices, and a signs and wonders ministry during coffee, they might, quite justifiably, feel just a little bit threatened. Threatened people, like threatened animals, can be very dangerous, so we need to make sure that we don't make them feel too insecure, but leave them as many points of contact with the past as we can.

(ii) Do it intelligently

Know what you are trying to do. I find it helpful to think in terms of three change levels and three change methods. The levels are those of ideas, structures and people. It is very easy to change your ideas, and relatively easy to change structures, given a positively disposed church council or whatever. But changing people is a much more difficult task. It must be done, however, if the change is to be anything but superficial, and a much higher proportion of time and energy must be put into it. If you are throwing everything you've got into changing structures, getting motions passed by the council, and so on, you may well be misdirecting your attention, and would perhaps be better off spending time with people, especially those who oppose you. In getting alongside them and listening to their complaints, you will be investing positively for the future as well as loving them in a practical way.

Three methods of change have been named: conversion, subversion and persuasion. All three are important and effective, but some may be more useful at times than others. Conversion is the deliberate attempt to win people over to your point of view by making changes in the hope that they will like what they see and decide that it's not as bad as they thought it would be. It is certainly valid at times to give people the opportunity, often against their better judgement, to 'suck it and see', and people will often be surprised at the positive way in which it works out. In a former parish we took the decision to introduce music sung by a small worship group during the administration of Communion. Since this was normally the domain of the robed choir, we could only do it during August when they were on holiday, but even then there was some fierce opposition as people thought this was the thin end of the wedge towards a 'charismatic' Parish Communion. However, when we went ahead and did it anyway, some of the most vocal critics were won over by the beauty and simplicity of the worship songs, and the sensitive and unobtrusive way in which they were sung. This became an important link between the weird, over-the-top activities of the extra evening service and the mainstream life of the church, as people realised that perhaps it was more harmless than their fantasies had led them to believe.

Two things are important to note here: the first is that this method is particularly good for those who are motivated in their opposition primarily by emotional rather than rational factors. They *feel* they won't like the changes, and no amount of talking will persuade them otherwise. Instead they need the opportunity to experience the new, so that they will hopefully feel good about it. This leads on to the second point which concerns the value of experimental periods. Generally speaking, people will not object too strongly to something if it is only to happen for a short time. Their hope is often that at the end of the experiment the vote will go resoundingly against change, and the whole issue will be buried once and for all; yours is that after experiencing the new, people will realise its value and want to make it permanent. Therefore whenever you can (and certainly every time you do anything new in worship), set up an experimental period of change and review it at the end of the period.

It worried me during the liturgical upheaval of the seventies in the Church of England that so many churches rejected (or accepted) new liturgies without such a trial period. Liturgy needs to get under your skin to be fully effective in worship, and it can't get very far under in less than three months, especially when the previous texts had been under the C of E's collective skin (and probably the individual skin of some) for the last 310 years. So give your new worship a chance, if the church will let you. Some may be changed by the experience, and if at the end the vote goes against change, change back. Not only is this fair, but it also builds up confidence in you for further possible experiments in the future. People will realise that when you say 'experiment' you mean it, and you're not just trying to get something in by the back door.

Subversion is a much more devious way of effecting change, but one which certainly does have a place in church life. It was Juan Carlos Ortiz who said that some churches are so dead that you need to begin underground! Subversion is the attempt to build up factors in the life of the church which are positively disposed towards the change for which you are working, and to weaken those against it. It is done quite simply by making priorities. We all make priorities, usually on the basis of what we enjoy or see as the most useful ways in which to spend our working time, so why not let's admit it and work consciously for positive change? You may find that you increasingly give more time in prayer and preparation to your new service than you do to the existing one. There is no need to feel guilty about this, since you are only giving priority to the areas where you can see the Spirit at work the most; in other words those areas to which God is giving most priority. You need to guard against two dangers, of course: no area of work must become shoddy and unprepared, and nobody must be made to feel second best or neglected. Trying not to leave awkward people out while trying to invest time in those who share your vision is like walking a tight-rope, but it can be done.

Persuasion is the attempt to take people with you before you go anywhere at all. Before making any changes, you need to have convinced at least a significant majority of people of the value of the change you are proposing, so that you will have their support when you do actually do something. People are involved in the thinking and planning from the earliest stages, and your job is to teach and educate them into your way of thinking. Those who are against the change get a lot of your time as you listen to their questions and hesitations. You may find your plans being modified in the light of the wisdom of those who oppose you. They have no stars in their eyes and can see possible pitfalls more clearly than you can. The traditionalists may not have much to say on a rational level, but at least they will feel listened to and cared for. You may even find some of them change as they feel your concern. This method is the ideal one in many cases, but its drawbacks are that it is time consuming and therefore frustrating, and, as we have seen, will work most effectively with those who are working on a rational agenda.

As I've said, each of these methods has its place. You were probably doing them instinctively already, but it is useful to identify and name what it is that you're doing so that you can do it more consciously and effectively.

(iii) Do it corporately

Intrinsic in what I've said so far is the idea that you want people to change with you. This may not, however, be true in all cases, and from the way some leaders go about things you'd get the impression that they don't really care whether people like it or not. They go running off ahead, doing everything they want to, in the hope that some of the people might catch up, but not minding too much if they don't. In fact any change will only be as effective as the support it receives from others in terms of quantity and quality, and so it must have at least some corporate nature.

A useful first stage is to identify people who will be with you. I believe that in many churches there are people hungry for a greater reality of God, especially in worship. If what you are proposing has the mark of the Spirit on it, there will be those who recognise in your words the words of Jesus. Like the sheep following the Good Shepherd, they will hear his voice and respond, and will give you their loyalty and support. These people will receive your first time priority as you meet, pray and worship together. With a strong group behind you, you can begin to work for change.

The first way is to begin to influence the corridors of power in your church. Depending on the decision-making method you use, you may at least be able to vote in an experimental period of some new type of worship or liturgy. But the second way is even more powerful and uses the principle of 'spillage'. You simply begin to do what it is you want to do in your small group in the hope that it will spill over into other areas of the church's life, such that people want the change rather than feeling it is being foisted upon them. Our singing during the administration of Communion is one example of this in action. Maybe you can think of ways in your own church to do something similar. Simply beginning to worship more freely in home groups or at a mid-week prayer meeting may so touch people's hearts that they are soon longing for the same depth and quality of worship on Sundays. There is not the same emotional resistance to change on weeknights as there is on Sundays for 'proper' services, so if you can win the battle mid-week you are on much stronger ground when you begin to change services.

When things go well and begin to move, the group can be strengthened since it has an inclusive character, not an exclusive, élitist one. And when things go badly and attacks and problems come, you can derive great strength and comfort from one another. It may also be true that this group can be strengthened by evangelism, since new Christians will immediately be attracted to the areas of greatest life in the church. Those older in the faith will be threatened by this, and may need care and help to feel that they are still important and valued.

When the time comes for political change of a major nature, for example the introduction of a new act of worship, you will follow the normal pattern of decision making for your church. Some leaders prefer to wait until there is a virtually unanimous vote, while others are happy to take things on a simple majority. In some churches there is no council as such, and matters are decided by the whole church or a group of elders. Whatever your model, it is important that you stick to it so that decisions are made in the traditional way. If the vote goes against you, it will test your qualities of love to the utmost, but you really do need to hear what people are saying and try to get inside the fears and hesitations they have. Until you deal satisfactorily with these, you will progress only at the cost of relationships within the church. Everyone concerned needs a lot of patience. Rome wasn't built in a day, and neither will the kingdom be in your patch.

Sometimes God will use defeat on church councils to tell

you that the timing for a particular project is not right. In one church I know, the minister was convinced that the way ahead involved a major reorganisation not just of the Sunday worship but also the whole pastoral structure of the church. Yet the elders turned the idea down very quickly and very decisively. Two years later, when the idea still hadn't gone away, he tried again. This time things were more favourable, the plan was more carefully thought through, and discussions began to test the idea on the whole church. The minister knew that he'd finally hit the jackpot when an old man, who was well known for being the most traditional person in the church, said in a meeting, 'Why do we have to keep talking about this over and over again? Why can't we just get on with it?' They did, and it appears to be working well. A thoughtful and prayerful leader will often have ideas before their time has come; it is a wise leader who sees defeat not as a final deathblow to an idea but as an invitation from God to refine it and sharpen it up. God uses defeat and disappointment to turn good ideas into the best ones.

Sometimes though, perhaps even most times, division will result from your attempts to change things. This should not be surprising; Jesus himself didn't exactly manage without it, even among those who were following him faithfully, but he was never afraid of it. In the early days of charismatic renewal, when so many churches were split down the middle over issues like tongues, opponents were frequently to be heard wagging their fingers and saying, 'See, it can't be right, because the Spirit is the Spirit of unity, and he can't possibly cause division.' This, it seems to me, is distinctly unbiblical. The Spirit, like Jesus, always divides. He divides people into those who are willing to go with him, and those who would rather stay where they are and quench and resist him. Sometimes it is the sad duty of a church leader to say, 'Well, I'm sorry, but this is where we believe God is calling us to as a church, and as a church we must obey him. If you can't come along with us that's sad, but we're going anyway.' This is a sad duty, and must never become an occasion for gloating in triumph, or for some kind of witch-hunt. It must be the Spirit who divides, not the leadership. And if at all possible, good relations must be kept with those with whom we disagree. The church ought to be a witness to the world of how people can disagree in love. Many people have left our church over the years for a variety of reasons, but they are still counted as friends. That is how it ought to be.

Change is never easy. In the world as well as in the church it has been said that perpetual change is here to stay. But it can be made slightly easier by an understanding of these principles. I have hardly mentioned the single most important factor in change: prayer. Whether it's the popular 'Lord, change him or get rid of him' prayer, the praying around the council members before a meeting, weeping before the Lord as he gives you a glimpse of *his* view of the church, prayer is vital if we are to effect anything of lasting value. And above all prayer is vital for us if we are to be sure that we've got it right. The last thing we'd want to be guilty of is trying to foist our own good ideas on the church, even if we have read them in a respectable book like this one. But if we can say with confidence to our church, 'It seemed good to the Holy Spirit and to me,' we can go about working for that change, knowing that we are wanting God's best for them.

CHAPTER FOURTEEN

HANDLING CHANGE

II. For the Congregation

WE'VE LOOKED AT CHANGE from the point of view of the leader wanting to change things about his congregation. Let's move on now to look at the other side of the coin, where the congregation, or more commonly some of them, are wanting to move on in worship but are being thwarted by the leadership. There are probably far more people in this position than in the other, and I do need to say right at the start that the prognosis here is nowhere near as good as for the reverse situation. I believe that the single biggest factor in determining the state of any local church is the minister, vicar or other person in overall charge. Until he or she changes, there will be little or no effective change anywhere. In one sense this is easier, because the fight is much more focused; it's far less vague praying, 'Lord, change him or get rid of him,' about the vicar than it is about the congregation, but in most other respects you have a very difficult fight on your hands. Nevertheless, let's have a look at some principles. Lest I seem too disrespectful, remember that I write as a church leader, but also as a member, because in the dim and distant past I was an ordinary weekly pew-filler suffering because of clerical incompetence, similar, no doubt, to the incompetence I now exhibit.

First of all, you need to understand your leader. In many cases he (or she) is a highly-trained and qualified professional, and has experience in church leadership of which he is justifiably proud. He understand things, and above all he has been trained and has gained experience in being in control at all times. David Pytches says that Anglican clergy are trained always to be two steps ahead of the Holy Spirit, and this may well be right about other denominations too. The leader knows that his job is to lead his people in their relationship with the Lord and their worship of him, and he is seeking to the best of his ability to do just that. But then some of his congregation start to get weird ideas. His immediate reaction is to stamp on things before they get out of control and start to cause trouble. He has people's best interests at heart, and genuinely wants to avoid seeing them fall into error or danger.

Then, of course, he may have tried it already. When I was a a student at York University, my father was most alarmed to read in his newspaper about a survey that revealed that 80% of students at the university had experimented with smoking marijuana. This sounded phenomenally high, but on reflection I reckoned it was pretty accurate if you included all the people who, like myself, had tried one joint and never touched anything again since. It was just something you did as a student in those days, but probably less than 1% of them are still involved in drugs today.

I believe there is something of the same dynamic in renewal. It is now pretty impossible for someone to have moved in ecclesiastical circles for more than a few weeks without having had some exposure to things charismatic. Some leaders even became involved themselves for a while, but now regard it as a phase which they passed through in more youthful and gullible times. For whatever reason, but most likely because of immature behaviour by other 'charismatics', they now regard the whole thing as a rather dangerous aberration from Christian orthodoxy. Understandably, when they see their flock falling into the same error they become alarmed, and try to restore sense to the proceedings. Add to this one or two of the vast number of horror stories which circulate in anti-charismatic circles, a tablespoon of split churches, half a cup of over-the-top worship and a pinch of messed-up deliverances, and you have a recipe designed to give a large dose of indigestion at the very mention of the word 'charismatic'.

In my early days of renewal, my friends and I could spot in anti-charismatics what we used to call 'the big BE' from 200 yards away. 'BE' stood for Bad Experience, and it was amazing how many people had had one, how often they talked about it, and how they managed to speak in such a way that you just knew Bad Experiences had to have a capital 'B' and a capital 'E'. Like it or not, we have to realise that many people have been put off renewal and all that goes with it through the bad behaviour of others. To win them back even to a friendly toleration of it will be an extremely hard job, requiring the breaking down of many barriers.

What is undoubtedly true of the renewal movement is also true of just about anything in the church which is designed to allow a greater degree of openness to God and immediacy of experience of the Spirit. Worship is no exception to this, and there are many horror stories of inane, mindless worship sessions, probably not all of them apocryphal. Worship could be described as spiritually on show, and all that people find difficult about renewal can be seen focused sharply in the worship of charismatics. It is one thing to be aware that there are some charismatics in your church somewhere, but when they start sticking their hands in the air during the *Sanctus* there's no escaping them.

Finally, some leaders will just be plain frightened. While others will genuinely disagree with what you are trying to do on biblical or doctrinal grounds, some will actually be working on a much more personal emotional basis. Those who are well defended emotionally may fear the extravagant and extrovert style of worship which they associate with renewal, preferring something which requires much less embarrassing behaviour. Some may prefer their God to be much more safe and predictable than that of the charismatics, and most would be scared stiff of the sort of things happening in their church which they have heard about from signs and wonders conferences. These difficulties on personal rather than theological grounds would be easy to deal with were it not for the fact that people seldom acknowledge them. The sort of people who typically have problems in this direction are the last sort of people who would admit to it, and so tend to wrap up their hesitations in much safer theological issues. It takes a certain amount of discernment to discover whether the leader who won't touch renewal because it says in Psalm 73 verse 9 that possession of the earth will be taken over by the *tongues* of the wicked genuinely believes that from the bottom of his heart, or is actually afraid because he once saw someone pushed over at a Pentecostal healing meeting. It is rather like the diagram from the last chapter; in opposing renewal (as well as just about anything else) some people work from a rational or theological base and some from an emotional base. They each need to be approached differently, and so it is important to know just what sort of person you are approaching.

So where might your leader be in all that? Wherever it is, he will need a lot from you if he is to change, and you will need to understand him very clearly. Those things which our instinct tells us to do in such situations are often the least helpful.

Let me go through seven principles, then, which may be important in changing your leader.

1. Submission—don't disobey

Your leader may be misguided if he forbids prophecy during church services, but he will be downright angry if you go ahead and do it anyway, and rightly so. The apostles may have felt it right to disobey the authorities because they couldn't help but speak of the things they'd seen and heard, but that doesn't give you an excuse. You are not dealing with anti-Christian political intrigue, but with appointed church leaders who have been given authority for and pastoral care over you. You needn't feel that your leader has the right to control everything which goes on in private between consenting adults, but when it comes to public worship and other official church activities, you should be in submission to him. Nothing is more certain to ruin your case and your reputation with your leadership than this sort of disobedience, and it should not occur. Many of his fears and fantasies may be about indiscipline and what he regards as over-the-top behaviour. Your job is to demonstrate that you are, in fact, a rational human being capable of understanding simple directions and obeying them.

2. Respect—don't assassinate

It makes me shudder to hear the way some Christians talk about their leaders behind their backs. No one should be discussed in some of the ways I've heard, and especially not those given authority in the church. Whatever you may think, you have a duty to speak only out of loyalty and love. Your leader has some good points, even if you have to dig very deep indeed to find them, and it is of these that you should speak, not of his habits of annoying you and getting in your way. What you say about someone not only is affected by what you feel about them, it also affects what you feel. To get into the habit of running down your leadership whenever you get the opportunity is to run the risk of getting into negative habits in what you say to them and the way you act towards them. Just as it is a cardinal rule in the marriage relationship never to speak ill of your partner to others, so it is in the church with regard to your leadership.

A good antidote to the tendency to speak ill of someone is to go out of your way to find opportunities to speak good of them. A useful exercise is to look for things in the worship tradition of your leader that you can value and appreciate. You may have theological questions about Solemn Evensong and Benediction, but can you get in touch with the sense of awe and mystery, and the presence of God in majesty and splendour? Or you may find it hard to sit through forty-five minutes of exposition of the book of Obadiah every week of the twenty-three week series, but what is there for you to learn which can lift your heart in silent adoration and praise? Look hard for these things, and when you find them, tell him how much you value them. Do it humbly and genuinely; do it in a real attempt to build him up in love and to learn from him, but don't do it too much, or he may increase the number of Benedictions and extend the series by another nine weeks.

3. Dialogue—don't be a walkover

Having said all that, it is possible at times to let your leader know that you disagree with him. I know one church where renewal was preached against from the pulpit in the most specific terms, much to the chagrin of a few charismatic members of the congregation. In such a situation you have every right politely to let the leader know that you disagreed with him, and that you were frankly hurt by what he said, but that you still love him and will be loyal to him. If you can be prepared to give an account of the hope that is in you, and explain scripturally why you think what you do, it is bound to do your case good. Even if he ends up disagreeing with you, at least you will have shown that you are capable of thinking intelligently. This is important, since he will have heard if not used the phrase 'unthinking charismatic' on many occasions. I remember a clergyman, on glancing at a paper entitled 'A Theolgy of the Charismatic Movement' remarking cynically, 'I didn't think they had any theology!' This may have been true in the early sixties, although I doubt even that, but it is certainly not true nowadays.

The myth needs to be exploded; that is why I've taken three whole chapters at the start of this book to explore the theology behind this type of worship. Letting your leader know that you have a worked-out theology for what you're wanting will never do any harm, unless you do it in a way which is arrogant and threatening. That assumes, of course, that you do have a worked-out theology for what you're wanting. The onus is on you to be thoroughly equipped theologically. Even if you can't do it in Aramaic and Latin like he can, you should still have thought it all through intelligently.

4. Practical help—don't just talk

The support and loyalty which you have decided to give your leader should be expressed not just verbally and in submission to him, but also in practical ways. Another of his fantasies about charismatics may well be that they are too superspiritual, too heavenly minded, to be of any earthly use. This is another myth which needs to be exploded, and when there are chairs to be put out, tea-towels to be washed, or flowers to be arranged, you ought to be in the front of the queue of volunteers. There are other imaginative ways of giving practical help too. At Spring Harvest I once heard a church leader explaining that he was there because people in his church, knowing he was hesitant about renewal, had had a whip round and paid for him to go, just for a holiday, with no obligation actually to attend any of the seminars or meetings. By the end of the week he was thoroughly convinced—although I don't know whether it was the Spring Harvest teaching or the love and sensitivity of his people which touched him most.

Another piece of advice I would give could also be conveniently put under this heading: make sure your practical help and support is given throughout the activities of the church, and not just in your little group of like-minded people. Most churches have various organisations attached to them with greater and lesser degrees of commitment to the spiritual purposes of the church; uniformed organisations for children and young people, women's organisations, PCCs, men's fellowships, and so on. What can very easily happen is that if someone moves into an experience of renewal, they leave all those quasi-religious organisations behind, and spend all their time instead in the ghetto of their charismatic friends. If they can't get spaced out in worship at a meeting, they don't see the point in bothering to go. As new Christians join the church, they too are sucked into the 'right' organisations or groups, and are never exposed to the existing ones.

There is, of course, a sense in which people will gravitate to the place where the spiritual reality is greatest, and it is right that new Christians should be put where they will get the nourishment to help them grow. But at the same time the church as a whole, and the leadership in particular, will soon spot the 'holy huddle' mentality and the new life which the Spirit is giving will be discredited to some extent. Instead of the process of spillage which we talked about in the last chapter there will be a desiccating process by which goodwill and life are sucked out of the rest of the church and guarded jealously by a few initiates. There are only seven days in a week, but nevertheless you should work hard at being involved both in places where you would naturally choose to be, and also in those where you wouldn't. And when you do go to the other meetings, don't go in to 'witness' as enthusiastically as you can and at every single opportunity to your new 'experience', or you'll soon have everyone wishing you would go back to the ghetto. Go in as a friend and a servant. Let the love and worship in your heart spill naturally wherever you go. That'll be the best witness you could possibly give.

5. Commitment—don't give up

You need to face the fact that things are almost certainly going to take a long time, possibly even a very long time indeed. As humans, we all share to some degree a tendency to impatience, and our whole mood can go up and down considerably depending on whether or not we are getting what we want quickly enough. I once preached a sermon about the fact that we live in what has been called an age of 'instant gratification'; my title for the sermon was 'Aspirins and Access Cards'. I made the point that pain-killers are almost always sold not on the merits of how effectively they relieve pain, but how quickly. The Access slogan of the time also seemed to reflect the spirit of the age—'taking the waiting out of wanting'. Those of past generations, perhaps including our parents, grew up in times when you didn't expect to get it all your own way and all at once. If you wanted something you saved up for it, and if you couldn't afford it you didn't get it at all. You lived with unfulfilled wishes in your life because that was what life was like. But now we have a new generation which has been brought up to expect by right whatever it wants, and to expect it now. Credit cards and finance companies thrive, as more and more of us get what we want now but pay for it later.

What is true in the world of materialism is also true in many areas in the church with regard to prayer. It seems to me that the whole house-church phenomenon can be seen as a manifestation of this same spirit. In the past, if you didn't like the spiritual temperature of your church, you prayed for the vicar. Nowadays you give him three weeks, then zoom off to the 'community church' or 'Christian fellowship' down the road. I don't want to be unfair to the house-church movement, but it is certainly true to say that many of their members have come from other churches, and that when they left, any hope of spiritual renewal or revitalisation in worship within those churches left with them.

What I am saying is that changing your leadership, or rather seeing them changed by God, is often a long slow task which requires much commitment. There may be long periods, years even, with no perceptible sign of hope. As Christians we are called to stand out against the spirit of the age, and to be prepared for such fruitless times and the long hard slog which goes with them. I have mentioned one of the revivals in an earlier chapter; what I didn't mention was that the Hebrides were set on fire for the Lord after months of prayer meetings held three nights each week, as well as in the early mornings. Every other revival has had the same ingredient—lots and lots of regular committed prayer.

Perhaps the greatest example of this was the Evangelical

awakening begun in England by the Wesleys. This was fuelled to a large degree by the prayer of Count Zinzendorf and the Moravians in Germany. A prayer meeting started on 25 August 1727, and was still going on uninterrupted one hundred years later. It would be tragic if years of prayer had gone into a particular church situation with no apparent result, but during which God had been steadily at work in the leader's inner life, only to have half the congregation walk out two days before he finally gave in and opened himself up to the Spirit. A well-known saying goes, 'If at first you don't succeed, so much for sky-diving.' Well, with the Lord it needn't be like that. Persistence in prayer is the order of the day. And since worship is so much a spiritual activity, inspired by the Spirit and needing his help if it is to be worth anything at all, we really do need to cry out to the Lord for the renewal of our worship. It has been my experience that worship is brought to birth in churches after much agony and travail in prayer, and much grief and penitence over past spiritual dryness and liturgical formality. We can't work up this sort of prayer, but we can allow the Lord space to make it happen for us. This is where worship in small groups of like-minded folk can be so powerful. We don't just spill the experience over to others, but we also allow God to spill spiritual power and conviction into the church.

Is it never right, then, to leave a church which appears to be dead? Yes, of course at times it must be. I am certain that God does write off particular situations which are so spiritually dead that they can never again see life and growth and which have leaders so hard-hearted that they haven't noticed or don't care. I am sure that it is truly the work of the Spirit to raise up new churches in areas where the existing ones are doing nothing at all which is faithful to the gospel. I rejoice at the many people who have found new life in Christ through the independent churches; they

suddenly discovered that there was life, when all the existing churches had given them messages of decline and death.
My only argument is the ease with which people nip
around from one church to another.

It's a bit like divorce. In the old days, when divorce was
comparatively rare (in 1911 in the UK there were only 2.2
divorces per 1,000 marriages), people just got on with it
and put up with things. Some marriages were, no doubt,
unbearable, but many must have been made to work
because the couple really didn't have any option. But now
divorce is common (over 300 per 1,000 marriages in the
UK, and over 500 in some parts of the USA) because the
whole thing is so much easier. Add to this the 'instant
gratification' syndrome which we've mentioned already,
and it's easy to see why there is very little commitment to
making marriages work, or putting up with marriages
which seem to fall short of the soap-opera and advert ideals
which the media tell us are the norm. It's a vicious circle;
because of the few marriages which really ought to have
been ended, the floodgates have been opened and any old
marriage which is having a bad patch gets ended too. The
easier it gets, the more people decide to do it.

The same sort of thing is going on in the church as well.
It's very easy to find a new fellowship which will welcome
with open arms all those who are finding it tough going at
their own churches, so people who previously would have
worked and prayed at it now stop bothering and go and get
blessed somewhere else.

So how do you know when it is right to leave a church
and find a new one? I can answer that in two ways. My first
answer would be, 'When God tells you to.' This may
sound superspiritual, but it is in the last analysis the only
reliable guide. I believe that leaving a church should be a bit
like a divorce in that it should be agonised over and done
only with tremendous pain and sense of loss. Someone

who moves from one sexual partner to another with about as much emotion involved as when they change their socks only betrays the shallowness of their 'love'. So, I believe, do Christians who flit from church to church every time something goes a little bit wrong. If you haven't agonised in prayer over your decision, it's almost certainly not time to go yet.

Secondly, though, I would want to answer the question, 'When should I leave my church?' by saying, 'When you can't stay any longer.' In order for a marriage to be mended there needs to be a high degree of motivation and commitment on both sides. Marriage counsellors would tell you that they are wasting their time in most cases when either or both of the partners have lost the desire to keep the marriage alive to the extent that they are not willing to work at it any longer. Sometimes the same will be true of you and your church. When you can no longer love and respect the leader, and when he can no longer love or respect you; when you can no longer muster any faith at all that things are ever going to be different there; when the experience of worshipping there depresses rather than uplifts you; when the absence of God hits you in worship with the force that his presence ought to hit you, and when every moment spent there is miserable and drains you of spiritual energy, then is the time to go. For your own good you'd better find somewhere you can feel positive about.

I need to make it clear that those two answers are not the same thing. It's quite possible to leave a church because you feel you can't stay any longer and do so without God having told you to. Again, it's like divorce. You can almost hear the sigh of sadness as Jesus reluctantly admits that 'Moses permitted you to divorce your wives because your hearts were hard. But it was not this way from the beginning' (Mt 19:8). If you really have lost all motivation, you'd better go, but that's not my Father's intention for you. Sometimes, though, it will be right to go, and the way you feel and the way you hear God speaking will add together to confirm the rightness of such a move.

When you go, though, make sure it is with mixed feelings. You may feel delighted to be free at last from the slog and fruitless work, but make sure you remember that you are leaving behind a situation which may well be terminal. When God tells you to move, he may be switching off the life-support system for your church. If that doesn't grieve you considerably, there's something badly wrong. (You ought to feel even more grieved if you as the life-support system switch yourself off because you've run out of whatever it is that makes you go.) And when you get to your new church, don't go in with the illusion that it's going to be much different. At first it may appear to be the exact opposite of where you've come from, but after a while you'll discover that all the same problems are there. What happens to your commitment then?

I'm sorry to have taken up so much space in a chapter on helping your leaders to change, in talking about how to leave, but it is a vexed question about which most of the material written seems to be of the 'get-out-quick-and-join-the-true-faith' variety. I hope some of what I've said is helpful to those agonising over whether to go or stay.

6. Sensitivity—don't nag

One of the ways in which our impatience can easily show itself is in the desire to speed things up by our own constant reminders to our leadership that things really do need to be different. Those of us who are married know this by the name of 'nagging', and we also know how totally counterproductive it is. It's not only wives who can sound like dripping taps, but congregational members too. Part of loving and respecting your leader involves giving him space and even a bit of peace from time to time. He does know how you feel, and what is going on for you, perhaps only too well, and constant reminders about your needs and his own inadequacies will do nothing to endear to him either you or your case. Having discovered your feelings about worship, your preferences and your dislikes and the things you can't stand at any price, he doesn't need to hear it all again and again after every service.

7. Prayer—don't despair

When all is said and done, this is the only thing which will make any difference at all in the long run. However much you come up with persuasive scriptural arguments, however sparkling your lifestyle and however deep your love and loyalty, only a sovereign act of God in a man or woman's heart will change them. Thus prayer should be a real priority for you. Cry out to the Lord with specific, committed prayer for your church, its leadership and the renewal of its worshipping life.

This needn't be done behind your leader's back. If you are in a group which meets regularly to pray, why not tell him so, and ask if he could keep you informed about his particular needs so you could pray about them? It ought to be possible to do this in such a way that he feels chuffed and honoured rather than threatened and got at. As you begin to pray along the lines of his agenda as well as your own, you'll begin to get a clearer grasp of some of the pressures he faces. He may say that at the moment his biggest need is to get rid of those pestilential charismatics who are trying to take over his church and hijack the worship. Well, at least that'll help you to appreciate that you're not the only ones with problems and frustrations. Prayer ought to feed love, as well as vice versa, and the two together really can move mountains.

Another important lesson I have learned in the past about prayer is actually to do it! No doubt you've been to a 'prayer' meeting where you've had fifteen minutes of coffee and biscuits, a forty-minute sermon (otherwise known as a Bible study), half an hour of discussion, and then the Grace. This may be a slight exaggeration, but it's amazing how little time the church actually spends in specific prayer to her Lord. When we had an urgent need in my first parish a group of us committed ourselves to meet for prayer for one hour, from 9.30 to 10.30 pm every Monday. We'd start at 9.30, whether or not everyone had arrived, and we'd stop at 10.30, and then we'd all go home. There was plenty more time during the week for coffee and chat, but this was for prayer. I'm sure the Enemy knows the power of prayer against his strongholds, and has therefore done a pretty successful job in squeezing it out of church life. The weak, diluted version most of us exist on explains the poor state of the church. It's like trying to run Concorde on paraffin instead of aviation fuel.

I hope some of these things will be useful to you in your particular situation. Change management is a whole subject on its own, so I've only been able to scratch the surface of a very difficult and emotionally charged issue. I hope what I've said will come over not as a set of simplistic answers but rather as some avenues to explore in prayer and action. Much of this material will have applications wider than just the worshipping life of the church. The principles apply, no matter what you are trying to change. To go back to something I said in the last chapter, it's very easy to change your ideas, and with a bit of know-how and political intrigue it's possible to change some of the structures. (If there is a bit of a spiritual vacuum in the church, anyone with deeply held convictions can begin to get their way— that, after all, is how Hitler came to power.)

But the change which really counts is the changing of

people, and this can only take place when the Holy Spirit breaks in at the very deepest level, convicts of sin and resistance to God, and makes us new from the inside out. Whether we need this for the first time at conversion, for a subsequent inbreaking of the power of the Spirit, for other major breakthroughs along the line, or for the regular daily tune-in to the Father's will, we still need it, and so, perhaps, do our leaders. Renewed worship, or any other change in the life of the church, will only be as effective long term as the change that has gone on in the hearts of the worshippers. Change has been called (I forget by whom) 'the angel of the changeless God', and we do well to see it wherever possible as a friend and not as an enemy, and to go carefully but expectantly with it, rather than to resist it at all costs. Changing our worship will be a symptom of that attitude, not a cause of it.

In this book I have tried to be as practical as possible. I've tried to talk about techniques, skills and some of the things I've learned on my pilgrimage towards worship in a way which will help others to experience some of the same things and take some of the same decisions and actions. If your worship will be enriched through what I've said, everything I've put into the writing of this book will have been worth it. But I wouldn't like anyone to run away with the idea for one minute that worship is primarily a matter of technique. It would be disastrous if my book sold you that idea. Worship is a matter of the Spirit breathing his life into the meagre things we have to offer to God. And until he has first breathed his life into us, trying to worship will be a futile exercise.

One of the saddest things I've seen is the situation which arises when a church takes on board the accoutrements of renewal without the spiritual reality. It offends me deeply when worship songs are used for a jolly singalong at a church youth group, or as background music for some event or other which has nothing to do with worship. But it breaks my heart when the same churches and the same Christians spurn, mock and speak out against the renewal by the Holy Spirit out of which the songs were born, and within which they have been such powerful vehicles of praise and worship. Personal renewal and church renewal are the prerequisites for renewed worship, and it would upset me greatly if techniques were lifted from this book in an attempt to spice up the worship of a church which is not in touch with the reality of the Holy Spirit and his renewing power.

I see the charismatic issue as a central one for all of us involved in worship, since it is a very specific and at times dramatic example of opening oneself up to the Spirit for him to take control. It certainly is not a panacea, but the person who has opened up in that way is far more likely to risk further openness, and therefore far more likely to be open to change in areas like worship. I'm not saying charismatics are perfect; there are still plenty of them stuck firmly in the mud, but that attitude of constant openness to God and the new things he delights to do is one which it is good to cultivate, and which the real sense of the immediacy of the Spirit brought by the charismatic movement can aid no end. If you want to improve your worship, this book ought to help at least a little, but the real issue does not concern the leader's effectiveness in doing his stuff, but rather the relationship of the worshipping community with their God. If that is wrong, no amount of techniques will put their worship right, but good praxis in worship combined with a genuine love for God, a real desire to see Jesus glorified in his church, and an expectant openness to the Spirit can work wonders—literally!

SONGS QUOTED, WITH SOURCES

I have used the three volumes of *Songs of Fellowship* and their successors, *New Songs*, as the basic books for this list. However, some of the songs are not yet available in these books, and most of them can also be found elsewhere, for example in the various Spring Harvest song-books, or in collections by particular composers. It is impossible to produce an exhaustive index, so this is just a rough guide. You should also note that many songs appear in different arrangements and keys in different books. Make sure your worship group are all using the same version, or you could really be making a joyful noise!

Song	*Source*
Almighty God, our heavenly Father (Confession)	NS3, 2
Ascribe greatness to our God, the rock	SF2, 165/MP14
At Your feet we fall	SF2, 167
Be bold, be strong	NS1, 2
Change my heart, O God	SF3, 344/SV3
Create in me a clean heart	SF3, 351
Fling wide your doors	SJS p56

For this purpose	SF3,364/SJS p83
For Thou O Lord	SF2, 188/MP53
Glorious Father, we exalt You	NS3, 9
God of Glory	SF2, 197
He that is in us	MW p13
Holy, holy, holy is the Lord	SF2, 206/MP74
Holy is the Lord	SF3, 381/SV13
Hosanna	NS2, 9/SV14
I get so excited, Lord	SF1, 44
I give You all the honour	SF3, 387/SV18
I just want to praise You	SF3, 388/SV19
I love You, Lord	SF1, 49/MP87
I'm accepted, I'm forgiven	NS1, 6
In the presence of Your people	SF3, 400/MP108
In the tomb (Christ is risen)	NS1, 12/MW p21
I will build My church	SJS p66
I will enter His gates	SF1, 62/MP97
Jesus put this song into our hearts	NS1, 14/MW p20
Let God arise and let His enemies be scattered	SF3, 428/MW p17
Lord have mercy on us	MW p12
Lord, the light of Your love (Shine Jesus shine)	NS2, 24/SJS p86
Lord, You are so precious to me	NS1 17/MW p11
Majesty	SF2 257/MP151
Make way!	NS1, 20/MW p15
May the fragrance of Jesus	NS1, 21/MW p10
Meekness and majesty	NS1, 22/MW p12
O Lord, have mercy on me	SV41
O Lord our God (We will magnify)	SF2, 270
O Lord, the clouds are gathering	NS2, 29/SJS p88
O Lord, Your tenderness	NS1, 23/MW p11
Open your eyes, see the glory of the King	NS1, 24/SV42
Peace to you	TG p68
Rejoice, rejoice!	SF3, 478/MW p14

Restore, O Lord, the honour of Your name	SF2, 286/MP196
The Lord is my strength (Ex XV)	SF3, 495/SV46
Victory is on our lips and in our lives	SF1, 136/MP252
We are Your people	NS1, 32
We believe	NS1, 33/MW p19
Who can sound the depths of sorrow	SJS p96
You laid aside Your majesty	SF3, 527
You shall go out with joy	SF2, 330/MP281

Key

SF *Songs of Fellowship* volumes 1, 2 and 3 (Kingsway: Eastbourne, 1981, 1983, 1985).

NS *New Songs* volumes 1, 2 and 3 (Kingsway: Eastbourne, 1986, 1987, 1988).

MP *Mission Praise* (Marshall, Morgan and Scott: Basingstoke, 1983).

SV *Songs of the Vineyard* (Mercy/Kingsway: Eastbourne, 1987).

MW *Make Way! A Carnival of Praise* (Kingsway: Eastbourne, 1986).

SJS *Make Way! Shine Jesus Shine* (Make Way Music: London, 1988).

TG *Make Way! for Christmas—the Gift* (Make Way Music: London, 1988).

The Christian Music Association is at:

Glyndley Manor
Hailsham Road
Stone Cross
Pevensey
East Sussex
BN24 5BR

Delusion Or Dynamite?

by Gervais Angel

A shrewd, incisive look at the charismatic renewal.

This perceptive, thorough study is intended to help
us think more clearly about the amazing phenomenon
of charismatic renewal, especially in Britain. After a
substantial historical overview, Gervais Angel brings
the sharp focus of Scripture to bear on the renewal.
Can we identify events today with gifts listed in
Scripture? What does the exercise of a gift indicate
about a Christian's spiritual maturity? Rather than
telling us what to believe, he helps us to make up our
own minds.

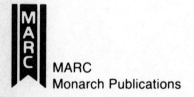

MARC
Monarch Publications

How To Have A Healing Ministry Without Making Your Church Sick

by C Peter Wagner

Should traditional evangelical churches remain apart from the charismatic renewal?

Peter Wagner believes that there have been three distinct 'waves' of God's Spirit in the twentieth century. The first was the Pentecostal movement, the second the charismatic movement. The third wave is now under way, as the Spirit manifests the same kind of power in traditional evangelical churches, but without requiring them to abandon their distinctive nature—to 'make themselves sick'.

As Dr Wagner analyses how the conservative evangelical churches are finding a new vitality of faith, he describes how, from being vehemently anti-charismatic, he has come to recognise the value of charismatic ministry and ultimately to exercise a significant healing gift himself, though without joining a charismatic church.

Dr Peter Wagner is Professor of Church Growth at Fuller Theological Seminary. He has written many books, including Your Spiritual Gifts Can Help Your Church Grow and Leading Your Church To Growth.

Monarch
Publications